Contents

Introduction

Lindon Barrett died tragically in 2008. His family, friends, and colleagues around the world are still mourning his untimely death, and we hope this book will contribute to this psychological work as well as continue Lindon's important intellectual work. Since 1999, when *Blackness and Value: Seeing Double* was published by Cambridge University Press, Lindon had been working on the present study of western modernity's construction of racial blackness. Those of us in regular correspondence with Lindon recall how excited he was about concluding a long, complicated research project. Several of his good friends recall how energized he was in the summer of 2008 about the completion of his manuscript. We had been at that stage with our own works and shared Lindon's enthusiasm, even ecstasy, to have at last finished work that had stretched over many years. Because Lindon had shared portions of his new book with many of his colleagues, students, and family, we also understood the trajectory of the project and thus could share his joyful anticipation of its completion.

None of us, however, had really read the entire manuscript, which understandably Lindon withheld from us until it was completed. When Lindon's friends and family organized his surviving scholarly work, they discovered that his laptop, on which the most current versions of the chapters of this book were stored, had been stolen. In the absence of Lindon's computer, we had only the hard copies of Lindon's recent work. These printed files included several different versions of four chapters of this book found in Lindon's apartment in Long Beach, California. During the academic year 2008–09, Winston James, Lindon's good friend and professor of history at the University of California, Irvine, went through these manuscripts, organizing the different versions of the book's chapters and separating them from essays in various stages of composition and revision that Lindon was preparing for publication elsewhere.

In June 2009, Winston and I met in Eastbluff, a residential neighborhood in Newport Beach, California, at Sage Restaurant, which was one of Lindon's favorites. After a pleasant lunch remembering our friend and discussing a plan to publish Lindon's book and other work, Winston handed me a large plastic bag, which contained all the versions of the book and any related materials Winston thought might help me in the task of assembling a publishable manuscript. The bag sat on the floor of my study for six months before I could approach its contents. I am a classic case of the procrastinating scholar, but in this case there was much more involved than just my usual delays. I dreaded the task, because I knew that Lindon's words would bring back visual, mental, and aural memories of our nearly twenty-year friendship.

I still recall the brilliantly clear, December day in 1989 at the Modern Language Association Convention in Washington, D.C., when Brook Thomas and I interviewed Lindon for the position he would begin at the University of California, Irvine, in the fall of 1990. A young scholar just finishing his PhD dissertation at the University of Pennsylvania, Lindon had distinguished himself from the hundreds of applications we had received from around the world. That day, Lindon convinced us of his rightness for our position in African American Literature in the Department of English and Comparative Literature by changing our thinking about African American modernism from a subset of American literature into a field that both subverted and transformed its encompassing discipline. It was the beginning of our long friendship, based on shared intellectual interests.

Happy as most of those memories are, I avoided them until December 2009, shortly after the fall semester had ended. As it turned out, the mental process of sorting through the manuscripts in the bag was not particularly complicated, despite my habitual impatience with editorial work. My psychological responses, however, were very complicated, and they surge up even now, nearly overcoming my ability to write about those first, painful days of unpacking Lindon's manuscripts.

There were several versions of each of the four textual chapters, but no extant version of an introduction. I am now convinced that Lindon had not yet written his introduction, waiting as many of us do to revise the entire manuscript before drafting an opening chapter that would forecast properly the relationships among the book's many parts. There were some variations in chapter titles but no evidence of parts or even loose pages from chapters other than these four. I am now convinced that these four chapters were the only chapters Lindon had written, even though he may have drafted other chapters or imagined certain essays published in or planned for scholarly journals to be possible parts of the final book.

I begin with a brief, descriptive catalogue of these chapters, in order to clarify some of the necessary editorial changes we have made in assembling this book and to explain my subsequent interpretation of Lindon's pioneering argument.

Chapter 1, "The Conceptual Impossibility of Racial Blackness: History, the Commodity, and Diasporic Modernity," traces modern conceptions of racial blackness from the beginnings of Euro-American imperialism in the Western Hemisphere through the seventeenth-century Atlantic slave trade and the mercantilist economy dependent on slavery up to the Federalist era (1780–1800) in early U.S. national politics. This chapter traces a historical trajectory—approximately 1500 to 1800—that links the origin of the U.S. nation (and its Constitutional avoidance of the immorality of its slave system) to European imperialism and the mercantilist economy supported by the slave trade.

Chapter 2, "Making the Flesh Word: Binomial Being and Representational Presence," focuses on the autobiography of Olaudah Equiano (1745?–1801), the African captured by slave traders in the Niger River region when he was ten years old, taken to the U.S. South, sold to a West Indian planter, who then worked aboard slave ships sailing between the Caribbean and England until he was nineteen. Buying his freedom, he continued his life as a merchant seaman and quartermaster for many years, working vigorously for the abolition of slavery, marrying an English woman, and serving as Commissary of Stores for freed slaves returning to Sierra Leone. His 1789 autobiography, *The Interesting Narrative of the Life of Olaudah Equiano, or Gustavus Vassa, the African*, is, of course, a famous account of the immorality of the slave trade, mercantilism's reliance on slavery, and the complicity of Equiano himself in the social, cultural, and economic consequences of this modern system. Equiano/Vassa's "binomial being" elaborates the social and psychological consequences of the Euro-American political economy of modernity outlined in the first chapter.

Chapter 3, "Captivity, Desire, Trade: The Forging of National Form," continues the discussion of Equiano/Vassa's autobiography, focusing on its role in the literary tradition as the most important eighteenth-century slave narrative in order for Lindon to set up the long tradition of the fugitive slave narrative in its pre-classic (prior to 1800), classic (1830–1865), and postbellum (1865 and later) versions. This chapter then turns to a number of fugitive slave narratives and related abolitionist texts from the classic period: William Grimes's *Narrative of the Life of William Grimes, the Runaway Slave* (1855); James Bradley's 1835 journalistic account of his own enslavement; David Walker's *Appeal to the Colored Citizens of the World, but in Particular, and Very Expressly to Those of the United States of*

America (1829); Frederick Douglass's *Narrative of the Life of Frederick Douglass, an American Slave, Written by Himself* (1845) and *My Bondage and My Freedom* (1855). These African American texts are interpreted in relation to the history of antebellum politics regarding slavery and abolition and such leading figures as William Lloyd Garrison, Ralph Waldo Emerson, and Anthony Burns, one of the first fugitives to test the Fugitive Slave Law (1850).

Chapter 4, "The Intimate Civic," is in several manuscript versions identified at the outset with the Roman numeral "V," suggesting this chapter was to be the *fifth*, rather than fourth, in the book's order. However, the preceding chapters are labeled I, II, and III, which seems to refute any claim that "The Intimate Civic" might have been conceived as chapter 5 *after* an "Introduction" was completed by Lindon (and thus numbered "Chapter 1"). Despite this break in sequence, "The Intimate Civic" appears to extend the argument of chapter 3. Just as chapter 3 begins with Equiano's autobiography, the central subject of chapter 2, so "The Intimate Civic" turns from the ways fugitive slave narratives negotiate political and legal rights to the personal and in some cases domestic issues facing African Americans in the antebellum period. Turning from Douglass's classic 1845 *Narrative* to Harriet Jacobs's *Incidents in the Life of a Slave Girl* (1861)—which receives central consideration in this chapter—Lindon also considers Mary Prince's *The History of Mary Prince, a West Indian Slave* (1831), Ellen and William Craft's *Running a Thousand Miles for Freedom* (1860), and James C. Pennington's *The Fugitive Blacksmith* (1849) as antebellum representations of how African American bodies connect both public and private rights in the struggle for the abolition of slavery and thus are foundational to the subsequent civil rights movement.

Chapter 5, "Modernism and the Affects of Racial Blackness," is not part of the book planned by Lindon. In addition to an introduction and conclusion, at least two other major sections seem to me to be conceptually missing from the book manuscript, both forecast by arguments in earlier chapters. Lindon concludes chapter 4 by commenting on how central the body would become to African American literature in the aftermath of Reconstruction and during the Jim Crow era, when laws would oppress, terrorize, and murder so many African Americans between the 1880s and 1940s. In the last pages of this chapter, Lindon refers specifically to Charles Chesnutt's *The House behind the Cedars* (1900), Pauline Hopkins's *Of One Blood* (1902–1903), James Weldon Johnson's *Autobiography of an Ex-Colored Man* (1912), and Nella Larsen's *Quicksand* (1928) and *Passing* (1929), as if anticipating their discussion in the next chapter, in which he would have carried the argument of the book through post-Reconstruction America to the beginnings of the Harlem Renaissance, the symbolic center of African American modernism. As readers of the book will notice, Lindon employs rhetorical transitions at the end of each of the first three chapters in which he identifies the literary works that will be discussed in the subsequent chapters. His list of the works at the end of chapter 3 (see above) thus seems to anticipate a lost or unwritten chapter 4 that focuses on the emergence of the Harlem Renaissance.

Among the few manuscripts, other than versions of the book chapters, included in the bag Winston gave me was "Modernism and the Affects of Racial Blackness," which focuses on the dispute between two important figures of the Harlem Renaissance: George Schuyler and Langston Hughes. Schuyler's critique of the African American avant-garde in his essay "The Negro-Art Hokum" (1926) and Hughes's response in "The Negro Artist and the Racial Mountain" (1926) provide a focus point to understand how African American artists and intellectuals imagined their relationship both to Western modernization and avant-garde cultural modernism.

It makes sense to me to include this substantial essay in *Racial Blackness and the Discontinuity of Western Modernity* even though it is unlikely he intended to use this essay as a chapter in this book. The essay does not adequately address the two most important historical and conceptual lacunae of the surviving manuscript: the late nineteenth- and early twentieth-century African American literary tradition (as well as the "third-stage" of the "fugitive slave narrative") and the cultural and geographically diverse modernist schools reductively treated under the heading of the Harlem Renaissance. Of course, recent scholarship divides these schools regionally into Harlem, Chicago, Los Angeles, and several other African American modernisms. Lindon's earlier discussion of nineteenth-century African American women writers, such as Harriet Jacobs, and his interest in the intersection of the racialization, sexualization, and gendering of the human body also suggest that this chapter (or perhaps chapters) would have dealt centrally with these issues. Although Schuyler and Hughes treat the U.S. social construction of race, neither author deals with gender or sexuality. We should not conclude, then, that the editorial addition of this essay as chapter 5 is in any way a proper substitution for what Lindon planned.

Because Lindon was in transition from one university position to another, many of us assumed there would be files of all the completed chapters in print or digital versions in the various recommendations required for his appointment at the University of California, Riverside, where Lindon moved in 2007, and in recent merit reviews at University of California, Irvine, where Lindon taught for nearly two decades. Katherine Kinney, Chair of English at UCR in 2009, was kind enough to search the departmental files, and Donna Iliescu, Program Manager when Lindon directed African American Studies at UCI, also searched her files. The graduate students at UCI who did so much to help his family and friends deal with the devastating news of his death have also been extremely helpful in searching their personal files and consulting with colleagues in hopes we might locate missing chapters. Katherine Kinney sent me a box of Lindon's manuscripts from UCR, and Janet Neary, who completed her PhD in English under Lindon's direction at UCI and is now an assistant professor at Hunter College, City University of New York, sent me several electronic files she and others had located. None of these sources, however, provided new material or information about Lindon's book. Of course, it is always possible that other versions, even new chapters, of this project will be discovered, but scholarship is also timely and subject to changes in methods and audiences. Lindon Barrett enjoyed a wide audience of interested scholars around the world. It thus seems appropriate to me and Dwight McBride, editor of this series, to publish this book, however incomplete, while those readers remain interested in Lindon's work. Neither of us would have been able to do this work without the assistance of Justin A. Joyce, a postdoctoral research scholar at Northwestern University, who digitized the hardcopy of the manuscript and copyedited it while also completing a PhD and beginning his scholarly career.

Lindon Barrett is one of the leading scholars and theorists in African American Studies. *Blackness and Value: Seeing Double* has contributed significantly to the reconceptualization of African American critical theory in the generation of scholars who succeeded influential figures like Henry Louis Gates Jr. and Houston Baker, formerly Lindon's Dissertation Chair at the University of Pennsylvania. Gates and Baker established themselves and contemporary African American Studies by adapting Continental theories to African American cultural texts. Lindon's generation learned from these influential scholars but went beyond them by identifying within African American culture its own theoretical, speculative, and philosophical resources.

Having initiated this work of revaluation in his first book, Lindon turned to an ambitious intellectual project for *Racial Blackness and the Discontinuity of Western Modernity*. Even in its unfinished state, the manuscript is an extraordinary accomplishment, because it provides a historically thick interpretation of how modern slavery and capitalism developed in conjunction. Traditionally considered a feudal institution, slavery and its concomitants—economic, political, and social racism—have gradually come to be understood as crucial tools in capitalism's control of class hierarchies and, of course, capital itself. Rather than simply accepting this conventional observation, Lindon returns to the Atlantic slave trade and its economic twin, seventeenth-century transatlantic mercantilism.

The phrase "Discontinuity of Western Modernity" in Lindon's title is indebted to Michel Foucault's theoretical conception of modernity as an epistemic rupture in European history, which Foucault traces back to the Renaissance. Despite recent revisionary efforts to interpret Foucault as an early critic of European imperialism and racism, Foucault actually has relatively little to say about both subjects. What W. E. B. Du Bois understood as modern racism, which Du Bois traced to Enlightenment reason, begins for Lindon with the division of the Americas in the imperial partitioning of the Western Hemisphere by European powers in the sixteenth century. Although Lindon does not cite the Argentine historian Rodolfo Kusch, the Mexican Marxists Enrique Dussel and Edmundo O'Gorman, and Walter Mignolo, he is following their groundbreaking equation of modernity with European imperial expansion, rather than any particular technological developments. In fact, the so-called "Conquest" had little to do with technical innovations in navigation, military arms, or maritime science; Columbus, Cortès, and Pizarro were relying on technologies known to Europeans since the later Middle Ages.

What motivated modernity was an economic, social, and political need for state legitimation, exemplified by Mignolo in the struggles of Ferdinand and Isabella to consolidate two small kingdoms, Castile and Aragon, into the modern Spanish state.[1] One crucial means of achieving such state legitimacy was to demonstrate a divinely ordained destiny of "ethnic" superiority—keeping in mind here the Greek root of "ethnos" as referring both to foreign and to state identities. Thus the expulsion of the "heathen" Moors from Iberia and the "discovery" of "primitive" peoples in Africa, the Western Hemisphere, and subsequently around the globe provided economic and ideological means of legitimating fledgling states, like Portugal and Spain and England, whose royal sovereignties would lay the foundations for their subsequent nations.

Within this logic, "racial blackness" is "impossible" in two very different senses. If we are thinking reasonably, then "racial blackness" as a category of inferiority makes no rational sense, if only because of the radical diversity of the peoples so designated in the European imperial imaginary. Of course, "racial blackness" is socially constructed and in obviously ignorant ways, so that Arawaks in the Caribbean and sub-Saharan Africans were equated by European conquerors and slave traders. The coalition of peoples Du Bois designates in his phrase "Equatorial Brown Belt" is clearly intended to suggest a critical response to the Euro-American construction of "racial blackness" as a global category. In the second sense, "racial blackness" is "impossible" to think within the West, because non-Europeans have been structurally excluded from the regime of Reason and thus by perverse logic are "incapable" of its protocols. Mignolo notes that the sixteenth- and seventeenth-century Spanish were so intent on defining "Indios" as "barbaric" that they destroyed systematically the pictographic texts of the Mexicas/Aztecs—the vast store of "books" the Spanish burned and otherwise banned as works of the Devil, which had they survived would have testified to a different regime of Reason, capable of its own elaborate (and often just as terrifying) semiotic codes.[2]

The preposterous equation of peoples as different as Africans and "Indians" as "sín razon" reduced them to the legal status of commodities so that they might be genocidally "worked to death." For instance, the Spaniards literally worked to death "Indians" in mines, such as the silver mines of Potosí in the Andes, so rapidly—a depopulation accelerated by the spread of European diseases—as to require the importation of African slave labor. Yet it was not just such horrible exigency that gave rise to modern racism, but the a priori demand of an economic system that distinguished between rulers and the ruled, between "owners" and "owned," later between capitalists and workers. Despite the "discontinuity of Western modernity," once initiated such modernity has a genealogy that can be understood only by studying the integral roles of slavery and racism.

It is thus not at all surprising that the vigorously anticolonial nations that would emerge in the Western Hemisphere in the late eighteenth and early nineteenth centuries should proclaim loudly their hatred of European colonialism while promptly competing with and imitating their former masters. From Hamilton and Jefferson's Federalism to Bolívar's English-style plan for Gran Colombia, what Benedict Anderson terms the "Creole Pioneers" of these new nations refined the racial categories of their colonial rulers, even as they framed their own Constitutions and protection of civil rights on freedom from colonial slavery and equality for all.[3] Such a long, transnational history of modern racism's role in Euro-American imperialism and capitalism explains that the failure of the U.S. founders to abolish slavery is by no means an oversight or exception but is integral to the phantasmatic structure of the modern U.S. nation.

Under what conditions, then, can the "fugitive" and then "emancipated" subject of this racial regime "represent" himself or herself? In chapter 2, Lindon turns to the "binomial being" occupied by Equiano of Niger and Vassa of Great Britain, using this "double consciousness" as an index of the ontological and epistemological problems facing the racialized subject from the Enlightenment to the present. The socially and economically imposed schizophrenia Equiano/Vassa represents as his "being" is compounded and multiplied in the variety of "fugitive slave narratives" in the "classic period" (1830–1865). The focus of chapter 3, "Captivity, Desire, Trade: The Forging of National Form," is less on these remarkable narratives than it is on the extraordinarily contradictory legal, economic, and political means employed by the U.S. state to control and suppress the bids for basic human rights represented in these fugitive slave narratives and complementary efforts to abolish slavery.

The antebellum period is defined by a series of congressional acts and legal decisions—ranging from the Missouri Compromise of 1820 to the Compromise of 1850 and its rider, the Fugitive Slave Bill, to the Kansas-Nebraska Act of 1854 and the Supreme Court's Dred Scott Decision of 1857. Like the crazy quilt of federal Indian laws in the nineteenth and twentieth centuries, the state's efforts to regulate "racial blackness" betray how the concept itself (its "impossibility") subverts all U.S. efforts to claim protection of "inalienable human rights." Instead, civil society is maintained only by the violence of slavery and postbellum racial terror, whereby aspirants to basic human rights are violently kept in their places.

What Foucault considers the modern state's regime of "disciplining and punishing" its citizen-subjects applies with even greater violence to those "minoritized" and rendered "eccentric" even when granted the status of what Etienne Balibar terms "citizen subjects."[4] For Foucault the practices of disciplining subjects involves the formation of personal habits, much as parents might discipline their children in an effort to get those children to conform to behavioral norms. In terms of African Americans struggling for basic human rights in the nineteenth-century United States, such discipline involves adaptation to white, middle-class conventions of personal and family life; conventions utilized by a slavocracy that did everything possible to deprive African Americans under its violent regimes. Thus Jacobs ends her account of Linda Brent's struggle for freedom in *Incidents in the Life of a Slave Girl* by refusing to "marry" Linda Brent in some respectable fashion, reminding us how Brent had indeed found in her marriage to Mr. Sands simply another betrayal at the family level equivalent to the broader betrayal of African Americans by slavery as an institution. Whereas Douglass ends his 1845 *Narrative* by proudly displaying his wedding certificate and aspiring to white, middle-class respectability in the North, Jacobs exposes the racism that poisons northern social relations and makes "family life" an impossible, even undesirable choice.[5]

We are brought, then, to the enduring problem—or in Du Bois's famous formulation, "what it *feels like* to be a problem"—not only of how the African American can represent himself or herself in this "American world," but how he/she is related to its prevailing, essential "modernity."[6] The subtitle of Paul Gilroy's *The Black Atlantic* is "Modernity and Double Consciousness," and in addition to Gilroy's interpretation of Du Bois's use of the key concept of "double consciousness" in *The Souls of Black Folk* (1903), Gilroy wants to show how the "double consciousness" of the "racialized subject"—that "impossible" subject, after all, who cannot even be *imagined* in his or her subjectivity by Western modernity—has contributed as much, perhaps even more, to a genuine modernization of the world than his or her oppressors.[7]

This subject would have been the focus of Lindon's unfinished work on the Harlem Renaissance, in which the problem of *how* to represent the racialized subject's relationship to modernity would have been central. We see some of this work in "Modernism and the Affects of Racial Blackness," the essay on Schuyler's and Hughes's different views of how African Americans ought to respond to the cultural avant-garde. Contrasting George Schuyler's criticism in "The Negro Art-Hokum" of the avant-garde pretensions of the Harlem Renaissance with Langston Hughes's "The Negro Artist and the Racial Mountain" and its advocacy of a distinctly African American cultural modernism, Lindon suggests what fuller chapters on fin de siècle African American literature and the Harlem Renaissance would have demonstrated. Whereas Schuyler champions adaptation to "American" bourgeois conventionality—what Existentialism would criticize as *la vie quotidienne*, perhaps exemplified by white-bread America of the 1950s—Hughes struggles to define an African American modernism that would challenge modernization (and its racial regimes) in ways far more challenging than the most avant-garde styles of Pound, Eliot, Stein, the Cubists, and the Surrealists. Lindon argues that in works like *Not without Laughter* (1930) and *The Ways of White Folks* (1934), Hughes endorses a utopian ideal of African American social relations—recognizing how its cultural vitality and political commitments have so often been stereotyped and primitivized—that would counter the entropic tendency of a Euro-American modernity doomed by its racial logic and the ghosts of its imperial genealogy. When I write "ghosts," I do so following Lindon's use of ghosts as a metaphorical recalling of the millions who suffered and died during the Middle Passage and centuries of slavery and racism in the Americas.

Of course, the debate between Schuyler and Hughes hardly represents the enormous diversity of cultural, political, economic, and personal views we now know are designated inadequately as the Harlem Renaissance. An informed and committed queer theorist, Lindon certainly would have wanted to include the challenges posed both to modernity and middle-class African American heteronormativity by queer African Americans, like Claude McKay, as well as the queer intersection of white and African American communities, such as Carl Van Vechten facilitated, enabling possible transformations of modern conventionality and its racial categories. Years later in *Mumbo Jumbo*, Ishmael Reed would mock the American version of *la vie quotidienne* as the "Atonist conspiracy," punning on white atonal tendencies—an inability to hear as much as to see other cultures—and Egyptian Atonism as the first sign of a troubling Western monotheism.[8] Far more seriously, Lindon would have interpreted the cultural and political richness of African American modernism as an alternative to the modern America that would lead us into such Cold War follies as Korea and Vietnam and such neo-imperial disasters as wars in the Persian Gulf and Afghanistan, as well as such foolishness as the Edsel, the Hula Hoop, and credit default swaps.

Lindon's book will have a major influence on contemporary debates regarding modern capitalism and its reliance on what David Theo Goldberg has termed "the racial state."[9] At the time of this writing, as regulation of Wall Street slowly makes its way through Congress with its provisions gradually eroded by lobbyists for the banking industry, the more pressing issues of the recent financial meltdown go unnoticed and unattended. We have forgotten already that the contemporary mortgage crisis has its roots in the Clinton administration's efforts to increase home ownership among low-income, especially minority citizens, many of whom were formerly "redlined" out of affordable markets. Relaxing various rules governing home mortgage qualification, the Clinton administration unwittingly allowed the financial industry to invent a dizzying array of incomprehensible lending instruments, as well as to falsify credit and employment records to qualify borrowers incapable of repaying such home loans. Conservatives have sought to place the blame on borrowers who signed and thus should be responsible for such loans, but such scapegoating seems foolhardy at best when the textual ambiguities of an adjustable-rate mortgage at the height of the mortgage lending bubble outdo the most challenging poststructuralist theory.

Lindon's book tells us nothing practical about financial derivatives, credit default swaps, or the bankruptcies of Bear Stearns and Lehmann Brothers, but instead offers a broader theoretical and philosophical interpretation of how the Capitalist State continues to commodify human beings, perhaps no longer in overt forms of slavery but certainly by way of an economic class system whose fantastic disparities are maintained by a profusion of cultural productions holding us in its thrall. Slavery was not an oversight of the founding fathers, subsequently corrected in that second revolution, the U.S. Civil War and abolition; slavery remains an integral part of a capitalist system dependent on racial, sexual, and class hierarchies to maintain its power. If the United States is indeed the leader of the modern world system as our occupations of Iraq and Afghanistan seem to confirm, then the United States, not South Africa (Goldberg's principal example), is the perverse model for the modern racial state. Lindon Barrett's *Racial Blackness and the Discontinuity of Western Modernity* helps us understand the modern history that brought the United States to this situation, even as we congratulate ourselves for having elected our first "African American" president. The critical task of *reforming* such a social, political, and economic fantasy is another, even more difficult challenge.

John Carlos Rowe

Notes

1. Walter Mignolo, *The Darker Side of the Renaissance: Literacy, Territoriality, and Colonization*, 2nd ed. (Ann Arbor: University of Michigan Press, 2003), 126–27.

2. *Ibid.*, 162.

3. Benedict Anderson, *Imagined Communities: Reflections on the Origin and Spread of Nationalism*, rev. ed. (London: Verso, 2006), 49–68.

4. Michel Foucault, *Discipline and Punish: The Birth of the Prison* (New York: Random House, 1977); Etienne Balibar, "Citizen Subject," *Who Comes after the Subject?* ed. Eduardo Cadava, Peter Connor, and Jean-Luc Nancy (London: Routledge, 1991), 48–59.

5. John Carlos Rowe, *At Emerson's Tomb: The Politics of Classic American Literature* (New York: Columbia University Press, 1997), 143.

6. W. E. B. Du Bois, *The Souls of Black Folk* (New York: Penguin, 1989), 13.

7. Paul Gilroy, *The Black Atlantic: Modernity and Double Consciousness* (Cambridge: Harvard University Press, 1993), 111–45.

8. Ishmael Reed, *Mumbo Jumbo* (New York: Bantam, 1973).

9. David Theo Goldberg, *The Racial State* (Oxford: Blackwell, 2001).

Racial Blackness and the Discontinuity of Western Modernity

CHAPTER 1

The Conceptual Impossibility of Racial Blackness

History, the Commodity, and Diasporic Modernity

One formula for specifying Western modernity is: the historical environment that reports the threshold between the materiality of the body and the abstracted forces of sociopolitical coordination as the trace of subjectivity—the discursive constituting the relays of these relations. Michel Foucault presents this model by offering the concept of the episteme, the concept by which "[discontinuity] . . . has now become one of the basic elements of historical analysis."[1] In short, the historical disjunction of Western modernity remains its emphatic characteristic.

Assuming this model, in *The Anatomy of Power: European Constructions of the African Body*, psychologist Alexander Butchart emphasizes the later turn of Foucault's work. However, Butchart identifies the historical disjunction of modernity in the co-implications of the ostensibly rational, classifactory discipline of the modern episteme with the emergent circumstances of the intercontinental exchange adamantly conscripting African and African-derived bodies for the formalization of the interwoven economic, social, political, and subjective articulations of modernity. Subtending the argument is the recognition that the partitioning and reorganization of the hemisphere of the Americas constitutes the fundamental, ongoing event of Western modernity. This event begins earnestly in the sixteenth century and remains the extended geopolitical episode that, as dramatically as it revises systems of world trade and the mechanics of state powers, revises the materiality of the body and the relations of the body to the discursive mechanisms by which it is socially apprehended and managed in the modern exclusive paradigms of personhood. Although the geographic, political-economic, and socio-psychic palimpsest is intricate, what is certain is that these coordinated transformations remain as racialized as they are far-flung.

The parallel micropolitical and macropolitical progresses of Western modernity illustrate the point. While human corporeality emerges at the micropolitical level as a discrete catalogue serving as well as obfuscating the economic and social management of mass populations, at the macropolitical level the transforming and emergent metropoles along the Atlantic coastlines of Europe and the "New World" forge their exemplary modern profiles by means of the immense surplus values depending on the depletion and the disordering of the political jurisdictions along the Senegambian, Guinean, and west-central African coastlines as well as the stark regimes of enforced labor in the Americas. In the words of the historian Walter Rodney, the peculiarity is the criterion by which almost no "human suffering was too high to pay for the monetary gain from trade in slaves and from the extension of capitalist production into the New World."[2] Insofar as racial blackness forms the historical and enabling point of "dis/integration" for the paradigms of Western modernity and, in this way, seems an eccentricity of the modern, the violent historical forging of the African diasporic communities of the Americas discloses the conceptual impossibility to be, on the contrary, the reported beneficence of modern "civic animation," the consolidated macropolitical and micropolitical determinations by which the modern remains viable. For at stake originally as the "modern" is the animation of a conceptual form—the commodity—as the principle of economic (and general) rationality, in the face of the already fully animate individual and collective forms—in human proportions—of racial blackness. The perplexity is, at once, phantasmatic, geopolitical, economic, and racial, because the impossibility of racial blackness seeming to lie within the limits of the economic fundament of the modern West as well as the limits of modern social and psychic rudiments belies the signal importance of the emergent circumstances of the concept of racial blackness: the rise of the Atlantic system of trade on which the articulation of the modern depends.

Butchart, introducing his argument, writes: "Foucault argued that all methods of knowing the human body related to it not as a means of discovery against an object waiting to be known, but as a productive power towards an object that is its effect. The concept defining this productive relationship between method and object is 'disciplinary power.'"[3] The argument understands that the infrequently examined *proposition* of racial blackness is fully insinuated in the historical contingencies developing disciplinary power for, as Butchart states, "[r]oughly coinciding with the European colonization of Africa, the age of Renaissance thought gave way from the mid-seventeenth century to the age of Classification."[4] The Foucauldian declension that Butchart executes specifies racial blackness as fundamental to the cognitive and cultural events recasting Western notions of the body from "a complex interplay of invisible elements, virtues, and spirits that united it to the irreducible 'soul' and inscribed their signatures in the body's members" to "a collection of overtly perceptible external organs—noses, teeth, hands, the skin, the feet, the genitalia, the breasts and so on" and subsequently "a three-dimensional anatomical interior possessed of organs such as the heart, the lungs, the spleen, the kidney or the brain."[5] This thesis takes for granted the European Renaissance and Enlightenment as residuals of the material as well as conceptual relations that place the emergent economies of the Atlantic arena as the chief concern of European acquisitiveness and contemplation, admitting, furthermore, that the materialities of African and African diasporic peoples are crucial to the interwoven economic, epistemological, and political constructions inaugurating the modern West. Put most simply, the material catalogue of the body as a conceptual point coincides with the material catalogue of the body as an emphatically consequential racial point.

Butchart's argument replicates and extends two preeminent principles of Foucault's theoretical paradigm: the "constructivist" conceptual turn that analytically equivocates the body as simply sentience and, second, the epistemic character of the notion of "disciplinary power," its consolidations signaling the modern historical disjunction. Cultural theorist Francis Barker in *The Tremulous Private Body* provides a summation of the first principle, the "constructivist" conception of the body:

> However necessary it may be to isolate the body for analytical purposes, the body in question is not a hypostasized object, still less a simple biological mechanism of given desires and needs acted on externally by controls and enticements, but a relation of liaisons which are material, discursive, psychic, sexual, but without stop or centre. It would be better to speak of a certain "bodiliness" than of "the body." It is the instance of a suturing of discourse and desire to the organism . . . and thus fully social in its being and in its ideological valency. Rather than an extra-historical residue, invariant and mute, this body is as ready for coding and decoding, as intelligible both in its presence and its absence, as any of the more frequently recognized historical objects. The site of an operation of power, of an exercise of meaning.[6]

These constructivist tenets aim to isolate the appearance of the body in the discourses that instantiate disciplinary power, the developmental line that provides the temporal aspect of the Foucauldian paradigm. In *Race and the Education of Desire: Foucault's History of Sexuality and the Colonial Order of Things*, anthropologist and historian Ann Stoler profoundly reconfigures this temporal aspect by considering at the same time the openly spatial aspects of the European imperial expansion co-extensive with the historical elaboration of disciplinary power. In this way, Stoler turns the Foucauldian paradigm to an analytical posture that must insist that race be considered effectively. The aim, she states, "is not to isolate racism's originary moment, much less to claim that all racisms are fundamentally the same. On the contrary," she explains further, "I grant slippage among the projects that modernity, the enlightenment and bourgeois liberalism embraced to make another sort of point, one that appreciates both how racial thinking harnesses itself to varied progressive projects and shapes the social taxonomies defining who will be excluded from them."[7]

Rather than self-evident forms of worldly agency, the human subject and the human body are precisely the enabling and exclusionary inventions of the modern episteme. To follow Butchart, the "epistemic space and the disjunction between epistemes cannot be explained through recourse to the human subject as a given and the human body as a constant."[8] Put differently, as René Descartes argues with revolutionary effect in the mid-seventeenth-century in *Meditations on First Philosophy*, the human subject is not a "natural" phenomenon at all, but rather the confounding, animating abstraction always ascertainable by its contradistinction to the natural, as most immediately represented by the material agency of the human body. The period of this re-imagination is also the period of the annexation of the Americas and the policies governing the opportunities to raise and traffic enormous quantities of goods in the new arena of the Atlantic economies, which transform the significance of the premodern axes of long-distance trade. The economic values of the emergent Atlantic economies abruptly eclipse those of the traffic of the Baltic Sea primarily in timber and fish, the trade in primarily the luxury items of fabrics and spices (including sugar) exchanged across the Mediterranean Sea, as well as the transfers of silk, lacquerware, coral, pearls, horses, wool, linen, and aromatics moving across the Indian Ocean as well as through the vast intercontinental arena of the silk roads. The newly promoted European desires for sugar and other tropical products that circulate in transatlantic relays following the fifteenth century formalize in the seventeenth and eighteenth centuries the enormous trade circuit termed the triangular trade, fusing the formerly disparate economies of the Americas, Western Europe, and the West African coast from Senegambia, Sierra Leone, the Windward and Gold Coasts, and the Bight of Benin, to Benguela beyond the Bight of Biafra, jurisdictions inhabited by Akans, Angolans, Ashante, Bambara, Igbo, Kongolese, Kru, Mandigas, Mende, Oyo, Vais, Yoruba, and others, who are hard pressed by the demands of the European modernity. In the triangular circuit of the new Atlantic economies, European manufactured objects are disposed of on the African coast in trade for slaves, who are shipped across the Atlantic as the requisite labor force for the massive production of the cash crops that in the final segment of the circuit are traded under the nationally protectionist policies of the European metropoles to serve the re-articulated desires of mass populations.

Because Foucauldian notions of disciplinary power diminish conceptualizations of modern power in terms of openly repressive forces, these circumstances mark the limit, or necessary point of supplementation, in Foucauldian paradigms—an issue that is increasingly recognized. For example, literary critic Lora Romero and postcolonial theorist Achille Mbembe eschew also what Butchart has called the "recourse to the human subject as a given and the human body as a constant,"[9] not primarily to codify affirmative systems of knowledge as does Foucault, but to disclose the profound structures of violence embedded in the modern epistemic break. Lora Romero in *Home Fronts*, her examination of nineteenth-century U.S. literary domesticity and sentimentality, observes:

> Conceiving modern power as the power to administer life rather than the power to inflict death would seem to require ignoring the genocidal animus which has characterized Western interaction with both Jews and people of color in the modern era. By emphasizing production, Foucauldian theory would seem unable to account for the racial holocausts that have punctuated the modern era and hence would seem necessarily to marginalize (if not to erase altogether) an important part of the history of Jews and the Third World."[10]

In the article "Necropolitics," Achille Mbembe draws the concatenation of the slave trade, plantation slavery, and the colony to define the fundamental insinuation of race with the abstract reason of Western modernity, and writes: "In fact, in most instances, the selection of races, the prohibition of mixed marriages, forced sterilization, even the extermination of vanquished peoples are to find their testing ground in the colonial world. Here we see the first syntheses between massacre and bureaucracy, that incarnation of Western rationality."[11] These refinements of the already revisionary approaches of Foucault to the historiography and the macro- and micropolitical relays of Western modern geopolitical power highlight the material and psychic violences of modernity that the epistemologies of modernity (more and less begrudgingly) refuse to acknowledge as fundamental to their articulation. In addition, Mbembe makes the point in relation to the work of Karl Marx—the preeminent materialist challenge to the idealist tendencies of Western thought: "That *race* (or for that matter *racism*) figures so prominently in the [historical] calculus of biopower is entirely justifiable. After all, more so than class-thinking (the ideology that defines history as an economic struggle of classes), race has been the ever present shadow in Western political thought and practice, especially when it comes to imagining the inhumanity of, or rule over, foreign peoples."[12] The racialized body and, in particular, the African and African diasporic body (conflated under the sign of racial blackness), provide these keen material determinants of Western modernity that are nonetheless rarely acknowledged in those terms.

The conceptual obfuscation, or upshot, is that the economic boon secured and re-secured by Europe and its outposts at each node of the Atlantic system of trade, the boon radically augmenting European diets, shipping, and markets, massively introduces sub-Saharan Africans and their descendants into the European "New World" or, differently put, into the newest mechanism of European viability and, as forcefully, into individual and collective European imaginations. In the study *A History of the European Economy, 1000–2000*, economic historian François Crouzet glosses these transformations as follows:

> Indeed, it has been maintained that Europe enriched itself and accumulated capital, thanks to its superiority in military and business technology, at the expense of the rest of the world, through the looting and mining of precious metals in America; the cultivation of plantations in the West Indies and the southern continental colonies by slaves (slavery is a theft of labor), on land stolen from Native Americans; and the gains of the slave trade. Though slavery is by no means specific to European expansion (it had existed for millennia in many regions, including Africa), the slave trade from Africa is a critical problem. It was established to provide manpower for plantations (mainly sugar plantations) in America. As plantations' slaves generally suffered a heavy demographic deficit, with a large excess of deaths over births, an increasing and massive transatlantic forced migration of labor took place: it is accepted that 11 to 12 million Africans were forcibly deported across the Atlantic from the 1400s to the 1800s. (About the same number was carried across the Indian Ocean by Muslim traders, but over a longer period). The average death rate during those voyages was 14 percent.[13]

The effect of these economic transformations exceeds simple economic principles, witnessed, for example, by the more empirical turn of the aesthetic evident in seventeenth-century Dutch still-life painting or, as dramatically, the development of the leviathan national bureaucracies calculating and intervening in the new circulation of the escalating Atlantic economic values.

The phantasmatic contours of modern subjectivity are insinuated also in these effects. Historian David Eltis, in the article "Europeans and the Rise and Fall of African Slavery: An Interpretation," draws this compound economic and imaginative impress disposing sub-Saharan Africans and their descendants in the European modernity. Historian David Northrup's *Africa's Discovery of Europe: 1450–1850* provides a cognate of Eltis's argument, because of the longstanding cultural and commercial relations between European and African peoples that the Atlantic slave trade revises starkly. Nonetheless, rehearsing in particular the unpursued and potentially far greater economic promise of European enslavement in the Americas, Eltis queries "which groups are considered eligible for enslavement" in the mercantilist era and its aftermath.[14] He proposes that the "crux of the matter is shipping costs, which comprised by far the greater part of the price of any form of imported bonded labor in the Americas."[15] The scope of Eltis's argument, rather than bound by national jurisdictions, is international, in order to demonstrate "that economic motivation should be assigned a subsidiary role in the rise and fall of the exclusively African-based bondage that Europeans carried across the Atlantic."[16] The shorter voyage from Europe to the Americas, the less closely packed ships of these routes, the lower mortality and morbidity rates in North as opposed to South Atlantic transportation, and the accessibility to European convict labor given that major European population centers abut navigable waterways, Eltis argues, attest to the far-from-complete role of economics in the arraignment of mercantilist labor forces. Rather, Eltis states, "The most cursory examination of relative costs suggests that European slaves should have been preferred to either European indentured labor or African slaves."[17]

The confluence of imagination, economics, and race is plain: "The most that can be said by way of comparison is that the spread of African slavery in the Americas coincided with the spread of forced labor in punishment systems within Europe (transportation in the English case). But no one was in any doubt about the distinctions between the two."[18] The ultimate point is that the "absence of European slaves, like the dog that did not bark, is perhaps the clue to understanding the slave trade and the system it supported."[19] The more than simply economic question foregrounds the imagination of the European subject, as well as attendant political and material forces, the quandary being "that the peoples with the most advanced capitalist culture, the Dutch and the English, were also the Europeans least likely to subject their own citizens to enforced labor," circumstances disclosing that "the celebration of British liberties—more specifically, liberties for Englishmen—depended on African slavery."[20]

Drawing a circumference around the entire Atlantic circuit, Eltis's argument extrapolates in important ways the thesis of historian Edmund Morgan's *American Slavery, American Freedom: The Ordeal of Colonial Virginia*, broadening the thesis so as to encompass the psychic and political subjectivity of modernizing Europe generally. In sum, the thesis of Morgan's classic examination of colonial Virginia is "not . . . that belief in republican ideology had to rest on slavery, but only that in Virginia (and probably in other southern colonies) it did."[21]

Eltis's more general rendition of the principle bears noting: If, in the episode of mercantile capitalism, the "early modern Europeans shifted property rights in labor toward the individual and away from the community,"[22] then, as clearly, these reorganizations shift property rights in labor (as well as in epistemological and cultural systems) across continental divisions: toward Europe and the Americas and away from the west coast of Africa. The Atlantic accessibility of the African continent provides the means for dismantling the longstanding systems of property rights, of commercial trade, legal and penal systems, and intercultural contact of the self-governing jurisdictions arrayed along the broad continental swath in which, in the words of economists Henry Gemery and Jan Hogendorn, "few—perhaps no—West African peoples appear to have been living on the very margin of subsistence during the eighteenth century . . . [for] research almost always seems to disclose some surplus output and some interregional trade even in the most isolated areas."[23] In short, the modern transfer of rights toward the European(ized) individual and away from the community has patent inverse effects on the eastern and western arcs of the Atlantic rim. Summarily stated, the fact that the modern "individual" and its revolutionary civic and political protocols did not precede the transfer of rights from the community to the individual, or from the eastern to the western arcs of the Atlantic, reveals plainly the powerful turns of the imagination that accrue along the western rim of the Atlantic in the modernizing centers of Europe and its outposts—fully in tandem with the vast economic values in question.

The modernity of individual psychic positions is forged from the very same enterprise as the modernity of mercantilist agendas as well as their revised, dramatic, and exorbitant nationalisms. For these reasons, the conceit of racial blackness, which indiscriminately catalogues dark-skinned Africans and their descendants, can be understood as a powerful analog of the complex of commodity fetishism. That is, the extended quarantining of the African-derived population largely and effectively promotes key turns of the imagination that naturalize the gulf between the social conditions of the labor yielding the commodity for exchange and the failure of the commodity to resemble those conditions in the exchange—in other words, the dissemblance by which it is not as readily apparent that what passes as rational economic transactions always dispossess some of the parties attendant to the exchange. In the most routine protocols of the Atlantic economies, the difference of phenotypes hyperbolically redacts the diacritical positions on either side of the commodity form, positions opposed as production and consumption. The difference of phenotypes in these turns of mind *naturalizes* the co-implicated subjective and economic feints of commodity fetishism, which is to say, the misperception that "producers" and "consumers" contend equally within the interests of modern market relations. These turns of the imagination are racialized in key, stark ways for the modern West, because of the radical modern dispositions of populations according to continental origin. These radical dispositions dichotomize Europe and Africa, consumption and production, supervision and subordination, reason and unreason as indices of race within the modern circumstances of unprecedented demographic proximities. On this point historian Robin Blackburn notes, importantly: "Although data on the immigration of free persons to the Americas are much less precise, it seems probable that enslaved African immigrants to the New World outnumbered Europeans by about four or five to one during the eighteenth century."[24]

This is to say that, as opposed to the occurrences in Europe and the Americas, the personal securities of the populations of the various polities along the coast of West Africa "evaporated to facilitate a trade that was a constant threat to their existence."[25] For instance, Senegambia, the northernmost coastal region disrupted in the vast triangulation of the Atlantic economies, includes the polities of the Bijangos, Mande, and Mandingas, among others, and, although it is the region that supplies the least number of enslaved conscripts to the expansion of capital accumulation, it nonetheless registers fully the effects of the international violence. Beyond the widespread warfare that does not arise necessarily from—but necessarily inflames—regional political animosities, a variety of legal and extralegal threats reorganizes and frustrates quotidian life across the Senegambia: Various systems of land tenure, based on land stewardship by the nobility (Papels) or reciprocal labor (Balantas), are compromised; penal systems are recalculated in order to broaden and expedite the possibilities of seizure for enslavement; the means of exploiting personal and class rivalries expand enormously; the enticements to lawlessness, such as kidnapping, alter both personal and organized political calculations. Most important, drawing the region into even greater entanglements with the European and "New World" ideally infinite arena of ideally infinite exchange, the enveloping threat to travel and unfamiliar intercourse weakens the internal commercial relations of the Senegambia. The disruption of the political economies along the lower Guinea and west-central coasts, territories of the Angolans, Kongolese, Oyo, Yoruba, and others, is even more acute, providing "ample proof that the economic pull of the American market could force a fundamental change within Africa."[26] The volume, rapidity, and high consequence of the overwhelming transfer of the African labor forces to the western rim of the Atlantic is noted by historian Paul Lovejoy:

> The largest exporting region in the early seventeenth century is west-central Africa, which continued sending thousands of slaves a year to the Americas, thus consolidating a pattern that began a century earlier. Senegambia and Benin maintained their relatively modest share of the trade as well, each providing about a thousand slaves a year. Slaves came from elsewhere too. The really dramatic expansion of the Atlantic trade began after 1650, and from then slave exports affected ever larger parts of Africa, not just the Kongo region. In the last fifty years of the seventeenth century, more slaves were sold to Europeans on the Atlantic coast than in the previous two hundred years combined. This phenomenal growth was a response to the spread of plantation slavery in the Americas. From the 1640s through the 1660s, sugar spread from Brazil to the lesser Antilles—Barbados, Martinique, Guadeloupe, St. Kitts, Antigua—and these new colonies acquired tens of thousands of slaves. The figure of the third quarter of the seventeenth century was double the previous twenty-five year period, averaging 17,700 per year, while in the last quarter, almost 30,000 slaves

> were exported annually. By now sugar plantations were being established on Jamaica and Saint Domingue, which rapidly became the two largest producers of sugar. As a result, the dramatic surge in slave exports continued into the eighteenth century, reaching figures in the order of 61,000 slaves per year for the whole century.[27]

Moreover, it is important to understand that the violence of the Atlantic conscription is neither random nor absolute. Lovejoy notes the closely deliberative aspects of the undermining of the political jurisdictions of the coast: "The introduction of new crops from the Americas increased food production and thereby helped to maintain population levels despite the export of slaves. Advances in commercial institutions including credit facilities, currency, bulking, and regularized transportation, assisted in the movement of slaves."[28] In short, while the intrusive transatlantic contact "implies disorder in the social framework wherever the external trade was important, the effective organization of slave supply required that political violence be contained within boundaries that would permit the sale of slaves abroad."[29] On this point, Achille Mbembe's acknowledgment of the relations between massacre, bureaucracy, and Western rationality is trenchant. The phantasmatic quality of these equations, directly yielding the social policies naturalizing "race," and finally also exceeding any manifest economic rationalizations, re-order the most fundamental conceptual systems of medieval European societies and their predecessors.

The certainty is that "[t]he export of about 11.3 million slaves from 1500 to 1800, including the astronomical increase between 1650 and 1800 in the Atlantic sector, could not have occurred without the transformation of the African political economy."[30] This fact is corroborated by Gemery and Hogendorn, who construct a hypothetical West African economy as it might have existed outside of the slave trade in order to make a comparison with the actual economic outcomes of the episode. They measure the net economic loss to the region based on five factors: the levels of subsistence production under both economies, the average surplus production per person above subsistence requirements, the longer working life of those transported to and enslaved in the Americas, morality during slave acquisition and delivery prior to the transatlantic transportation, and the greater economic contributions of the younger, more productive, more highly conscripted groups of the labor force. They write: "Any one of these independent factors . . . would in itself convert the net impact of the slave trade into an economic loss for West Africa. The implication is overwhelming that when these factors are taken in combination, the economic costs of the trade exceeded its gains on an overall basis. Let us reemphasize that this conclusion is reached without any reference to the massive intangible costs of the trade."[31]

The crucial criterion or conceit in these circumstances—racial blackness—proves the decisive point of nullification in the geopolitical, economic, and phantasmatic confluence that ultimately betrays the large co-extensiveness of the modern market, which can be defined as the ideally infinite arena of ideally infinite exchange, and modern subjectivity, which can be defined as the animating series of relays reconciling the body to the demands and yields of the material and social environment, which in modernity always already supports the exorbitant formation of the abstract marketplace. This is to say, the epistemic discontinuity identified by the Foucauldian paradigm exceeds the explanatory power of that paradigm insofar as discursive archives are adamantly foregrounded as the genealogical index of the discontinuity, rather than the revolutionary economic principles deeply co-implicated with the epistemologies and interpellations of the modern.

One possible revision of Foucauldian theory might stand as follows: Premodern sovereign power positions finally the visage, figure, and personage of the monarch (occasionally rendered as a divinely and spectacularly destructive principle) as the phantasm investing the imperative toward social order of even the most distantly situated subordinates of the sovereign. Modern disciplinary power, on the contrary, figures the alternative phantasm investing the imperative toward social order of even its most distantly situated subordinates as the more acutely abstract and more acutely determined force of "capital," a principle of sustenance and destruction never having—in either the micropolitical or macropolitical situation—easy singularity or anthropomorphic spectacularity, like the monarch. If the epistemic rule of sovereign power specifies the social order as a manifest descending dynamic, then, inaugurated in coincidence with the episode of European mercantile capitalism, disciplinary power specifies the social order as a less manifest, multiply refracted diffusion of power upheld by all the agents enmeshed in the distributive networks of "capital." This transformation, in one aspect, refigures the cultural lineaments of the "body," securing it as the mechanism coveted for the work of "capital," and yielding, as one of its most productive corollaries, the "ontological" condition of racial blackness as one key index of the body as a new material catalogue. Both channels—the imagination and commerce—transact these points of modern understanding that remain far from merely reasonable.

Because, therefore, the modern appearance of African and African-derived bodies must be reckoned in the concomitant economic and epistemological terms, the neo-Marxist paradigms address well the limitations of the Foucauldian paradigm. For these models detect and theorize the inexorable structures of domination and exploitation codifying the modern and, therefore, openly inflect the communicative, commercial, and social alterations accelerating after the European Renaissance—its anthropomorphic, market, and psychic rationalities—with the strict material and imaginative violences on which they depend and tend to accelerate. As already suggested, the concept of commodity fetishism proves exemplary. In the article "Marxian Value Theory and the Problem of the Subject," economists Jack Amariglio and Antonio Callari argue that the concept of commodity fetishism provides a succinct rendition of the Marxist codification of subjectivity. "Marx," they write, "has had a theory of the subject, the theory of commodity fetishism. To the extent that it attempts to conjoin the analysis of commodity production and circulation with a discussion of 'ideology,' commodity fetishism does discuss the peculiar subjectivity typical of capitalist social formations."[32] In particular, Amariglio and Callari point out that the Marxist understanding of "socially necessary labor time" as the essential value masked in commodity fetishism clarifies the subjectivizing force of the modern market, which is to say, the imperatives "naturalizing" the difference between the social conditions of the labor yielding the commodity and the failure of the commodity to resemble those conditions in the exchange. In this way, "the act of exchange is not simply the site of an economic process but also one of the key locations within capitalism where a symbolic order is particularly constituted and learned."[33] The concept of commodity fetishism describes the phantasmatic torque of rational exchanges so as to abrogate, in the words of Amariglio and Callari, the "unnecessary gulf [that] has come to exist between two important areas of theoretical work in contemporary Marxism, with the theory of value (the economics, if you will) on one side and the nature and role of subjectivity (an antieconomism) on the other."[34] The ideally infinite arena of ideally infinite exchange of the modern abstracted market forms the most efficient nexus of material and conceptual exchange. In the historical trajectory, the cultural trajectory, and the trajectories of subjection, commodity fetishism depends on and stands for the fantastic impossibility by means of which not only the possible seems coherent but, more important, the force of the actual seems coherent. This nexus is racial in character insofar as the phantasmatic, geopolitical, and economic coincidence yields the modern declensions of humanity and subhumanity. The attendant disclosure is that "the history of European people on both sides of the Atlantic indicates that responsiveness to the market economy cannot be taken for granted, for it reflects values and ideas even more than material conditions."[35]

In the signal study *Black Marxism: The Making of the Black Radical Tradition*, political scientist Cedric Robinson emphasizes, in particular, the role of race in the entangled economic and subjectivizing trajectory of Western modernity: "The creation of the Negro was obviously at the cost of immense expenditures of psychic and intellectual energies in the West. The exercise was obligatory. It was an effort commensurate with the importance Black labor power possessed for the world economy sculpted and dominated by the ruling and mercantile classes of Western Europe."[36] Robinson employs the term "racial capitalism" to foreground analytically the brutalization of African-derived persons in the development of quintessentially modern systems of exchange, material and otherwise: "The development, organization and expansion of capitalist society pursued essentially racial directions, so too did social ideology. As a material force, then, it could be expected that racialism would inevitably permeate the social structures emergent from capitalism. I have used the term 'racial capitalism' to refer to this development and the subsequent structure as an historical agency."[37] The early modern fortunes of sugar as a commodity provide the fundamental illustration of the structural and historical imperatives designated by the concept "racial capitalism" as well as the psychic (dis)identifications paradigmatic for the social relations of "racial capitalism": "The invention of the Negro was proceeding apace with the growth of slave labor. Somewhat paradoxically, the more that Africans and their descendants assimilated cultural materials from colonial society, the less human they became in the minds of the colonists."[38]

The process begins with the increasing feasibility of Portuguese voyages farther and farther south along the sloping African coast, and when, in 1434, the Portuguese sailor Gil Eannes travels decisively past Cape Bojador, still far above the Senegal River, these voyages prompt innovations in sailing technologies, ushering in the era of "the lateen-rigged caravel . . . after 1440 because of the urgent need to assure seamen's safe return from voyages taking them ever farther southward."[39] Reaching the mouth of the Senegal River in 1444, the Portuguese adventurer Denis Dias encounters the Azanaghi on the northern bank and the Wolof and the Serers on the southern, a voyage that begins to gain access for Portugal to the richest gold mines in West Africa. Nonetheless, earlier in the century, the Portuguese seizures of Madeira and the Canary Islands, along the African coastline, provide the crucial events for reorienting the international trade in commodities to the Atlantic Ocean, as well as transforming, for Europeans, the meaning of the cultural contacts between Africans and Europeans.

The term "racial capitalism" designates this paradigmatic economic and sociological imbrication, fashioning the modern determinations and circulations of commodities, structuring, in turn, the principles of modern social animation, or subjectivity, that Amariglio and Callari theorize through the Marxist framework. For the introduction of sugar cane cultivation to Madeira and the Canary Islands transforms the interactions along the African coast. While by the 1450s the Portuguese trade in slaves has been regularized with the Wolof in exchange for "woolen and linen cloth, silver, tapestry, and grain,"[40] so that by 1460 there are enough Africans in Lisbon to form "a Brotherhood of The Virgin of the Rosary, a specifically black community,"[41] the successful plantation of sugar in Madeira by 1452 and in the Canary Islands in 1484 exacerbate the demand for and use of slave labor. By the early sixteenth century, the Portuguese Cape Verde Islands, parallel to the mouth of the Senegal River, serve primarily "to hold slaves from the African coast facing them, and the islands established a protectorate over the region for that purpose."[42] In *The Slave Trade: The Story of the Atlantic Slave Trade, 1440–1870*, historian Hugh Thomas notes the early recognition of the economic promise of "Santiago in the Cape Verde Islands whose settlers had gained for themselves the right to collect slaves from the coast of Africa facing the archipelago. They soon extended their range to include the Wolofs on the river Senegal. Because of its good security, Santiago would become the biggest slave depot ('factory') of the sixteenth century, and the various tiny Portuguese bases on the coast—on, for example, the river Cacheu—became in effect colonies of that island."[43] The commodification of sugar through the expediency of enslaved African-derived labor forces reforms the Portuguese encroachments along the African coast in the fifteenth and sixteenth centuries, and, moreover, also powerfully determines the overabundant, new economic activity that would circumnavigate the Atlantic subsequently.

The cultivation of sugar for international markets occurs, prior to the Atlantic centers of production, in the eastern Mediterranean. Anthropologist Sidney Mintz in *Sweetness and Power: The Place of Sugar in Modern History* recognizes three phases in the international trade in sugar: "From the Mediterranean basin, sugar was supplied to North Africa, the Middle East, and Europe for many centuries. Production there ceased only when production in the New World colonies became dominant, after the late sixteenth century. During the Mediterranean epoch, Western Europe very slowly became accustomed to sugar. From the Mediterranean, the industry then shifted to the Atlantic islands of Spain and Portugal, including Madeira, the Canaries, and São Tomé; but this relatively brief phase came to an end when the American industries began to grow."[44] The historical and geographic relay in the commodification of sugar for international markets does not stand as a direct correlate to the processes introducing African-derived persons into the economic and civil networks derived from Atlantic traffic; however, by the end of the eighteenth century, the commodification of this product represents the preeminent market activity defining the Atlantic trade. In particular, it remains the catalyst for British economic and imperial ascendance in the "New World."

> The first crop in the New World to win a market for itself was tobacco, an American domesticate, swiftly transformed from a rare upper-class luxury into a working-class necessity. Tobacco made headway even against royal disapproval,

> and became part of the consumption of ordinary folk by the seventeenth century. But by the end of that century, sugar was outpacing tobacco in both the British and French West Indies; by 1700 the value of sugar reaching England and Wales was double that of tobacco. The shift from tobacco to sugar was initially even more pronounced in the French Caribbean colonies than in the British, though in the long term the French market for sugar never attained the scale of the British market.[45]

In the eastern Caribbean, Barbados—which is seized by the British in 1627—already by the 1840s is the exemplary site of British sugar production, for the supplanting of tobacco by sugar as the primary cash crop amounts to a "switch from a crop with minimum European market value to a crop with maximum European market value making the Barbados planters rich overnight. They consolidated their small farms into large plantations manned by black slaves imported from Africa,"[46] notes historian Richard Dunn, who observes further: "From the very beginning the island colonists developed their own life-style, and once they converted from tobacco to sugar, everything was bent by their eager embrace of African slavery."[47] The point is not that the political economy and social relations of Madeira and the Canary Islands are transmitted directly to the "New World" but, rather, that the commodification of sugar for an expanding market abutting the Atlantic Ocean reforms the tenor of European contact with the peoples along the African coast in ways that forecast the massive introduction of African-derived populations into the emerging societies of the Atlantic world. Differently put, at its most basic, Western modernity amounts to the novel quotidian world established by the ready availability of commodities far beyond their sites of production, most important initially the largely tropical items cocoa, coffee, cotton, sugar, and tobacco, all products that stress the equally novel demand for the commodification of mass, coerced, African-derived laborers. The establishment of these modern commodity chains constitutes "racialization" as a signal proposition for their viability.

The developments in sugar production bolster the Portuguese descent along the West African coast. "Individual entrepreneurs were encouraged to establish sugar-cane (and other) plantations on the Atlantic islands, manned with African slaves and destined to produce for Portugal and other European markets, because their presence safeguarded the extension of Portuguese trade routes around Africa and toward the Orient."[48] Additional support comes from the 1480 treaty between Portugal and Spain, in which "in return for Portugal's surrender of all claims to the throne of Spain, the queen of Castile recognized the Portuguese monopoly in Africa: Indeed, the Spaniards also accepted Portuguese control of commerce in Fez, Madeira, the Azores, and the Cape Verde Islands."[49] In 1481, the year the Portuguese Prince João becomes King, this expansion along the African coast grows to include the trading castle Elmina, "the first substantial European building in the tropics."[50] In 1486 the Portuguese begin to settle the equatorial island of São Tomé, across from the river Gabon in the Gulf of Guinea, and which becomes another center for the growth of sugar cane using African slave labor, that is, one further precursor to the widespread plantation slavery to mark the western regions of the Atlantic arena.

Further signaling the increasing significance of the European dispersal into the Atlantic world, Pope Alexander VI specifies an imaginary line 277 leagues west of the Cape Verde Islands so as to specify a Spanish zone of influence west of the imaginary line and a Portuguese zone of influence east of the imaginary line, as set out in the Treaty of Tordesillas, even though the division is disputed into the late eighteenth century. This final decade of the fifteenth century is the age of Christopher Columbus, who lives for a time on Madeira amidst its slave labor and sugar production, and who has direct family ties to the Portuguese aristocracy, expanding their domination into the Atlantic. It is important to note that the Portuguese imperial ambitions yield steadfast movement along the Atlantic African coast prior to Christopher Columbus's extension of Spanish imperial sway into the Americas. By 1471–72 João de Santarém and Pêro Escobar venture as far as São Tomé, situated off the coast between the mouths of the Niger and the Congo Rivers, as the African coast turns south for thousands of miles; by 1483 Rui de Sequeira reaches the Congo River, at approximately the midpoint of the continental length; by 1484 Diogo Cão attains Cape Cruz near the southern tip of the continent; by 1487 Bartolomeu Dias embarks down the coast in search of a route to India, a journey on which he rounds the tip of the continent and sails along the east African coast. By 1499, however, on the other side of the Atlantic Ocean, Spain is beginning to consolidate its American empire, replacing Christopher Columbus as the governor-general of Hispaniola—the land mass partitioned now as Haiti and the Dominican Republic—with Nicolás de Ovando, who by 1509 retires from his post an eminent success: "He had completed the subjugation of the entire island; had established fifteen permanent, strategically located towns; had boosted the production of gold, dye wood, and local provisions; and had converted the failing, sporadic attempts of Columbus into permanent settlements. With Ovando's effort, Spain truly arrived in the Americas."[51] Spanish settlement on Cuba is achieved as early as 1502 and by 1514 the conquest of the island is completed under the military leadership of Diego Velázquez, his campaign beginning in 1511. The Spanish quickly intrude into Puerto Rico by 1508 led by Ponce de León, seize Jamaica in 1509 led by Juan de Esquivel, and enter Florida led by Ponce de León by 1511. The campaigns of Hernán Cortés in Mexico begin in 1519, and by 1531–32 Francisco Pizarro overcomes the Peruvian Empire of the Incas. Already on the South American coast by 1500, the Portuguese begin growing sugar cane almost immediately, the first sugar technician ordered for Brazil by 1516.

Early in the sixteenth century, then, the European predations on the opposite side of the ocean from the African coastline already begin to clarify the novel opportunities for extending the profitability of coerced African-derived laborers: "Ponce de León . . . took some Africans with him in the conquest of Puerto Rico in 1508; and, two years later, Geronimo de Bruselas, presumably a Fleming, who worked as a founder of precious metals on that island, was given authority to import two black slaves there to assist his labors."[52] By the end of the first decade of the sixteenth century, King Ferdinand, with Spain claiming the Greater Antilles, begins to recognize the inadequacy of the sanctioned raids on the indigenous Caribbean populations mounted to alleviate the chronic demand for labor in the new settlements. He authorizes in January 1510 the transport of fifty slaves to Hispaniola and the transport of two hundred more slaves in February. The fiscal values of trading in African-derived persons become considerable, at this point, to the "New World" planter and merchant interests as well as the interests of the modern sovereign state because, from this point, the trade in slaves is regulated bureaucratically, responding to the demand for labor in the Western Atlantic, yet also generating state revenues through taxation and the licenses awarded for the state-sanctioned trade in African-derived laborers.

Led by Spain, the European incursions have decimating consequences for the indigenous inhabitants of the Western Atlantic. In *The Making of New World Slavery: From the Baroque to the Modern 1492–1800*, historian Robin Blackburn reports:

> The population of the Americas was perhaps 50 million in 1500, with some estimates much higher, but barely 8 million in 1600. In the Caribbean the original population of the larger islands resisted enslavement, suffered from disease and overwork, and was either destroyed or driven to seek refuge out of reach of the conquerors. The populations of the islands of the Lesser Antilles, mainly peoples known as *Caribes*, resisted effectively enough to dissuade the Spanish from bothering to colonize them. The population of Mexico and Central America fell from 8–15 million in 1520 to a low point of 1.5 million by the middle of the next century. In the Andes, the other area of intensive cultivation and high density, the population fell from 9 million or more in the 1540s to under a million by the next century.[53]

The sweeping evacuation of the peoples and cultures of the hemisphere underscores that the establishment of the mass commodity markets auguring Western modernity mandates the selective destruction of people and natural forces, destructiveness developing to include the coordinated persecution of West African peoples. Cedric Robinson's term "racial capitalism" credits analytically this organizational dynamic of modern world trade for, historically, the violent acquisitiveness of capitalist logic destroys alternative cultural logics and, strategically, the phenotypically distinct populations, most routinely developing and maintaining less commercially rapacious systems. In illustration, the supplanting of the indigenous peoples of the Americas with a population of transported, coerced laborers proves increasingly the upshot of the Spanish and Portuguese presence in the Americas extending from the Caribbean basin.

In 1518, Charles V, the new eighteen-year-old Spanish king, responding to the entreaties of colonists on Hispaniola and to the recommendations of his advisors, who include Rodriguez de Fonseca, grants the Flemish courtier Lorenzo de Gorrevod permission "to import no fewer than four thousand blacks, brought direct from Africa, if need be, into the new territories of the Spanish empire."[54] Interested primarily in the market value of the permission, Lorenzo de Gorrevod sells the grant to Juan López de Recalde, treasurer of the increasingly important *Casa de Contracion*. "The monarchs determined that all trade with America should be centralized and kept under strict surveillance, and to this end they established the *Casa de Contracion* [which may be interpreted as Department of Trade] at Seville in 1504, through which all shipping bound to the Indies had to be cleared and all goods and bullion in American trade registered."[55] Juan López de Recalde, using Alonso Gutiérrez, the treasurer of Madrid, as an intermediary, resells the permission for twenty-five thousand ducats to a firm of Genovese merchants, who ultimately secure the means of executing the permission:

> The merchants, in turn, resold the permission, probably illegally, to individuals who were in a better position to effect the purchase and transportation of Guinea slaves to the Americas—Portuguese sea captains, sailors, and factors—making a profit on their investment of some 275,000 ducats. This experience demonstrated that the slave trade had become such a lucrative business that even speculating middlemen could make handsome profits. By 1528, Charles realized that there could be a profit for the Crown. He sold the monopoly, then regarded as an asiento, to two front men for a powerful German banking firm, Heinrich Ehinger and Hieronymous Seiler. With the monopoly, the Spanish Crown tried to fix both the flow of Africans—about 1,000 per year—and the selling price at the point of delivery—about 40 ducats per pieza, or unit of labor roughly equivalent to a physically healthy adult male slave. Unfortunately, the American colonists found, not for the last time in their history, that both the legal number and the legal price could be breached with impunity.[56]

The very different transoceanic and intracontinental circuits sponsored by these transactions deserve notice, for the venture of transferring sub-Saharan peoples across the Atlantic correlates to the clearer articulation of the fiscal circuit (and cultural identity) "Europe," the fundamental concept of Western modernity. The massive coordination—formal and informal, legal and extralegal—required to seize the western Atlantic and the collaboration necessary for the Atlantic transfer of Africans is extensive. The commercial relations attenuated through the American hemisphere in this way draw and redraw the political economic entanglements as well as the greater or lesser sense of shared destiny of the north Atlantic global region. This is to say that, paradigmatically, the "first major consignment of slaves for the Americas was thus in every sense a European enterprise: the grant of the Flemish-born emperor was to a Savoyard, who sold his rights, through a Castilian, to Genoese merchants—who, in turn, would, of course, have to arrange for the Portuguese to deliver the slaves. For no Spanish ship could legally go to Guinea, the monarchs of the two countries were then allies, and anyway, only the Portuguese could supply slaves in that quantity."[57] By the end of the sixteenth century, the Dutch, the English, and the French acquire growing stakes in the Atlantic enterprise and, beyond the fiscal sedimentations, there are, as acknowledged by Sidney Mintz, more diffuse effects to extending the market relations of the north Atlantic territories into tropical and subtropical locations: "Chaucer's references to sugar are scant; they mainly stress its rarity and preciousness. By Shakespeare's time, the references have multiplied, and though they remain concentrated upon rare substances, the imagery flowing from them is highly diversified."[58] The currencies of the imagination in the north Atlantic territories alter by the end of the sixteenth century.

However, in the middle of the sixteenth century, the Americas do not hold the greatest demand for enslaved Africans, about which time, writes Hugh Thomas, "[f]ive thousand went to the North Atlantic islands [Madeira, etc.] and 7,500 to Europe. Probably a mere 12,500 went to Spanish America and a trickle only to Brazil."[59] By the closing decades of the century, though, the Portuguese imperial connections between Angola, Congo, and the Brazilian coast are responsible by themselves for the transfer of forty to fifty thousand enslaved African laborers:

> In these years, Brazil was showing herself to be São Tomé's successor as Europe's most important sugar supplier, just as São Tomé had succeeded Madeira, the Canaries, and the Mediterranean islands. Brazil—that is, a narrow coastal strip of it—had about 120 sugar mills by 1600 and was probably the richest European colony. She was also an international enterprise: Italian sugar equipment was to be seen, artisans from the Canary Islands and Madeira had been deliberately brought out and, as early as the 1540s, Cibaldo and Cristóvao Lins, Lisbon representatives of the Fuggers of Augsburg were marketing as well as producing sugar. Dutch merchants often provided the ships to carry the sugar home to Europe, as well as the capital for many of the plantations. Then it was the great market of Amsterdam which sold much of the sugar—still principally considered as medically desirable, rather than as a sweetener, since tea, coffee, and chocolate, which seemed in their early days of fashionableness to need sugar for taste, had not appeared on the European scene.[60]

The unification of the Portuguese and Spanish states in 1580 (until 1640) under Philip II of Spain reaffirms the Iberian hold on the "New World," as well as begins to define the principles of mercantilism, providing the template for international capital late into the eighteenth century. Philip II, as the rivalries among the north Atlantic states intensify, is keen to exclude foreign trade, the Dutch and English specifically, from the imperial traffic and revenues restructuring the significance of the Americas. France's Jean Ango, of Dieppe, whose captains seize Hernán Cortés's treasure fleet of 1522, receives as early as 1530 royal sanction to plunder Portuguese shipping, and by 1539 France begins to supplant Portugal in the trade for grain along the Senegal and Gambia Rivers. João Affonso, a Portuguese native sailing as Jean Alphonse for France, is one of the pioneers of the triangular trade, navigating from the Guinea coast to French Rio de Janeiro before returning to the north Atlantic. The English adventurer John Hawkins appears along the Guinea coast in the 1530s and the Brazilian coast in 1532. In the 1550s, sailing for the English, John Lok, Antonio Anes Pintado, another renegade Portuguese adventurer, William Towerson, and Thomas Wyndham successfully reach the West African coast—developments troublesome enough to prompt King João III to reassert the Portuguese monopoly of Africa by papal grant. In 1562, John Hawkins, the son of William Hawkins, initiates the British slave trade by illegally selling transported Africans in Hispaniola, which inspires a successful second adventure in 1564, and a third in 1568 with Francis Drake that ends in defeat by a Spanish fleet. In 1572, the Portuguese grant the English the right to peaceful trade in gold along the African coast, but not in slaves.

Although not so at first, the English and French encroachments on the Iberian Atlantic hemisphere finally are the most consequential. The "international economy that had been dominated for centuries by the cities of northern Italy and had then seen the brief scintillation of south Germany and Castile, was to be led for the next three hundred years by the economic powers of the west; by the Dutch briefly, and then overtaking the Dutch in the course of the seventeenth century, by the English and the French."[61] Frenchmen begin to settle in the northern regions of the North American continent in 1541, the Brazilian coast by 1555, and Saint-Christophe and Tortuga in the Caribbean in 1625. In 1635 François Fouquet, a Parisian merchant, forms Company of the Isles of America. The English arrive in Virginia in 1607 and begin to hold Bermuda in 1609, Barbados in 1624, and Antigua, Nevis, and Montserrat by 1632.

Initially, the Dutch, who by the 1570s trade regularly with Brazil and who secure by 1600 "half the carrying trade between Brazil and Europe,"[62] have the greatest success interceding into the Iberian Atlantic commerce. Dutch intervention along the West African coast begins in the 1590s, following the capture of the sea captain Bernard Ericks by the Portuguese on his way to Brazil. Ericks's confinement on the island of Principe, north of São Tomé, is a misadventure acquainting him with the trade along the African coast, knowledge soon resulting in the Dutch trading in gold, ivory, and eventually also enslaved laborers. The maritime advance of the Dutch is more consequential, at first, than the intrigues of the English and French, because the merchant wealth increasingly concentrated in the Dutch seaboard provinces of Zeeland and, particularly, Holland, by the latter sixteenth century represents the greatest number of seagoing ships in Europe. In addition to urbanizing cities like Amsterdam and Haarlem with an influx of foreigners from within and without the Netherlands drawn by work and comparatively high wages, the wealth generated in Holland and Zeeland is transferred, also with urbanizing effects, to the outer provinces by tax transfers used to maintain important town garrisons on the frontiers of the republic. In the years from 1570 to 1647 the population of Amsterdam grows from 30,000 to 140,000, for example. The expedient interprovincial system accounts largely for the military repudiations of the Spanish in the latter decades of the sixteenth century. The novel, successful forms of national organization and international intrigue in the northern Low Countries are sustained after the 1590s by the vast Dutch international mercantile system of trading generated initially by the bulk trading (grain, timber, fish, salt) of the northern trading route. When, at the close of the sixteenth century, Phillip II lifts the Spanish embargo against Dutch commerce in the peninsula, the Dutch become leading traders also in the "rich trades" as well—spices, sugar, and the other colonial items trafficked through Spain and Portugal. As this peninsular trade fuels Dutch expansion so that Phillip III reimposes the embargo in 1621, the Dutch work to sustain their own direct routes to these commodities, east and west. The result is "Dutch world trade primacy, based on the Dutch entrepôt role, after 1590, as a general reservoir of commodities of all types, and from all parts of the world, both high-value and bulk, and an incomparable mass of shipping with which to bring goods in and out lasted almost a century and a half."[63] By the mid-seventeenth century, the Dutch secure "a monopoly of the world supply of cinnamon,"[64] for instance. This is to say that Amsterdam and the northern Netherlands in early modern Europe are the prime sites for the incipient routine civic coordinations of foreign and local peoples, international goods, urbanization, and republican order, all effects of revolutionary mercantile prosperity. The historian P. C. Emmer in the essay "The Dutch and the Making of the Second Atlantic System" contends that the Dutch were instrumental in combining the production technology of the first [Spanish and Portuguese] Atlantic system with the capitalism of the second Atlantic system. As a result, the major production areas of tropical cash crops shifted from Brazil to the Caribbean and to the southern regions of North America."[65]

The Dutch trouble the Atlantic holdings of the Portuguese, particularly. In 1610, an already existing company of Dutch investors becomes the Guinea Company and builds within two years a trading castle, named finally Fort Nassau, fifteen miles east of the renowned Portuguese castle Elmina. In 1617, the Dutch purchase from the Portuguese the island of Gorée. In 1621, a Council of Nineteen restructures the Dutch West India Company, founded in 1607, and the Dutch intervention into the Atlantic gains much greater initiative. In 1624, the Dutch capture and control Northern Brazil, which, however, they must relinquish in 1654. In the 1630s, the Dutch acquire the Caribbean islands of Curaçao, Saint Eustatius, and Saint Thomas for use as entrepôts rather than sites of production, and in a surprise naval attack in 1637 capture the fortress Elmina from the Portuguese. In 1641, the Dutch expel the Portuguese from their trading stations along the African coast at Luanda, São Tomé, and Benguela, and in 1642 with the surrender of Fort Axim, the Dutch virtually vanquish the Portuguese from the African trade they had dominated for two hundred years. Accordingly, in the middle decades of the seventeenth century, the Dutch gain control of the African slave trade. From 1613 to 1664, the Dutch also manage the colony New Amsterdam on Manhattan Island, at which point the English claim the colony as New York. The Swedes and the Danes, early in the seventeenth century, also attempt to organize interventions into the growing commerce associated with the Americas without, however, becoming major players in the intrigues of the Americas. Still, by the end of the seventeenth century, writes the historian Franklin Knight, it was impossible that "the internal affairs of the rival European states be separated any longer from their overseas involvement—and much of that involvement was in the Caribbean. Peace in Europe and peace 'beyond the line' of amity became integrally related."[66]

By the 1640s, with the onset of the sugar boom in Barbados and the Caribbean, the Brazilian economy begins to diversify, particularly with the discovery of gold in Minas Gerais in 1698, and the Caribbean becomes the premier point of supply for the exponentially expanding north Atlantic markets for sugar. The new mass availability of a variety of tropical products for European populations—cocoa, coffee, tea—has immediate effects on the quotidian world of the North Atlantic, bringing revolutionary change to the European social world since the "success of tea, like the less resounding successes of coffee and chocolate, was also the success of sugar."[67] The advent of tropical staples as commonplaces in European households and public life galvanizes the transportation of enslaved Africans to the American hemisphere. After the calculated consolidation at this point of the enormous British market for sugar, for "a century and a half after 1660, the English dominated all forms of ocean transportation of people," reports historian David Eltis in *The Rise of African Slavery in the Americas*. "They carried more slaves across the Atlantic than any other nation and shipped more convicts, indentured servants, and probably more fare-paying passengers as well."[68] By 1655, after failing to seize Hispaniola, the English capture Jamaica from the Spanish, the island serving initially as a buccaneering base for further raids against the Spanish, but by 1720 sugar production on Jamaica, "close to the size of Connecticut, or ten times the combined area of Barbados, St. Christopher, Nevis, Antigua, and Montserrat," surpasses sugar production from Barbados.[69] In 1651 British interests founded a new Guinea Company in London, and London-based ships enter into regular trade in enslaved African laborers. The formation of the Royal Adventurers into Africa follows in 1660, a trading company that, by 1663, includes Charles I, the Duke of York, John Locke, and Samuel Pepys among its shareholders. The English capture from the Dutch the formerly Portuguese possessions the Cape Verde islands, the Cape coast, and then (we have noted) in North America, New Amsterdam on Manhattan island, which is renamed for the Duke of York, the leading shareholder in the Atlantic initiative.

The augmented British trade includes slaves, gold, ivory, wax, hides, wood, and grain (pepper). Nonetheless, the financial troubles of the Royal Adventurers into Africa result in the formation of the subsidiary concern the Gambia Adventurers by the late 1660s—financial troubles that are overcome, however, by the final decades of the century, when the "RAC traded over sixteen thousand slaves between 1690 and 1700."[70] By the end of the century, it is impossible to restrain the many British interlopers encroaching on the supposedly one-thousand-year monopoly granted the Royal African Adventurers, interlopers subsequently to become known as "Ten Percenters" because the legal access to the slave trade granted in 1698 requires from them an ad valorem tax that is placed on all goods exports to Africa in trade, in order to subsidize the British forts maintained along the African coast that are indispensable to the traffic in slaves. "Ten Percenters would carry 75,000 slaves between 1698 and 1707, as against 18,000 by the RAC."[71] Further still, beginning in 1701, when the Portuguese still hold the Spanish *asiento* (the official contract to transport African laborers to Spanish America), the War of Spanish Succession bolsters British supremacy in the Atlantic trade routes. When Philip V, born in France, grandson of the King of France, ascends to the Spanish throne, the new government pays one million pesos to Portuguese merchants holding the contract to relinquish it, and the French Guinea Company receives a ten-year monopoly on supplying the Spanish empire with slaves, from 1702 to 1712. Portugal, England, and the Hapsburgs align themselves against the Bourbon monarchs of France and Spain who, as a result, cancel the payment to the Portuguese. The 1713 Treaty of Utrecht that ends the war concedes the right of the British to supply slaves to the Spanish Americas, concedes them as well Gibraltar and Minorca in the Mediterranean, and Newfoundland and Nova Scotia in North America.

Meanwhile, the French production of sugar is also escalating. The 1697 Treaty of Ryswick grants France the western territory of Hispaniola-St. Domingue, later to become Haiti. The most important French holdings in the Caribbean at the beginning of the eighteenth century, then, are Guadeloupe, Martinique, and St. Domingue. Following 1713, the French pursue sugar production on St. Domingue, "10,714 square miles compared with 4,411 square miles for Jamaica,"[72] more quickly than the production of sugar accelerates on Jamaica, outpacing the British in sugar cultivation by 1735, when "French sugar was not only more plentiful, but cheaper, and probably better."[73] Whereas British sugar production fortifies and foremost relies on the insatiable domestic market in the metropole, French production services international European markets.[74] "[I]n 1787 Saint Domingue's sugar output reached 87,000 tons," Robin Blackburn observes, "compared with an output of around 49,000 tons in Jamaica in the same year."[75] But, further still, to underwrite the massive cultivation of sugar for the demands of the north Atlantic markets, in the eighteenth century the French engage most earnestly in the corollary trade in enslaved African laborers. Hugh Thomas writes: "Between 1721 and 1730, the French shipped fewer slaves than either the British or the Portuguese, but they still were responsible for carrying at least 85,000. During the 1730s, the French were busier. They probably shipped over 100,000 slaves. Between 1738 and 1745, Nantes alone would carry 55,000 slaves in 180 ships, the chief buyers being the *nouveau riche* planters of Saint-Domingue (about three-quarters of the total) and Martinique (about a fifth)."[76]

Undeniably, by the end of the seventeenth century the entanglements of the three regions of the Atlantic generate regimes of competitiveness and exploitation that make international commodity chains a fundamental priority for the sovereignties of Europe. The policies that these governments charter to contour the Atlantic commodity chains constitute the first phase of modern capital accumulation, mercantilism, the outlines of which arise at the opening of the sixteenth century, when Spain attempts to safeguard the economic boons of its American empire, as increasingly the principal European powers covet the Americas. At this moment, in open exercises of international political influence, Spain attempts to enforce the access of foreign agents to the trade generated by Spanish America, as witnessed, for example, by the imposing and lifting of the embargos against the Dutch. The changing assignation of the *asiento*, the license to supply the enslaved laborers of Spanish America, highly lucrative since 1518, provides another example. Still, the paramount articulations of mercantile capitalism remain the 1660 British Navigation Acts and the 1673 French *l'exclusif*. The Navigation Acts provide British colonial tobacco and sugar the monopolization of the British domestic market, and *l'exclusif* similarly restricts foreign powers from the French colonial trade; the interests of both measures are the establishment of national monopolies on the shipping, refining, and marketing of American hemispheric products as well as monopolizing the continental trade supplying the respective American colonies. Historian Arthur L. Stinchcombe in *Sugar Island Slavery in the*

Age of the Enlightenment: The Political Economy of the Caribbean World summarizes the aims of mercantilism: "The primary purpose of . . . mercantilist policy seems generally to have been to make the trade easily taxable, to get advance payment for the monopoly privileges, and to make the colonies pay for the projection of empire power into the interimperial system. The exports of the colonies were, then, to some degree protected from foreign competition, and merchants from the metropole were given monopolies (of varying weight and importance) of the supply of both slaves and other goods to the colonies."[77]

One effect of this is that the regional hemispheric trade in the Americas remains either hindered or outlawed—subordinated directly to the international dictates of imperial advantage. Whereas, subsequently, industrial capital sets the priority to be the organization of production in tandem with the free movement of commodities in international markets, mercantile capitalism distinctly organizes the international channels of trade and distribution. In this way, trade between the proximate islands as well as with the mainland, despite whatever immediate local advantages or disadvantages, depends on the sanctionings and curtailments of trade set by far-distant centers of authority. Finally, the imperial coordination also rehearses the modern forms of political sovereignty that coalesce initially in the American hemisphere, as well as the exclusive modern forms of civic subjection forged in the phantasmatic palimpsest of economics, race, and unprecedented demographies: "By the early 1650s, as a result of the sugar revolution, Barbados had achieved a population density greater than that of any comparable area in the English-speaking world except London."[78] In the same way as the economic activity burgeoning from the Atlantic arena precipitates an arduous task of management that more fully articulates the collectivity "Europe," it also generates unimagined forms of political sovereignty. The emphatically modern historical break of the British mainland colonies from their national origins is evident in the imperatives of mercantilism, reflected in its concerns with state jurisdiction, international trade, and sovereign intervention. Ralph Davis notes the importance of imperial intrigue and the local, interregional American trade in the novel political direction taken by the British mainland colonies:

> After 1760, when the French were driven from North America—a situation formalized at the peace of 1673—the situation was entirely changed. Thereafter direct economic loss from the imperial connection had no indirect compensation in the form of free protection from the French, and the loss grew rapidly with the widening of American resources. By removing the one essential function of the imperial connection, namely protection by one great European power against the other one that had a foothold in the American continent, success in war removed the need for that connection. It removed a restraint within which anti-imperial feeling had had to operate, so that it became possible for all the

> minor reasons for breaking the connection, political and economic, real and false, to make themselves felt, reinforcing the great and substantial reason that the need for it was gone, and with it the justification.[79]

Beyond redrawing routinely the national territories of the American hemisphere, the mercantilist era of capitalism also profoundly expands the concept of national sovereignty from paradigms conceiving the nation as the extension of divinely invested personhood to the national experiment in the British mainland colonies constituted on the abstract secular processes of socioeconomic management. The mercantilist upshot, in a phrase, is not merely fiscal and material. Rather, by the 1770s, the radical new forms of abstraction underlying the unprecedented independence of the mainland colonies broadly restate the formula and figure of Atlantic collective animation—the nation—the expressly stated new formula and figure being the proposition of the people, a concomitantly material and administrative catalogue, as opposed to the subordinated citizenry united by the punitive, premodern, sovereign specularity theorized by Michel Foucault. Arising from undisguised attentiveness to the meanings and mechanisms of voluminous international trade, the imagination and documentation of the new sovereign jurisdiction is foremost as the site of socioeconomic execution and administration, and in this way, among others, the mainland independence clarifies dramatically the more than material significance of the modern Atlantic commerce and markets. From the sixteenth to the eighteenth centuries, the modern Western nation-state holds the monarch as the mechanism of government, as government comes increasingly to mean commercial oversight in a trajectory, however, that supplants the monarch with the figurative people as the mechanism of government. Nonetheless, as detailed by David Eltis in "Europeans and the Rise and Fall of African Slavery: An Interpretation," the hyperbolic recalculation of the people in the dramatic permutation of modern political community is not equivalent to the general welfare, the particular steadfast principle adamantly exercised in relation to African-derived persons who are, by the extraordinary contrivances of international coordination, held as profitable materially and psychically.

In the long-gathering intrigue prefacing the decisive realignment of Western commercial powers, only the products of the labor of African-derived persons, far more so than the subjectivities and adequate welfare of African-derived persons, are most legible. On this point, the economic activities associated with the modern production of sugar are exemplary again. The longstanding uneasiness, as Sidney Mintz writes, is that the mercantilist routes of trade remain severely breached:

> There grew up, in effect, two so-called triangles of trade, both of which arose in the seventeenth century and matured in the eighteenth. The first and most

> famous triangle linked Britain to Africa and the New World: Finished goods were sold to Africa, African slaves to the Americas, and American tropical commodities (especially sugar) to the mother country and her importing neighbors. The second triangle functioned in a manner contradictory to the mercantilist ideal. From New England went rum to Africa, whence slaves to the West Indies, whence molasses back to New England (with which to make rum). The maturation of this second triangle put the New England colonies on a political collision course with Britain, but the underlying problems were economic, taking on political import precisely because they brought divergent economic interests to confrontation.[80]

The alienation of the labor of African-derived populations is taken for granted in the military, political, and trading exploits that reorder the international landscape of the eighteenth century. In these arrangements, African-derived populations, under duress, remit the broad well-being of their communities for the maintenance and augmentation of other jurisdictions coveting the remittance. That is, contrary to imperial intentions, mercantile capitalism defines unexpected spheres of acute economic competition that, at the level of quotidian animation, depend on the puzzle, dilemma, or fully contrived performance rehearsing the misrecognition, the unaccountability, that the modernization of civic presence proposes distinctly that human animation fails the criteria of human being: the pragmatic modern meaning of the mass introduction and presence of African-derived persons in the circuits of Atlantic commerce and the "New World." This uncertain premise of modern civic animation admits human presence, rather, in the void between the new conceptual viability of the body as a material catalogue and the new, expansive mechanisms of the socio-political extraction of surplus value—the novel, steadfast priority of the reconceived Western nation-state. The installation is affective, epistemological, but, most important, intricately ideological in its foreclosures because, if the historical period of mercantilism begins to set economic policy as the urgent sovereign task, and if the proposed inhabitation of civic presence, if not human presence, alters accordingly, then, as assuredly, the phenotypical and economic scoring of the Atlantic cartography primarily elaborate these transformations and, in these circumstances, the political concept of the people is fraught.

The subjectivizing premise of the modern nation-state, the assumption of basic or fundamental cohesiveness, obscures the more openly destructive imperatives crafting modern national formations. The beguiling and basic national proposal, the proposal of an ineffable "psychological bond that joins a people and differentiates it, in the subconscious convictions of its members, from all other people in a most vital way," credits the nation as a centrifugal, if not fully cohesive, entity.[81] However, the wide reverberations of national formations (and re-formations) in the mercantilist era do not apply foremost or finally to the Western communities redrawn within (and as) the modern national territories but, as fully, to the distinctly specified bearers of the "socially necessary labor time" in the transforming Atlantic world, who are never readily calculable within the civic populations of the Americas. In 1882 Ernest Renan writes famously: A "nation is a soul, a spiritual principle,"[82] the outcome of a "great aggregation of men, [who] with healthy spirit and warmth of heart, creates a moral conscience which is called a nation."[83] There is no recognition in the formula, however, of the destructive forces of modern national formation. The violence in question, unlike the apparent cohesion it makes possible, never merely is equivalent to, or circumscribed by, the national formation. Instead of innate sets of psychological bonds or easily calculated moral gestures, the modern nation-state details the necessity of the micropolitical re-description—in addition to the macropolitical reformulation—of social power: the intricate ideological feat in question. These re-descriptions of power—defined by political economist Susan Strange as "the ability of a person or group of persons to affect [the] outcomes that their preferences take precedence over the preferences of others"[84]—fix the always vulnerable margins between the conceptual and the inconceivable and, in particular, in the Atlantic arena the proximities to and the attenuations of the violence yielding the various new terms of national sovereignty increasingly redefined by the European occupation of the Americas. The inadequacy of the "national" rubric for effectively scoring this violence is plain, because, "[s]imply put, people from one continent forced those from a second continent to produce a narrow range of consumer goods in a third—having first found the third's native population inadequate to their purpose."[85] Because the modern—nationally situated—subject comprises the hiatus in these arrangements, the modernizing racial trajectory of the West is implicated in the revolutionary certainty that functional human being—individual and especially collective—is inseparable from the ideally infinite arena of ideally infinite exchange, an arena that even the broadest legislative, military, and rhetorical resources fail to master as often as not. The complex is a matter of subjectivity, the full reach of which—paradoxically—is never the discrete subject but, rather, turns of the (ideally collective) imagination by which discrete subjection reforms and adheres to the foundations of the socius, which are increasingly, following the sixteenth century, the coveted processes and values of transatlantic (and global) commodity circulation. The abstracted international arena of exchange constitutes a rarified intersubjective template questionable, as by the mainland colonists in the late eighteenth century, for example, only under the most pressed of circumstances. Differently put, the full measure of the trajectory of mercantile capitalism and its modernizing transfers of economic values and peoples rests in the subtleties and protocols that establish human congress as inseparable from the exchanges (and feints) of the unwieldy abstracted market.

The resulting macropolitical effect—the nation—and the micropolitical effect—the ineffability of "the people" as the collective representation of individual subjects—reveal that, to reiterate Amariglio and Callari, "the act of exchange is not simply the site of an economic process but also one of the key locations within capitalism where a symbolic order is particularly constituted and learned."[86] Beyond the macropolitical reorganizations, the affective principle, the feint, remains the apparent discrete viability—whether national or individual—that betrays, in fact, the competitions over and the complements of the ideally infinite arena of ideally infinite exchange. The subjectivizing complex of Enlightenment "nations" and "nationalisms," contingent on the feint of commodity fetishism, sponsors the misperception of the nation as foremost or essentially a cohesive or coherent "imagined community," in the well-known phrase of Benedict Anderson. By the end of the third decade of the nineteenth century, the number of novel military and administrative jurisdictions emergent in the "New World" includes Haiti (1803), Argentina (1816), Chile (1881), Venezuela (1820), Mexico (1821), Great Columbian (1822), Bolivia (1825), Paraguay (1826), and Uruguay (1828), as an outgrowth of the competition over the economic values trafficked through the Atlantic theatre.[87]

Thus, at the conclusion of the eighteenth century, the incipient United States, as the sign of emphatic modernity, outlines new nation as territories as well as new conceptual forms, events reflecting the new interrelated lineaments of the commodity form, the human subject, and the bureaucratic nation-state that mark in their entanglements vast economic and political possibilities. Historian John Brewer in *The Sinews of Power* summarizes mercantile capital as, rather than a coherent set of policies, an "era in which the relationship between state power and international trade was seen as a problem of exceptional importance, one which was normally formulated as a debate between the interventionist obligations of rulers rather than a matter of free trade," a summary sketching the essential points of the intrigue between Britain and the mainland seaboard territories.[88] The British Sugar Act of 1764 that imposes tariffs on the seaboard colonies, resulting in the enormous, economically crucial smuggling between the colonies and the Caribbean basin, and the 1773 Stamp Act, lowering these tariffs in order to make British intervention into the smuggling more viable, are important points of escalation in the transatlantic tensions prefacing the independence of the colonies and the scrupulous alignments of economic and social life in the description of modern national agency:

> The birth of the North American republic had a large impact on the plantation-related trade of the rest of the Americas. United States exports to the French, Spanish, Portuguese, and Dutch colonies reached nearly £1 million annually in 1790–92, representing 24 percent of the total. The tonnage of U.S. shipping

> registered as engaged in overseas commerce totaled 346,000 tons, twice that of the tonnage of British shipping involved in the Atlantic trade, in 1770; by 1801 the tonnage of U.S. commercial shipping more than doubled to 718,400. Merchants from New York, Boston and Philadelphia traded with all parts of the Caribbean and Americas in sugar, cotton, coffee, cacao, and indigo, much of which was then re-exported to Europe. They offered powerful economic as well as ideological encouragement to creole aspirations to American independence. The total export trade of the United States grew fivefold in the period 1790 to 1807, swelled by its role as entrepôt for the plantation produce of the Americas, to reach $60 million (over £10 million).[89]

The paramount measures of mercantilism are the British Navigation Acts and the French *exclusif*, aiming to ensure that the tropical products cocoa, coffee, indigo, rum, sugar, and tobacco (as well as gold and silver) extracted from "New World" outposts by means of African-derived labor are shipped exclusively on the vessels of their respective metropolitan centers, then refined and marketed in those metropolitan territories by their national agents and industries. The point Brewer demonstrates in the seventeenth- and eighteenth-century histories of England in *The Sinews of Power* is that, shaping the international flow of goods and wealth by means of intercontinental markets, mercantilism fosters and reinforces modern forms of nationality as bureaucratic, administrative entities. Mercantilist principles, exacerbating the economic jealousies that are the principal dynamic of the Atlantic economies, eschew feudal concepts of national agency as well as the longstanding terms of quotidian, collective self-conception. Historian Andrew Cayton observes, "Indeed, many saw the efforts of nationally oriented men to attach people to the new republic as essentially radical innovations designed to undermine traditional social relationships. Not only were Federalists elevating imperial authority above local authority. By privileging abstract impersonal principles above particular personal ties, they were redefining the nature of social and political relationships."[90]

The articulation of the new, dramatic national independence clarifies both the enormous material boon, as well as the subjectivizing turns of the imagination emergent from the codification of the Atlantic economies—a historical progress describing the co-implicated terms of the macropolitical and the micropolitical.

It bears restating that the force in question is macropolitical, which is to say broadly historical and supranational, enforcing the economic circuits imbricating the West African, "New World," and European polities and the adamant diacriticism of race following the sixteenth century. After the opening of the sixteenth century, "in less than one hundred years the world's economic situation had altered completely," writes historian Harry A. Gailey. "Negro slaves, who were of only nominal value in 1500, had become indispensable to the maintenance and development of this new plantation economy."[91] Concomitantly, the force in question is micropolitical, which is to say it insinuates and enforces, to quote historian Joyce Appleby, the interpellation of a "model of economic life that borrowed its order from . . . the newly conceptualized nature of predictable regularity. As this economy absorbed more and more of the attention of men and women it supplied a new identity for them. By the end of the eighteenth century the individual with wide-ranging needs and abstract rights appeared to challenge the citizen with concrete obligations and prescribed privileges."[92] For these reasons, it is important to acknowledge that in the British mainland colonies "African slaves, if taken together . . . [form] the largest single group of non-English-speaking migrants to enter the North American colonies in the pre-Revolutionary era."[93] The historical progress reveals that, rather than foremost the vectors of human coherence, the modernity of the national formations, especially in the Americas, provides foremost the novel, beguiling means by which individual and communal detachments are created, channeled, and exploited in the transcontinental arrangements yielding unprecedented demographic proximities. The matter is not economic simply but, rather, involves, as specifically, the turns of the imagination that demand the impossibility—violently secured—of racial blackness being a feature of openly recognized human being.

This is to say, the profound conceptual problems, yet pronounced political efficacy, of the figure of "the people" are unmistakable in the finally supranational intrigue of the independence of the seaboard colonies and subsequent U.S. Federalist era. The U.S. Federalist era ranges from the 1780s, fomenting the debate over supplanting the Articles of Confederation with a new constitution, to the election of Thomas Jefferson to the U.S. presidency in 1800. Still, this is to say further that, in the matter of nation-building, the aporetic force in question is not simply the military drama of the U.S. Revolutionary War, but the effects of the African-derived "socially necessary labor time" on which the modern Atlantic market and its various national articulations (and re-articulations) depend. The material and conceptual effects of the African-derived "socially necessary labor-time" redoubles the incongruity of the local, federal, and individual renditions of "the people" that mark the political urgencies of the Federalist era. The developing historiography of the U.S. Federalist era draws out the perplexity of the figure of "the people" forming the national register of the independent British mainland colonies. Historian Robert Shalhope, in the article "Republicanism and Early American Historiography," outlines the work of Bernard Bailyn, Gordon Wood, and J. G. A. Pocock, and their formation of the historiographical "republican synthesis," or the related set of convictions that, insofar as early U.S. history "revealed a continual struggle between the spheres of liberty and power, the American Revolutionaries quickly formed a consensus in which the concept of republicanism epitomized the new social and political world they believed they had created."[94] Shalhope positions principally the scholarship of Joyce Appleby against the contentions of the "republican synthesis," so as to describe a "major weakness of earlier analyses of republicanism . . . namely, a focus on political and constitutional issues to the detriment of economic analysis."[95] What is clear from the discrepant perspectives, Shalhope contends, is that the "American Revolution created a single political nation but certainly did not fashion a cohesive national community."[96] Appleby, in her own consideration of the historiographical tensions, "Republicanism in Old and New Contexts," forthrightly rejects the earlier "insistence that the classical republican paradigm controlled how eighteenth-century men reacted to change," claiming the historical record demonstrates, instead, that the colonial elite "living with sensibilities formed in an agrarian society and struggling to interpret change with an ideology pivoting on the pre-eminent importance of stasis could only be disconcerted by the intrusive vigor of the [effects of the] market."[97] To this end, in the article "'Baubles of Britain': The American and Consumer Revolutions of the Eighteenth Century," historian T. H. Breen outlines pointedly the shortcomings or the explanatory limits, of the historiographical investments of the "republican synthesis":

> Intellectual historians encounter a different, though equally thorny, set of problems. They transform the American Revolution into a mental event. From this perspective, it does not matter much whether the ideas that the colonists espoused are classic liberal concepts of rights and property, radical country notions of power and virtue or evangelical Calvinist beliefs about sin and covenants. Whatever the dominant ideology may have been, we find that a bundle of political abstractions has persuaded colonists living in scattered regions of America of the righteousness of their cause, driving them during the 1760s and 1770s to take ever more radical positions until eventually they were forced by the logic of their original assumptions to break with Great Britain. Unfortunately, intellectual historians provide no clear link between the everyday world of the men and women who actually became patriots and the ideas that they articulated. We are thus hard-pressed to comprehend how in 1774 wealthy Chesapeake planters and poor Boston artisans—to cite two obvious examples—could possibly have come to share a political mentality. We do not know how these ideas were transmitted through colonial society from class to class, from community to community.[98]

In short, as much as the "republican synthesis" advances ideal propositions of historical and narrative continuity, it cannot account for the way in which radically distinct geographical populations as well as social classes arrived at the collective apprehension of a national "people," revolutionary acts of imagination yielding the "mobilization of strangers in a revolutionary cause [that] eroded the stubborn localism of an earlier period."[99] This episode that produces finally the federal compact, more so than a political theoretical inheritance, turns on novel economic and conceptual priorities.

Brief considerations of the roles of the three authors of the composite *Federalist*, which famously appeals in the 1780s for the new national compact, begins to illustrate the point. The three exemplary figures are Alexander Hamilton, who is the successful architect of federal economic policy within the first administrations; John Jay, who is the New York lawyer and, like Alexander Hamilton, one of the representatives from New York at the constitutional convention and who in *The Federalist* pens nativist appeals for the new national agency; and James Madison, who is the instrumental figure in the 1787 constitutional convention. The architectural economic strategies of Alexander Hamilton underscore the immediate conceptual force the relays of commodity exchange hold for the national endeavor. The nativist appeals of John Jay betray the occlusions of the international complex equally necessary to the endeavor. The role of James Madison highlights the representational quandary, yet nonetheless political efficacy, of the rhetorical figure of the people. The imbrications of their positions are fundamental to and productive of the enterprise they conceive and debate.

Alexander Hamilton—"the colossal genius of the new system,"[100] notwithstanding James Madison's more preeminent role in the details of constitution-making—recognizes keenly the neo-mercantilist dilemma of the incipient national union: "Believing economic independence was inseparable from political freedom, Hamilton was alarmed by American dependence on British imports. He opposed commercial coercion, fearing that the young nation would be devastated by such a contest. His less confrontational design envisioned ridding the United States of British economic domination by developing American manufacturing. He concluded that American technological backwardness stood in the way of American manufactures and urged the federal government to launch an aggressive campaign to acquire England's protected industrial secrets."[101] In the policies sponsored by Hamilton, the "intrusive vigor of the market" is undisguised: the pursuit of public credit for the federal agency, the establishment of the national bank, the championing of domestic taxation in support of public credit, the redrawing of economic relations with Britain while at the same time supporting rival domestic manufacturing by flouting British patent laws, the championing of a well-funded national military in the service of international force, the elimination of the federal land-grant program in fear of losing skilled immigrant workers to the more open South and West—in effect, the twinning of the fortunes of the new republic with the interests and influence of financiers, bankers, merchants, manufacturers, and land speculators. Jeffersonian opposition to these inaugural federal policies is intense, as is the resolve of the governing Federalists under the presidency of John Adams in the few years before the 1800 presidential election of Thomas Jefferson. The observations of Lance Banning concerning the tense political atmosphere of the early national union are apt: "Twice in a period of two years [the Federalists'] maneuvers brought the nation to the brink of disunion and civil war. Their attempt during the Quasi-War with France to muzzle the opposition with the Alien and Seditions Acts in 1798 moved Jefferson, in the Kentucky Resolutions, to advocate nullification. Two years later, in response to the Federalists' Burr maneuver, Republican leaders in Virginia and Pennsylvania considered raising an army and marching on the nation's capital to place Jefferson at the helm."[102]

It is important to note that a significant part of the Jeffersonian opposition to the programs of Alexander Hamilton and the initial Federalist administrations draws on the popular opposition to the expansion of the national military in support of international influence, the policy dependent on formalizing domestic taxation as the perpetual supplement to the revenues collectible from customs and tariffs. The lineaments of mercantilist programs remain in these programs, for they instate the prerogatives of the bureaucratic federal agency in the stead of the prerogatives formerly uniquely attached to the divine investiture embodied in the monarch, as historian Francis Jennings suggests: "With money, a king could hire armies to enforce his edicts. The centralized nation-state developed in tandem with the body of merchants and bankers whose money could be alienated by taxes for use as the king desired."[103] However, the local colonial populations "as their representatives in Congress made clear, and some of them also made clear out of doors, were not prepared to pay taxes to support a powerful military and aggressive posture in foreign affairs."[104] The policies and impress of the first federal administrations compromise plainly, then, the straightforward, simple figurativeness of the people, particularly, as "[i]n principle, central government was antithetical to liberty, which most Americans associated with local self-rule."[105]

The question of the independent powers of the federal agency subordinates to the international coordination of economic values the individual subjections and subjects on which it depends for its representative basis. Historian James Ferguson in the article "Political Economy, Public Liberty, and the Formation of the Constitution" places the question of the powers of the federal agency in the international context that determines it more completely. Ferguson outlines that, before the complications of the initial intrigues of the independent seaboard states, "an analogous political economic process affected British development."[106] The Bank of England, in order to underwrite more ample business credit as well as provide more efficient means of general exchange, is established in 1694, establishing as well as British innovation of the funded debt, the innovation that provides the national government access to immense funds with the exceedingly generous license that "no pledge was given ever to repay the principal."[107] The effect—also considered by Brewer in *The Sinews of Power*—is that "[t]he ability to borrow, limited only by having to pay interest, was the crucial factor in Britain's victories in eighteenth-century wars."[108] In Britain and subsequently the independent seaboard states, the alternatives to the expanding system of commercial credit are repudiated. In England, the scheme to employ land banks, which base credit in real property, is forestalled, and in the North American states, the greater powers of federal taxation finally override the policies of "currency finance," in which governments raise capital by issuing their own paper money or certificates redeemable at a later date and, since guaranteed by the government agency, exchangeable as currency. These policies, undertaken separately by the newly independent states, would allow them to assume the federal debt accumulated in the Revolutionary War and, thus, curtail the powers of the new federal agency. The retention of the national debt at the federal level, the crucial measure of the viability of the new federal agency effectively bestowing much wider federal authority, allays the quandary paramount to the Federalist vision, the concern that the "Union was a league of states rather than a national system because Congress lacked the power of taxation."[109] The quizzical specification of the people that is the rhetorical hallmark of the struggle remains deeply troubled—ultimately overwhelmed as a viable appeal—since "[i]n the closing years of the Revolution, the Nationalists under the aegis of such leaders as Robert Morris, Gouverneur Morris, and Alexander Hamilton started a secondary revolution directed against the political-economic establishment of the American states."[110] The federal agency garners its sovereignty by diminishing the former, wider prerogatives of the more local state agencies.

These indeterminacies of the federated or national people, to follow the perspective of Appleby, betray ultimately that "[n]o concepts existed for analyzing a trading system that had not only moved beyond the confines of political boundaries but had created wealth essential to the conduct of politics. There was no classical language for understanding a commercial system that was public, progressive, and orderly. However appealing civic humanism was to English gentlemen involved in public issues, it did not help persons who sought to understand the private transactions that were determining the shape and direction of the Anglo-American economy.[111]

Further still, beyond the discrepancy of the local and federal imperatives, the new proposition of individual national identity discloses the subjectivizing—rather than merely the individual—puzzle brought into being by the exigencies of the Atlantic economies. New York jurist John Jay, one of the negotiators of the 1783 Treaty of Paris arranging independence from Britain, the first chief justice of the U.S. Supreme Court, as well as governor of New York, advocates the principle of nativism in support of the new national identity. He presses for the prerequisite of presidential native birth, and in *Federalist* #2 misstates hyperbolically the cultural unity and common sensibilities of the internationally disparate population of the independent mainland states: "This country and this people seem to have been made for each other, and it appears as if it were the design of Providence that an inheritance so proper and convenient for a band of brethren, united to each other by the strongest ties, should never be split into a number of unsocial, jealous, and alien sovereignties."[112] The hyperbole is undisguised since, in fact, Jay is intimately familiar with "the already ethnically and religiously cosmopolitan New York City and was himself three-eighths French and five-eighths Dutch, without any English ancestry."[113] In other words, Jay, as does Hamilton, understands the scrupulous set of international dynamics and equipoise on which the experiment of the new nationality depends. This comprehension is evidenced as much in his characterization of the radically diverse and changing human landscape of the independent states as "one united people,"[114] as in his role in negotiating the 1794 Jay Treaty that brings further economic and political rapprochements with Britain, thereby imperiling U.S. relations with Britain's chief European rival, France. The translation of the unprecedented ethnic and racial coordinations of the mainland states into "a people descended from the same ancestors, speaking the same language, professing the same religion, attached to the same principles of government, very similar in their manner and customs" patently re-imagines the diverse immigration to the mainland territories and their dynamic social atmosphere.[115] Bernard Bailyn in *The Peopling of British North America: An Introduction* describes the late-eighteenth-century immigration to the North American mainland, revealing the extremities of Jay's entreaties to the singularity of the new individual national identity:

> The migration to America in the fifteen years between the end of the Seven Years War and the Revolution was remarkable by the standards of the time. Between the end of warfare in the mainland colonies and the disruption of empire in 1775, over 55,000 Protestant and Irish emigrated to America, over 40,000 Scots, and over 30,000 Englishmen—a total of approximately 125,000 from the British Isles—in addition to at least 12,000 from the German states and Switzerland who entered the port of Philadelphia, and 84,500 enslaved Africans imported to the southern colonies. This grand total of about 221,500 arrivals in the fifteen-year period (a conservative figure, yet almost 10 percent of the entire estimated population of mainland America in 1775) meant an average *annual* influx of approximately 15,000 people, which was close to the total estimated population of Boston during these years; and, except, for the slaves, the great majority of these tens of thousands of newcomers crowded initially into a few small port towns, almost all of them south of New England.[116]

In short, as do its local and federal assignments, the new subjective assignment of nationality remains as conceptually fraught as it is effective. Indeed, as historian Carol Berkin points out, from its inception in 1664, New York City in particular is notable for the motley diversity of its cultural life, immigration patterns, languages, and populations. She writes of the peaceful change from Dutch to British governance of the colonial outpost, noting, "The Dutch tolerance of diversity within the colony also seemed to be acceptable to the new English proprietor. Indeed, between 1665 and 1685, the colony became a religious refuge for the Scottish Presbyterians, English Quakers, and French Huguenots. By the time James ascended to the throne of England in 1685, New York was a thriving colony of fifteen thousand, representing the greatest variety of faiths, races, and ethnic backgrounds the English colonial word had yet seen."[117]

Particularly because Virginia lawyer James Madison registers and calculates keenly the representational antagonisms of the concept of the people, he holds a highly exemplary role in these political and subjectivizing revolutions. Madison's insights into the delicacy of re-imagining the federal compact in the 1780s, as "state rivalries blocked formation of a common front against British trade policies," are galvanizing for the new national viability.[118] Historian Jack Rakove observes, "Far more than was the case at the state level of politics, where the task of correcting the errors incorporated in the first constitutions seemed open-ended, reform of the confederation could proceed only through the pursuit of a carefully delineated agenda. So at least it seemed to James Madison, the most thoughtful and eventually the most influential of these reformers, and to the relatively small circle of like-minded men who shared his interest in national political problems."[119] In the unraveling intrigue, Madison is the leading proponent of the U.S. Constitution, serving as the "chief spokesman at the Federal Convention for a radically new plan of government . . . subsequently champion[ing] the Constitution as 'Publius' in *The Federalist* and as a delegate to the Virginia ratifying convention . . . [and further bringing] the process of constitution-making to a successful close by guiding through the First Congress the amendments that became the Bill of Rights."[120]

In the article, "The Negative on State Laws: James Madison, the Constitution, and the Crisis of Republican Government," historian Charles Hobson remarks James Madison's motives for, fluctuating opinions of, as well as compromises accepted in the specific form of government taken by the United States. The two severest blows at the 1787 convention to Madison's political vision are the rejection of the proposals "for proportional representation in both houses of the legislature and . . . to give the national legislature a 'negative,' or veto, over the laws of the states."[121] James Madison is intent to diminish the local influences represented by the states in deference to the more completely abstracted generality of national influence. For—as registered by the insistent fears of the smaller states, like Delaware, New Jersey, and Rhode Island, of the larger states, like Massachusetts,

Pennsylvania, and Virginia—forms of interstate conflict and commercial rivalry precipitate in large part the move to the new federated combination, fears Madison rehearses throughout *Notes of the Debates in the Federal Convention of 1787*. The perspective of the smaller states is argued most strenuously by William Patterson of New Jersey, which is an agricultural state fated to supplement, through the excises and tariffs transacted at their busy ports, the welfare of its commercial neighbors New York and Pennsylvania. The federal agency authorized in the way Madison champions would meet more effectively these and other matters of interstate rivalry. In sum, the federal agency would be one with authority accruing not only over the several states but—by virtue of their national singularity—also, at best, over the newly re-ordered competition over the transatlantic flow of property and currency, as well as the rest of the vast North American continent. The envisioned interstate organization and comity aspires to this end above all. As recorded by Madison in the aforementioned *Notes*, John Dickinson, the successful lawyer, who is one of the representatives of Delaware and who achieves much of his social standing by marrying into "one of the first and wealthiest commercial families" of Philadelphia,[122] states the jurisdictional quandary plainly: "We must either submit the states to the danger of being injured by the power of the Nat'l Gov't or the latter to that of being injured by the states."[123] The concept of the national "people" is pinioned, rather than clarified or highlighted, in the metonymic tensions that trouble the "nation" and the "state" as coherent markers of identity, nonetheless, in the reportedly disinterested organization of social and political power. The proposal of the veto power that would discipline fully the local legislative determinations of the aggregate national populace redacts powerfully, this is to say, the conceptual peculiarity of the notion of the people.

It is important to grant that, as disclosed by the conclusion of *Notes on the Debates in the Federal Convention of 1787*, the unanimous approval of the new constitutional document is foremost symbolic and carefully orchestrated—particularly by Benjamin Franklin, Alexander Hamilton, and James Madison. If the magnitude of the U.S. federal powers is not as great as he first imagines, Madison recognizes nonetheless in the compromised document that is the product of the 1787 convention the adequate means to the bolder federation of the states. Hobson describes the trajectory of Madison's changes of perspective as follows: "[O]n the very eve of his debut in *The Federalist*, Madison was highly dissatisfied with, not to say, contemptuous of, the proposed government. The October 1787 letter [to Thomas Jefferson] was a strong dose of nationalism that contrasted sharply with 'Publius's' celebration of the Constitution and indeed with all of Madison's subsequent writings. After this full and candid critique he ceased his advocacy of the negative on state laws and never again spoke ill of the Constitution."[124]

The dilemma of the proposed veto—in which the notion of the "people" is vexed between the antagonisms of their state and federated renditions—provides an important measure of Madison's alterations, or alternately circumscriptions, of mind. That is, the federal veto might attenuate the influence of the larger states yet—as readily as it might exercise it—can do so in no final way. For, with or without the federal veto, given the strength of proportional representation obtaining in the first legislative chamber (attenuated in the Senate), the scheme retains the always potentially greater influence of the larger states—whether applied alternately as states or as elements of the larger conglomerate. It is unlikely that the representatives of large states would endorse policies directly injurious to the interests of their states, or veto (or sanction efforts to veto) policies directly bolstering the interests of their states. In tandem, particularly, Madison's defeated proposals of proportional representation in the Senate and the federal veto strengthens the position of the large states. Large states that would more fully constitute the legislative agency would also have a greater power to protect their interests by means clearly distinct from their local political renditions. In all the permutations of authority, the influence of the state of Virginia, the largest Revolutionary state and the state that James Madison represents, remains well disposed and, as much as the federal veto he champions obfuscates the looming influence of the large states, it exacerbates, in doing so, the vexations of the concept of the people. It is intriguing, on this point, to note that the first U.S. census, undertaken in 1790, "established that 18 percent of the American population was enslaved and 42 percent of all slaves lived in Virginia. In addition, it counted 59,557 free blacks, or 12.7 percent of a total black population of 757,181."[125]

The entreaties of Alexander Hamilton in support of the new federal compromise are instructive. In *Federalist #35*, beginning by outlining the dangers to government represented by the disparate interests of "the people," by its conclusion Hamilton redefines "the people" so as to conflate the concept virtually with the principles and effects of the market, the ideally infinite arena of ideally infinite exchange. Hamilton's focus is taxation: "There can be no doubt that in order to a judicious exercise of the power of taxation, it is necessary that the person in whose hands it is should be acquainted with the general genius, habits, and modes of thinking of the people at large and with the resources of the country. And this is all that can be reasonably meant by a knowledge of the interest and feelings of the people. In any other sense the proposition has either no meaning, or an absurd one."[126] Evidenced by the juxtaposition of "the general genius, habits, and modes of thinking of the people at large" and "the resources of the country," "the people," as a national formula for self-imagination, reveals that the appearance of cohesion is merely the beguiling or subjectivizing effect of the new relays of accumulation generated in the modernizing episode of mercantilism. Any notion that otherwise holds "the people" and the market as essentially distinguishable, Hamilton emphasizes, risks absurdity. Hamilton in *The Federalist*, as Madison did before the first congress, exposes "the people" as the device of elite colonial subjects forging their advantage and modernity in the revolutionary national expression.

Even as he is an important figure in the Jeffersonian opposition to the administration authorized by the new federal document, James Madison, having served in the Virginia state assembly from 1784 to 1787, arrives at the 1787 constitutional convention with the fear that "[i]n republics the majority made the laws but too often these laws, rather than reflecting the public good or general interest of the whole society, ratified the self interests of a dominant faction in that society—whether debtors, creditors, planters, merchants, manufacturers, members of a certain religious sect, inhabitants of a particular region, or some other political, economic, or cultural group. Whenever the opportunity presented itself, there was nothing to restrain a majority faction from seizing control of the government and imposing its designs on the minority."[127] Madison's motives for, fluctuating opinions of, as well as compromises accepted in the specific form of government taken by the United States turn always on the absolute representative impossibility of the figure of the people, even as it certifies and ideally humanizes the relays of wealth and power that in the late eighteenth century remain, as yet, radically or relatively unassumed (depending on perspective).

The unprecedented political opportunities and calculations on the North American seaboard and its environs ensures, to cite historian Lance Banning, that "[t]he era of the American Revolution was a period of political paranoia. Social and political events were seldom conceived to have causes apart from conscious purpose, and the purposes of any group organized to have an impact on government were automatically thought of as malignant."[128] Banning argues further in the article "Republican Ideology and the Triumph of the Constitution, 1789–1793" that the intense climate of the U.S. Revolutionary era yields the precipitous stature of the new, compromised constitutional document. In the aftermath of its framing, the constitutional document that James Madison worries over is seized as an exceptional resource in the political rivalries it licenses to unfold. "Paradoxically, then, it was the appearance of a deeply felt opposition to the policies of our first administration," Banning writes, "which assured the quick acceptance of the Constitution that had been committed to its care. More than the government itself, the opposition had to have an unchallengeable constitution on which to rely."[129] The new constitutional document is arrayed against the policies, in large part, of Alexander Hamilton, who represents New York at the 1787 convention and, as the first secretary of the treasury (resigning in 1795), is the triumphant strategist of the fledgling national economic policy:

> During the first year of the new government, while Jefferson made his way back from France, Madison acted as congressional leader of the forces who meant to assure a strong and independent executive power. He parted with the administration only on the questions of discrimination and national assumption of the debt, policies Virginians considered sectionally unjust. On these issues, however, both Madison and Jefferson were willing to compromise for the sake of federal union. The two Virginians did not move firmly into a more general opposition until they were confronted with Alexander Hamilton's proposal of a national bank. Then, already troubled by what seemed to them a growing sectional bias in the laws, they saw in the broad construction of federal powers which Hamilton advanced in support of the bank a powerful blow at the barriers against an indefinite expansion of federal authority and, with it, the enhancement of the dangerous power of a northern majority.[130]

Charles Hobson codifies the opposition as follows:

> Despite its extended sphere, the government proved more susceptible to faction than [James Madison] had foreseen in 1787. The threat of oppression, moreover, came not from a majority faction (whose dangers his previous warnings had dwelled on almost exclusively) but from a highly organized and influential "moneyed interest" that had somehow seized the reins of power and was adroitly maintaining its control through "corruption." To combat the Hamiltonian system of funded debts, banks, and encouragements for manufactures, Madison adopted a strategy of opposition that necessarily forced him to retreat from his high nationalism of 1787 (even to the point of flirting with the doctrine of "state interposition" in 1799).[131]

The exemplarity of James Madison, Alexander Hamilton, and John Jay is not to fix the feints of the rhetorical and nationalizing "people" as original to any personality but rather to underscore that as the sign of its emphatic modernity, the fledgling United States re-describes national territories and presents new conceptual paradigms, attending always to the immense transatlantic economic values generating the series of macropolitical confrontations for well over a century, as in the First and Second Anglo-Dutch Wars (1652–54, 1664–67), the Nine Years' War (1689–98), the War of Spanish Succession (1702–13), the War of Austrian Succession (1740–48), the Seven Years' Wars (1756–63), and the U.S. Revolutionary War (1776–83). The forthright glosses of the "people," as does the macropolitical context eliciting the concept, give modern forms of commercial exchange the priority shaping the renewed coordination of the former mainland colonies.

As the Federalist era demonstrates, the United States is, above all, a concept with its conceivability, effectively the matter of the turns of the imagination, resting finally on the programs of force that, as the fundamental characteristic of European modernity, fail the report of force. This conceptual turn is fundamental, as documented in the article "Slavery, Economics, and Congressional Politics, 1790," in which historian Howard Ohline outlines the constitutive role of the African-derived "socially necessary labor time" yielding—beyond the material artifacts of the Atlantic economies—the inaugural compromises and coalitions of the revised experiment in the seaboard nationality. Ohline examines the role of interest-group politics, "the tendency of individual congressmen to pursue the priorities of his constituents while shaping the policy of the nation as a whole,"[132] in order to argue that, "[a]fraid of alienating possible southern support for assumption of state debts, no northerner consistently supported the first abolitionist attempt to transform Revolutionary antislavery ideals into the explicit policy of the national government."[133] The political compromise in question arises when petitions to define congressional powers over slavery and Alexander Hamilton's recommendations concerning public credit are considered by the national representatives on the same agenda in 1790. The principle that "[h]umanity unconnected with material interest was not within the limits of republican legislative actions"—employed to refute the abolitionist entreaties of the Quakers, who have no immediate connections to slave property—is evident as well in the regional alliances producing the policies that foreclose both the assumption of the national debt by the states and federal abolitionist measures. "The reason that historians have failed to understand that northerners, too, were engaged in special-interest politics in 1790," Ohline writes, "is that they have looked at the issue entirely in terms of slavery versus antislavery."[134] Northern representatives and their commercial interests, who understand that, in "a country in which the operative fiscal systems were those of thirteen local and diverse entities, a federal debt was anomaly,"[135] understand also that "[l]oss of the debt portended disaster to the Nationalist movement. Without a debt there would be little reason to ask for the [federal] taxing power, since . . . paying the debt was about the only thing that Congress would need much money for."[136] Ohline summarizes as follows the national compromise and coalition of the distinct interest groups: "As republicanism helps one to understand why Americans accepted slavery in a society dedicated to freedom, special-interest politics helps one to understand why congressmen who claimed to be antislavery accepted slavery as they constructed a modern political system bound together by economic self-interest. The belief of northern congressmen that the national government should foster economic stability and growth created a functional relationship between slavery and economic measures."[137]

The legislative fiat on which the new guarantor of national viability—federal taxation—depends designates racial blackness as the political, if not human, point betraying the violent premises and conceptual dilemmas of modern political community. The modern civic proposition of self-coherence granting national identity as its most hyperbolic form proceeds from the conscription of sub-Saharan Africans and their descendants into the severest routines of the Atlantic commercial cycles, as well as the severest routines of individual and administrative European imaginations. Both actually and figuratively "the people" and the nation, historically and paradigmatically, depend on the massive production and movement of the cash crops cocoa, coffee, indigo, rum, sugar, and tobacco that elicits the international competition over the economic values of the Caribbean basin, competition sponsoring and orienting the first modern national formations. The reasoning in question forcefully determines racial blackness as the ideal, adamant recognition of African-derived peoples as if exploitable, indispensable, fully accounted quantities. The disposition of racial blackness is the impossible point of human conception in the enterprise—foreclosed as the unnamed violence of human visibility. Toni Morrison, from the vantage of the late twentieth century, is scrupulous, then, when she repeats, accordingly, that "[t]his is not a story to pass on."[138]

CHAPTER 2

Making the Flesh Word

Binomial Being and Representational Presence

Racial blackness, the primary enabling point of exclusion for the development of Western modernity, complicates the legibility of modern subjectivity. This point of civic animation, buoyed by international trade and markets, by the end of the eighteenth century would be the iconic referent of human presence—the novel animation drawn in the material and interpretative diffusions of the Atlantic commodity and cultural exchange represented, concomitantly, as discrete nomination. Racial blackness is the contrary nomination of the "great majority of immigrants to America up to the end of the eighteenth century, [who] were not Europeans whether free men, indentured servants or transported criminals—they were slaves. Men, women, and children from Africa . . . to the number of a million or so before 1700 and over six million during the eighteenth century."[1] The complication is an exposure, then, the exposure of the dilemma, the contrived performance, drawing the uncertain proposition that human animation fails the criteria of human being: the pragmatic meaning of the mass introduction and presence of African-derived persons in the modern Atlantic commerce and society. The unsteady performance has psychic, scripted, and social ruptures.

Historian David Brion Davis in *The Problem of Slavery in Western Culture* outlines the conceptual reorderings of racialization emergent broadly by the end of the eighteenth century, given the insinuating uncertainty of the specification of human being in the Atlantic world: "It was only in the eighteenth century, however, that discussions of American slavery acquired a prominent place in the standard works of history, jurisprudence, political economy, and moral philosophy. Firmly established by Montesquieu, Francis Hutcheson, William Robertson, Blackstone, Adam Smith, and Jefferson, the convention was sustained by leading thinkers of the nineteenth century."[2]

Nonetheless, if the theoretical reconciliation of Africanity and human being begins to prosper widely by the conclusion of the eighteenth century, the various circumstances of quotidian interactions in the Atlantic world already abundantly bear out the point. To open his study *Black Tacks: African American Seamen in the Age of Sail,* historian W. Jeffrey Bolster asks, "How could one understand early black America without recognizing that plantations were connected to a larger world of black people, as well as to world markets, by black seamen? And given seaports' historic function as crossroads for people and ideas, what roles had sailors played in the formation of black America?"[3] The same Atlantic channels on which modern international coordination transforms African-derived persons into figures of human animation failing the criteria of human being in the political calculations of the Western Atlantic also outline the plain limits of the fiat. The participation of African American men in the merchant marine force, accounting at the beginning of the nineteenth century for "about 18 percent of the contemporary American maritime labor force, then estimated at 100,000 strong,"[4] creates social worlds in which white sailors "confronted . . . a vibrant black culture that contradicted what they had been taught about racial inferiority"[5] as well as presses Western technology toward the service of African-derived communities, since "[s]ailors thus became for black people in the Atlantic world what newspapers and the royal mail service were for white elites: a mode of communication integrating local communities into the larger community of color, even as they revealed regional and local differences."[6] The black jacks in their persons and in their circum-Atlantic contacts openly rehearse forms of civic animation that belie the exclusive Western calculations of human presence essential, nonetheless, to configuring both the labor and commodities trafficked in the Atlantic commerce. Unaccountably, despite the foundational racial imperative following the sixteenth century, the black jacks routinely inhabit the exclusive forms of social agency reserved as the cognates of human presence: "Boisterous and contentious, freewheeling and egalitarian," writes Bolster, "eighteenth-century Atlantic maritime culture offered black men the opportunity to be accepted as individuals by white sailors, or to be joined in common cause 'claiming a Right' against the men and institutions that perpetuated their dependency."[7]

For African diasporic persons to assume plainly the technologies of modern civic animation in the Atlantic world is a consequential feat, and the textualized voices of former slaves in the Americas directly excite the controversies over reconsidering the original modern definition of political community. As noted by art historian Marcus Wood in *Blind Memory: Visual Representation of Slavery in England and America, 1780–1865*, by the 1770s, the waning of the mercantilist era, images of African diasporic persons already effectively circulate in the controversies:

> On 22 May 1787 the London Committee of the SEAST [Society Effecting the Abolition of the Slave Trade] was set up. They rapidly turned their attention to the systematic production of propaganda which drew on every available area of contemporary reprographic technology, and which was particularly inventive in terms of the way it generated visual propaganda. . . . The seal of SEAST with its representation of a kneeling enchained male African beneath the question 'Am I not a man and a brother?', was reproduced as the heading to a great number of anti-slavery publications appearing as stationary, in books, prints, oil paintings, newspaper headings and as a ceramic figurine. In its manifestation as a mass-produced Wedgwood ceramic medallion the image became so generally fashionable in the late 1780s and early 1790s as to be worn as a broach or hairpin by society ladies, and was incorporated into the lids of snuff boxes.[8]

Accordingly, when Atlantic sailor Gustavus Vassa—formerly the kidnapped and enslaved Olaudah Equiano—inhabits the emphatically modern genre of autobiography, with the publication of *The Interesting Narrative of the Life of Olaudah Equiano, or Gustavus Vassa, the African, Written by Himself*, the textual (and, additionally, political) event holds measurable consequence because, as recognized by the consensus of a disparate group of theorists, the genre of autobiography is emphatically modern, the product of the profoundly transformed ethos of European societies and their extensions following the Middle Ages. In "Conditions and Limits of Autobiography," an essay foundational to the criticism of the genre, literary theorist Georges Gusdorf describes immediately the modernity of autobiography and its nominal subject:

> First of all, it is necessary to point out that the genre of autobiography seems limited in time and in space: It has not always existed nor does it exist everywhere. If Augustine's *Confessions* offer us a brilliantly successful landmark right at the beginning, one nevertheless recognizes immediately that it is a late phenomenon in Western culture, coming at that moment when the Christian contribution was grafted onto classical traditions. Moreover, it would seem that autobiography is not to be found outside of our cultural area; one would say it expresses a concern peculiar to modern man, a concern that has been of good use in his systematic conquest of the universe . . .[9]

In other words, the genre discloses the subjectivizing discontinuities between classical and medieval European societies and modern European societies and their permutations: the discontinuity amounting to the "individual presence"—

the preeminent psychic and civic infrastructure, as well as cautionary index of the Atlantic modernity—rendered in detail by the textual artifact. The premise of autobiography reconvenes the figure of the human as the literal and authoritative exposition of the "individual" yet, rather than the redaction of any fundamental or necessary human identity, the most effective exposition of autobiography remains the apparent conflation of language and human being in the unique gesture of strict or remarkable fidelity assumed by the genre and assumed at the historically and geographically specific coordinates noted by Gusdorf.

Rather than a primarily anthropomorphic semblance, the emphatic modernity of autobiography reveals the accelerating civic attachments to the technologies of literacy more and more indelibly marking the ethos, mechanisms, and economies of the modern societies organized to sustain capital accumulation. In the era of mercantile capitalism, the diffusion of literacy clarifies the points of social cohesion that develop with the Atlantic systems of commodity and labor exchange, the reconceived points of social cohesion, obversely, sustaining the socioeconomic and geographic ruptures that racialize and populate the Americas at once.

Whereas Gusdorf glosses the particular "limit[s] in time and in space" that reveal the modernity of autobiography, the literary critic Robert Folkenflik in the "Introduction" to *The Culture of Autobiography* states them more forthrightly: "The first published use of the term *autobiography* in any language . . . occurred in the adjectival form in the preface to the 1789 edition of Ann Yearsley's *Poems* as an 'Autobiographical Narrative' of her strained relations with her patron."[10] Folkenflik also states the pronounced geographic specificity:

> The term *autobiography* and its synonym *self-biography*, having never been used in earlier periods, appeared in the late eighteenth century in several forms, in isolated instances in the seventies, eighties, and nineties, in both England and Germany with no sign that one use influenced another. The two terms not only were invented but reinvented during this period. In France, a more linguistically conservative country, the term first appeared in the *Dictionnaire de l'Académie française* (1836), defined there as 'biography made by hand, or manuscript,' and it did not appear in its accepted modern form until 1838, with the *Dictionnaire* putting it into its supplement in 1842.[11]

The genre of autobiography and its subject, then, imply the rehearsed (individual) progression of the narrative to be, nonetheless, the inevitable figure for the geographic and cultural specificities of Western Europe that would represent, as it turns out, the unfolding progression of the (collective) European diasporic individuals. Historian Karl Weintraub in *The Value of the Individual* reiterates this implied trajectory in terms that forthrightly recall the opening analysis of Gusdorf's signal essay: "At one end of the spectrum, one can posit a primitive tribal form of community with very little differentiation and near-complete identification of the individual with the socially given world; at the other pole stands a highly differentiated society in which each constitutive element is an individually different part of the whole."[12] The genre gains its peculiar modernity, its historical and geographic specificity, by codifying "individual presence" to be synonymous with human presence, and the equivalence is racializing, as Gusdorf demonstrates, when he imagines "the shock of traditional civilizations on coming into contact with Europeans. The old world is in the process of dying in the very interior of that consciousness that questions itself about its destiny, converted willy-nilly to the new life style that whites have brought from beyond the seas."[13] The peculiarity (from one perspective) or the occlusion (from another) is that the autobiographical subject is not anthropomorphic primarily, or at all.

To follow the postcolonial historiography of Dipesh Chakrabarty in "Provincializing Europe: Postcoloniality and the Critique of History," the peculiarity—subjective, textual, and conceptual at once—directly concerns the co-implication of writing and subjectivity and temporality, for "a historical construction of temporality (medieval/modern, separated by historical time), in other words, is precisely the axis along which the colonial subject splits itself [and to grant the premises of universalism also all modern subjects]. Or to put it differently, this split *is* history; writing history is performing this split over and over again."[14] Chakrabarty presents history as the sign of the subject situated in opposition to the premodern, a situation that the dynamic of literacy itself reiterates. That is, as writing formalizes the subject, at once, it formalizes the subject as a historical coordinate in the progressive temporality that fundamentally measures the distance as well as the increasing distance between the premodern and the modern.

Appearing in 1789, *The Interesting Narrative of the Life of Olaudah Equiano, or Gustavus Vassa, the African, Written by Himself* also credits the new role of alphabetic script beyond its role in the codification of information, as the apparent representation or rehearsal of authentic human being, but significantly under African diasporic authorship. The contradiction of civic animation (and its exclusive premise of humanity) that Gustavus Vassa, or Olaudah Equiano, embodies in his history with the merchant marine retains textual cognates. Slave narratives, remarking the breach between the premodern and the modern as violence rather than order, fail to reproduce the basic presumptions of modern subjectivity. The subjective, discursive, and conceptual disclosure—to borrow again from Dipesh Chakrabarty—"is not that Enlightenment rationalism is always unreasonable in itself but rather a matter of documenting how—through what historical process—its 'reason,' which was not always self-evident to everyone, has been made to look 'obvious' far beyond the ground where it originated."[15] One aspect of the disclosure is that the figure of the ex-slave narrator—corporeally and textually—seems only ostensibly "far beyond the ground where [modern rationalism] originated." Slave narratives dramatically disclose that African-derived persons and African-derived subjectivities stand as fundamental ciphers of the premodern—violently conscripted nonetheless for the emergence and the temporal progress of modernity. Insofar as the title *The Interesting Narrative of the Life of Olaudah Equiano, or Gustavus Vassa, the African, Written by Himself* juxtaposes two names as seemingly equivalent to the premodern and the modern, rather than the singularity understood to accrue as autobiographical identity, the disruptive binomialism redacts the formative violence of the modern that the narrative recasts, subsequently and progressively.

Because he names himself twice, the narrator of *The Interesting Narrative of the Life of Olaudah Equiano, or Gustavus Vassa, the African, Written by Himself* is a highly peculiar autobiographical figure, a curiosity pursued by literary critic Vincent Carretta in "Olaudah Equiano or Gustavus Vassa? New Light on an Eighteenth-Century Question of Identity." Carretta interrogates the caesura between "Olaudah Equiano" and "Gustavus Vassa," pursuing the question of the subjective referent of the early slave narrative by empirically checking against extant shipping records the dates that the narrator offers in the text in order to determine the veracity of the narrative events and ultimately to attempt to determine whether or not the narrator is born in Africa, as he claims, or in the "New World." Carretta writes: "From the evidence I have seen, the presence of the name Olaudah Equiano on the subscription proposal and title page of 1789 must have come as a revelation to friend and foe alike of Gustavus Vassa. They may have known that he claimed an African birth, but we have no proof yet that they knew of Olaudah Equiano before 1788."[16] The peculiarity is that the narrator lives in the Western world known by his Western name, even as the title announces in its juxtaposition of the two names the incompleteness of this identity. The issue, as with all slave narratives, also involves the political circumstances of the text's publication: "If an African could write and publish without the help or authorization of European intermediaries, and if he could attest from personal experience to the cruelty and inhumanity of the Middle Passage and slavery, he was prima facie evidence against the major arguments made by contemporaneous apologists for slavery."[17] In other words, African-derived voices emergent in the practices of modern literacy redact the historical violence of modernity in ways that make subjectivity, for the moment, unreadable, particularly given the adamant coordination of subjectivity with the literacy on which the modern depends.

The binomial title disrupts the premise, or feint, of the autobiographical subject, the clarity of the "individual," the premise shared with its cognate the modern civil subject, also enmeshed in the technologies of literacy. The duality of the self-declaration confounds the formulas of human presence that it would reiterate. In autobiography, the entanglement of nominalism, textuality, and the self-declaring subject yields the precarious ideal that one text yields one voice, the apparent hypostasis of quotidian human agency, the consubstantial phantom of the textual autobiographical subject. In the proposed dynamic of modern political community, the entanglement of nominalism, textuality, and the principles of legal contraction that seemingly supplant material violence with the exorbitance of regimentation and order, equivocates political community with "concern with needs of a generalized human individual conceived as nonsocial or presocial,"[18] a purely theoretical singularity. Still, as cognate indications of human presence, both remain elaborate paradigms of self-alienation that—if not ultimately fully resolved—seem calculable and determined. The self-alienation of the autobiographical narrative is the preeminent issue of autobiographical theory. The autobiographical writer translates historical and other experiential processes into a diegesis revealing not only the act of substitution but, more ineffably and implausibly, the essential individuality confirmed in realizing the substitution; the formula presents the presiding diegetic presence as the redaction of the writer without the text. The self-alienation of the necessary monad of modern political community is an enforced psychic proposition.

Arrayed among communities, markets, and nations, the subject is a relay and cipher in the diffuse technologies of obligation subtending the international economies of adamant commodity exchange, the contractual web broadly sustained by cursive script. However, the conceptual distress of the binomial title proposes human visibility in other terms, in terms that exceed these modern forms of routine self-possession, because the issue of self-possession is limited strictly according to the fiats of race, a prime civic force. Put otherwise, the paramount point to notice is that the opposite Africanity of the title accounts for its binomialism; this irregularity by which racial blackness conflates with textuality presents an anomalous figurative rendition of human being that, at once, nonetheless, seems to forfeit the figurativeness of human being as it is designed by the cultural and political logics of the Western Atlantic.

The disturbance of the title, then, rather than incidental, variously structures the text: its generic specification(s), narrative voice(s) and, particularly, its most closely detailed scene, the scene of manumission pivotal to the narrative. The distress of the title, for these reasons, insists on an extended exposition or formulation: The nominalism on which the equation of the autobiographical text and subjectivity depends is the point of distress in the binomial *The Interesting Narrative of the Life of Olaudah Equiano, or Gustavus Vassa, the African, Written by Himself*, conceptual distress calling into question the veracity of the "individual presence" associated with the autobiographical form. As an integral part of this solicitation—in the Derridean sense of the word—the binomialism registers the arbitration of literacy in the Atlantic lineaments of race, the divide along which the index of the premodern and modern is codified, as well as, finally, full human visibility in the Western Atlantic, which is to say, "the bureaucratic construction of citizenship, modern state, and bourgeois privacy that classical political philosophy has produced."[19] These claims to paramount human visibility in the Western Atlantic are transactional, and the scene of manumission re-scripts these transactional premises to a point of distress reminiscent of the distress of the title.*

In distinction to the marginal importance of literacy to the premodern, this standard formulation betrays the constitutive role of literacy in the consolidation of the modern. The political scientist C. B. Macpherson explains this sociopolitical condition by the term "possessive individualism":

> The theorist of autobiography Philippe Lejeune in "The Autobiographical Pact" famously claims the literary specificity of the genre precisely in its contractual nature, that there is only an implicit, imaginative contract guaranteeing the viability of the autobiographical subject. Philippe Lejeune states: "Making an agreement with the 'narratee' whose image he constructs, the autobiographer incites the real reader to enter into the game and gives the impression that an agreement has been signed by the two parties. But it is evident that the real reader can adopt modes of reading different from the one that is suggested to him, and especially that many published texts in no way include an explicit contract.[20]

Nonetheless, the modernity of autobiography also remains in the obverse features of the watershed transformations following the sixteenth century and the modern

* At this point, the original manuscript contains an introductory sentence regarding the well-known work of Henry Louis Gates, followed by an incomplete sentence that seems to be the opening of another, incomplete paragraph and a pair of words that served perhaps as notes or place markers from an earlier outline:

> In *The Signifying Monkey*, in his discussion of the trope of the talking book, the literary critic Henry Louis Gates outlines the emphatically skewed alignments on which the narrative turns and the title reflects.
> [. . .] in its direct conflation of the pre-modern and the modern performs in its necessary reference to cursive script the complexity of identity marked by the binominal title Vass is named several times.
> Modernity / pre-modernity

As Gates's Signifying Monkey is well known—and treated in detail in the following section—and because Barrett's further thoughts on the connection seem intended to buttress the points above regarding the importance of the binomial title and the way this dual naming structures the narrative, these incomplete sentences have been omitted from the final manuscript.

racial cognates of civic identity. Finally the textual, historical, and geocultural co-implications of European modernity restate the distinctiveness of the genre of autobiography.*

To return to our discussion of the narrative of Equiano/Vassa, we note that the distress is not confined to the title, however, for the juxtaposition of the two names forecasts strategies of protest central to the narrative that expose the international violence inextricably linked with the proposition of modern individual and autobiographical identity. The duplicity of the naming is reconstituted in the first three chapters of the narrative in particular, by the manipulation of narrative point of view. The perspective of Olaudah Equiano the African child predominates in the initial portions of the text over the perspective of Gustavus Vassa, the British/modern citizen-subject more or less reconciled to the conditions of the West. The narrative begins without the limits of the European world in the Bight of Benin, so that the juxtaposition of the points of view of "Olaudah Equiano" and "Gustavus Vassa" in plotting the narrative fosters numerous strategies of racial and cultural critique. Making this observation early in the criticism of the narrative, literary critic Valerie Smith in *Self-Discovery and Authority in Afro-American Narrative* notes: "Most of the narrative is told from Equiano's reasoned, equable, and worldly wise adult point of view. This tone, however, is interrupted on several occasions in the first third of the book by . . . his point of view as a young African boy."[21]

This point of view of Olaudah Equiano, representing the premodern view from without the European world, does not describe a world of disorder, but of clear social organization. This organization includes geographical/jurisdictional division: "Benin . . . extends along the coast about 170 miles, but runs back into the interior part of Africa to a distance hitherto I believe unexplored by any traveler, and seems only terminated at length by the empire of Abyssinia, near 1,500 miles from its beginning";[22] social rank/jurisprudence: "Those Embrenche, or chief men, decided disputes and punished crimes, for which purpose they always assembled together. The proceedings were generally short, and in most cases the law of retaliation prevailed";[23] marriage and monogamy: "The men however do not preserve the same constancy to their wives which they expect from them, for they indulge in a plurality, though seldom in more than two";[24] diet: "bullocks, goats, and poultry supply the greatest part of their food. These constitute likewise

* Here the original manuscript again contains what appear to be remnants of notes or a structuring outline that we have chosen not to include in the final manuscript, this time consisting of two names: Habermas/Davies. It seems that Barrett had intended to use these two scholars to transition from a discussion of the inherent modernity of autobiography back into a discussion of Equiano's narrative. The transitional phrase has been added to the opening of the next paragraph in an attempt to signal this return.

the principal wealth of the country and the chief articles of its commerce. The flesh is usually stewed in a pan; to make it savoury we sometimes use also pepper and other spices, and we have salt made of wood ashes. Our vegetables are mostly plaintains, eadas, yams, beans, and Indian corn";[25] dwellings: "These houses never exceed one storey in height; they are always built of wood or stakes driven into the ground, crossed with wattles, and neatly plastered within and without. The roof is thatched with reeds. Our day-houses are left open at the sides, but those in which we sleep are always covered, and plastered in the inside with a composition mixed with cow-dung to keep off the different insects which annoy us during the night. The walls and floors also of these are generally covered with mats";[26] commerce: "As we live in a country where nature is prodigal of her favours, our wants are few and easily supplied; of course we have few manufactures. They consist for the most part of calicoes, earthenware, ornaments, and instruments of war and husbandry. But these make no part of our commerce, the principal articles of which, as I have observed, are provisions."[27]

It is important to recognize how starkly the human presence discernable through the lineaments of these points of reference opposes the lineaments of the modern subject and the historical political order of the modern subject, in the words of Chakrabarty "the bureaucratic construction of citizenship, modern state, and bourgeois privacy that classical political philosophy has produced."[28] Further, it is important to note the frequency of pronouns of collective identity—"we," "our"—in the early sections of the narrative, that mark claims to and of community never fully reproduced or exceeded at any other point in the text. In short, "Olaudah Equiano" makes explicit the oddity of what is familiarly "European" as seen from the point of view he draws beyond the geography and customs of Europe.

As well as in the binomial title, the figure "Olaudah Equiano" functions in the narrative to mark the suspension between two cultural or epistemological orders. The opening features of the narrative undercut the European world that comes to predominate in the text; or, to put it differently, the discrepancy in the points of view is not merely a matter of individual perception but the recognition and articulation of the racialized, international systems of predation enacting and always reenacting the break between the premodern and the modern, and determining the course of the narrative. In the West African context "Equiano" means "vicissitude or fortunate; also one favored and having a loud voice and well-spoken," the narrator relates in the first chapter; but in the context of the Atlantic world to which the narrator is taken "Equiano" holds no meaning, as Carretta points out, except to question the "New World" and British identity that the narrator is forced to acquire. Carretta writes, to repeat the point: "From the evidence I have seen, the presence of the name Olaudah Equiano on the subscription proposal and title page of *The Interesting Narrative* in 1789 must have come as a revelation to friend and foe alike of Gustavus Vassa."[29] Like the unfamiliar African name, the opening episodes enact a suspension between African-derived personhood and the routinized systems of violent domination inaugurating Western modernity as well as sustaining its historical progress.

It is important to note that the opposing points of view reflect the irresolvable structural paradox of autobiographical identity, the unbridgeable distance between the narrating "I" and the narrated "I." "Olaudah Equiano" at the opening of the narrative corresponds most directly to the narrated "I," the recalled figure of the past understood to approximate fully the figure recounting the narrative, despite the fact that the narrative stands as the unequivocal evidence of the temporal and other differentiations between the two. "Gustavus Vassa" at this point in the narrative corresponds most directly to the narrating "I," the authorial figure of some present moment understood to be making the claims of identification with the figure emerging through the temporal and other differentiations between them, ironically forming the narrative. Gusdorf states the problem as "the [autobiographical] illusion [that] begins from the moment that the narrative confers a meaning on the event which, when it actually occurred, no doubt had several meanings or perhaps none. This postulating of a meaning dictates the choice of the facts to be retained and of the details to bring out or to dismiss according to the demands of the preconceived intelligibility."[30]

Still, the binomialism cannot be reduced strictly to this autobiographical riddle as it certifies modern subjectivity. The juxtaposition also redacts other divisions of the narrative, such as the generic distinctions that fracture it. The opening approximates the style and themes of the picaresque plot, a series of episodic events finally unified by the recurring appearance of the picaro or antihero surviving the series of adventures, while the conclusion approximates the style and themes of the spiritual autobiography or conversion narrative, the organizing principle being, as put by Foster, the belief that there is "no more praiseworthy quest than that for salvation."[31] The literary critic Angelo Costanzo in *Surprising Narrative: Olaudah Equiano and the Beginnings of Black Autobiography* emphasizes the sequence of these generic distinctions: "The narrative has a three-part structure. The first part deals with Equiano's capture in Africa and with his subsequent bondage. . . . [T]he second part deals with the purchase of his freedom, the turning point in his life . . . by means of which his physical freedom allows him to practice faithfully his newfound Christian religion. . . . Thus in the third part of the book he becomes more religious."[32] As Gustavus Vassa faces continuing trials and adventures across the Atlantic Ocean, the Mediterranean Sea, as well as a return to the African coast after his manumission, his characterizations of these events often become occasions for reflection on his circumstances, or for invocations of Providence. The opening perspective conveys bewilderment, confusion, and disgust, whereas the perspective in the latter sections of the narrative is more reflective in the open service of Christian testimony. For instance, chapter 10, the chapter recording Gustavus Vassa's spiritual conversion, is unremittingly intertextual, referring liberally to passages from The Book of Revelation, John, Acts, Job, and Canticles, as well as concluding with religious verses that Gustavus Vassa writes himself.

In other words, marking the generic fracture, the pivotal scene of manumission both coalesces and disfigures the presiding autobiographical identity by consolidating the autobiographer within the political structures of modernity but, at the same time, reiterating the emphatic self-difference signaled in the caesura between "Olaudah Equiano" and "Gustavus Vassa." That is, the scene of manumission depicts the legal and economic contract that most clearly guarantees the distinction in identity between "Olaudah Equiano" and "Gustavus Vassa," the narrated "I" and narrating "I" of the opening portions of the narrative; however, because of the distinction between the two figures, the scene reflects this legal and economic contraction as the most ostensible, orderly trace of the international predation establishing the opposition of the identities and the opposition of the premodern and the modern in the first place, as well as the developmental progression of this opposition providing the conceptual torque of modern temporality. The binomialism of the title, the distinct narrative points of view, and the generic divisions of the narrative, signal in turn, then, the fracture indelible to the modern identity of the narrator.

Coordinating the mutual information of these aspects of the narrative, the scene of manumission not only revises the narrator's status from chattel (or commodity) to nominally free citizen-subject, but it revises as well the earlier scene in which the narrator first acquires the name of the free citizen-subject "Gustavus Vassa"—if not the status of citizen-subject—a scene told from the perspective of Olaudah Equiano: "While I was on board this ship [traveling from the African coast], my captain and master named me *Gustavus Vassa*. I at that time began to understand him a little, and refused to be called so, and told him as well as I could that I would be called Jacob; but he said I should not and still called me Gustavus; and when I refused to answer to my new name, which at first I did, it gained me many a cuff; so at length I submitted and was obliged to bear the present name, by which I have been known ever since."[33] The manumission, like this earlier scene, highlights the visibility and familiarity of the name Gustavus Vassa but replaces the violence of the first transaction with the discursive order represented by the exchanged legal and fiscal instruments in its subsequent rendition of the narrator's identity as Gustavus Vassa. Restated, since the figure and the traces of

Olaudah Equiano in the narrative hold always the contrary interest of recording the forms of violence that sustain modernity, the scene of manumission troubles the conflation of the human, legal, and fiscal lineaments that it documents, even despite its more fortunate scripting of the narrator's cultural identity.

The trouble is worth pursuing: Olaudah Equiano renders the early scenes of human contact in the narrative as primarily scenes of affective exchange—for example, his attachment to his family (particularly his sister), his integration into other African communities after his kidnapping, his friendship with Richard Baker on the slaving ship, his disappointing encounter with his young playmate on arriving in Guernsey, England. He describes the inhabitants of his Ibo village by stating: "We are almost a nation of dancers, musicians, and poets."[34] Olaudah Equiano's first kidnapping and subsequent status as a slave provide the initial trauma of the text, and the trauma is his circulation in new and unfamiliar communities and forms of community, experiences he opposes immediately to his circulation as a commodity in the Atlantic system of trade. Olaudah Equiano's initial forms of enslavement reposition him locally and culturally yet still within the renditions of human interaction premised on affective relations, rather than the adamant, forbidding dynamics of modern commodity exchange, modernity *as* commodity exchange.

As a point of illustration, Olaudah Equiano recalls one of his earliest episodes of enslavement through the exchanges that take place over meals: "I could scarce help expressing my surprise that the young gentleman should suffer me, who was bound, to eat with him who was free; and not only so, but that he would not at any time either eat or drink till I had taken first, because I was the eldest, which was agreeable to our custom. Indeed, everything here, and all their treatment of me, made me forget that I was a slave. The language of these people resembled ours so nearly that we understood each other perfectly. They had also the very same customs as we."[35] In contrast, he recounts once on board the slaving ship: "One day they [the white sailors] had taken a number of fishes, and when they had killed and satisfied themselves with as many as they thought fit, to our astonishment who were on the deck, rather than give any of them to us to eat as we expected, they tossed the remaining fish into the sea again, although we begged and prayed for some as well as we could, but in vain; and some of my countrymen, being pressed by hunger, took an opportunity when they thought no one saw them of trying to get a little privately; but they were discovered, and the attempt procured them some very severe floggings."[36] These and other scenes of eating, by ironically commenting on each other like the scenes of naming and manumission, invert the customary valences of the premodern and the modern, Europe and Africa, as well as modern catalogues of racialization.

The episode of manumission does not turn so much on the clearly directed violence of the modern but on the coincident verbal and financial exchange transforming the status of the narrator. The scene draws, at once, affective exchange and the preeminent instruments of the exorbitant discursive order underwriting the Atlantic economies of exchange. These features no longer serve as markers of cultural differentiation but as points of coincidence: "When I went in I made my obeisance to my master, and with money in my hand, and many fears in my heart, I prayed him to be as good as his offer to me, when he was pleased to promise me my freedom as soon as I could purchase it. This speech seemed to confound him; he began to recoil: And my heart that instant sunk within me."[37] The episode is the most closely rendered in the narrative, drawn through the most extended exchange of dialogue and the series of reactions punctuating the dialogue in which, paradoxically, the narrator is both the object of commodification and the agent gaining possession of the commodity in the exchange. If being understood as an object of commodification is startling at the outset of the narrative, the narrator in this scene masters this once strange form of interaction, which is to say, the arbitrariness of personification and reification at the center of the re-imagination of world markets that produces and animates modernity, and the verbal, emotional, legal, and financial exchanges ensuing around this incident broker the distinction between "Olaudah Equiano" and "Gustavus Vassa." Holding paramount significance in the unfolding of the narrative, the scene renders commonplace the form of interaction entirely absent from the earliest portions of the text. In its reformulations, personhood and the community become derivatives of the abstracted notion of the market in which priority is given to the symbolic foremost as cursive script, as evidenced by the financial instruments and the legal contract essential to the scene. Yet, given the importance of the point of view of Olaudah Equiano to the narrative, the personhood and the community drawn in the scene contradict those of the market as the premodern, which is, on the contrary, the derivative of the community coalescing in the public physicality of marketplace that embodies always additional and privileged forms of social—and, therefore, symbolic—exchange. The caesura between the two names "Olaudah Equiano" and "Gustavus Vassa" holds the contradistinction.

The scene of manumission profoundly marks the narrator's increasing command of European-derived systems of culture and trade, documenting not only the change in legal condition but also the cultural transition that has been underway since the severest trauma of the narrative, the violent voyage across the Atlantic. The remarkable transformation, beyond the legal and fiscal ones, is "the shift in the way community is formulated as an object-ideal," in the words of cultural critic Hortense Spillers.[38] The revision, beyond the narrator's status from chattel (or commodity) to nominally free social subject, is the revision of the forms of human interaction and affective relations that introduce the narrative through Olaudah Equiano's characterization of the West African coast. The scene documents the narrator moving more adeptly into the system of commodity exchange responsible precisely for the greatest early traumas of the text, his encounter with European-derived persons and cultural practices. In the signal episode, the human contact and affective exchange remain inextricable from commodity and fiscal exchange: "When I got to the office and acquainted the Registrar with my errand he congratulated me on the occasion and told me he would draw up my manumission for half price, which was a guinea. I thanked him for his kindness, and having received it and paid him I hastened to my master to get him to sign it, that I might be fully released. Accordingly he signed the manumission that day, so that before night, I who had been a slave in the morning, trembling at the will of another, was become my own master and completely free."[39]

Olaudah Equiano describes the first rendition of his person as a commodity very differently: "The first object which saluted my eyes when I arrived on the coast was the sea, and a slave ship which was then riding at anchor and waiting for its cargo. These filled me with astonishment, which as soon converted into terror when I was carried on board. I was immediately handled and tossed up to see if I were sound by some of the crew, and I was now persuaded that I had gotten into a world of bad spirits."[40]

The caesura, then, between "Olaudah Equiano" and "Gustavus Vassa" signals the disruption of identity that nevertheless seems to produce the autobiographical identity itself. The figure of Gustavus Vassa, although an identity already acquired, most legibly and literally is rescripted at this point and, moreover, thenceforth governs the narrative most clearly. Put another way, in the transaction the conditions of captivity and desire and trade coalesce, in contrast to the earlier scene, in which the clear disjunction between captivity and Olaudah Equiano's desires are pronounced as violence. The pivotal appearance of the instruments of literacy ratifies the conflation of captivity, desire, and trade that supplants the earlier disjunctions between them articulated as the violence of the narrative. One signal effect is the concomitant fixing and confusing of the autobiographical identity, rendered through the concomitantly literary and historical trace of the predatory racial premises of modernity—if not in the significant order and hypostasis of cursive script of the transaction, script exceeding the autobiographical individuation it brokers because of the intercontinental violence it revises abruptly. "Olaudah Equiano" as well as the caesura between the two autobiographical names troubles this script, cursive and otherwise. For the ability to buy and sell people is a form of institutionalized violence rather than the ratification of social and epistemological order, particularly from the perspective of the people being commodified. The complexity is that the unfamiliar name registers the fact more certainly.

Atlantic Economies and the Self

These issues are confirmed textually and racially. Two roughly contemporary but profoundly distinct narratives published at the close of the eighteenth century underscore that the epistemological and economic alliances of the European modernity effectively formalize—in the construal of the phantasm of the individual—race. The narrative figures of Olaudah Equiano in *The Interesting Narrative of the Life of Olaudah Equiano, or Gustavus Vassa, the African, Written by Himself* and the Scottish physician Mungo Park in *Travels in the Interior Districts of Africa* (1800) literalize as racial premises the cultural premises of the phantasm of the individual. Olaudah Equiano in the first narrative "marshals the army of contemporary metaphors at his disposal to make a highly articulate argument against slavery on the basis of Christian morality"[41] and, in doing so, redacts dramatically the formula of "autos," "bios," and "graphe" in what the literary critic Henry Louis Gates in the study *The Signifying Monkey* terms as the topos of "the Talking Book." In the other narrative, Mungo Park records his attempt "to begin at the mouth of the Gambia River, to travel inland to the Niger to find out which direction it flowed, and return with as much information as he could about the country he had traveled through,"[42] disclosing the arbitration of the modern subjection as he must recast himself within the cultural contexts of the West African interior recasting the meaning of literacy. In the first narrative the figure of human presence is realized troublesomely in the figure of Olaudah Equiano and is sustained troublesomely in the figure of Mungo Park in the other. Both narratives take up the autobiographical charge to convey modern human presence as much as, if not more so than, the contexts they describe.

In the fourth chapter of his narrative after describing in the previous chapter his fear and astonishment at the cruelty rampant aboard the slaving ship abducting him from the African coast, Olaudah Equiano employs the image of the "Talking Book." The topos of "the Talking Book," as theorized by Gates, underscores that following the cultural reorganizations of Europe proceeding from the sixteenth century, one consistency "was that black people could become [human and sometimes civic] speaking subjects only by inscribing their voices in the written word,"[43] the upshot being that the topos constitutes "the ur-type of the Anglo-African tradition."[44] The topos dramatizes Olaudah Equiano's incomprehension of and astonishment at print culture, incomprehension of and astonishment at the extraordinary feint proposing the technologies of script to be equivalent conventionally to human presence. In the racialized incident, the rudimentary premise of the genre of autobiography is confounding: "I had often seen my master and Dick employed in reading, and I had a great curiosity to talk to the books as I thought they did. . . . I have often taken up a book and have talked to it and then put my ears to it, when alone, in hopes it would answer me; and I have been very much concerned when I found it silent."[45]

The scene states Olaudah Equiano's disbarment from the stark contrivance of the humanizing protocols of European modernity and its extensions, recapitulates his inhuman status in the European modernity, inhumanity rendered acutely by the brutality of the Middle Passage as well as the ideal abjection of the African diaspora proposed by the European diaspora. The autobiographical phantasm, the individual, is profoundly solicited—in the Derridean sense of the word—by the autobiographical figure dehumanized before the signs of literacy. The self-penned appearance is the curious appearance of race within the modern protocols.

In *Travels in the Interior Districts of Africa*, Mungo Park, having "contracted with a group known as the African Association,"[46] arrives at the mouth of the Gambia River hoping "to examine into the productions of a country so little known; and to become experimentally acquainted with the modes of life, and character of the natives,"[47] and in preparation he is "furnished with a letter of credit . . . for £200."[48] From the outset, then, the narrative represents the abiding individual presence in routine proximity to the formula that reconvenes foremost as human presence the individual, the market, and literacy. The contrivance fails Park because he travels through cultures in which neither the phantasm of the individual, literacy, nor the market receive the same import—even as they hold status in alternative systems of exchange and sociality:

> [T]hese [sheep's] horns were highly valued, as being easily convertible into portable sheaths, or cases, for containing and keeping secure certain charms or amulets called *saphies*, which the Negroes constantly wear about them. These saphies are prayers or rather sentences, from the Koran, which the Mohamedan priests write on scraps of paper and sell to the simple natives, who consider them to possess very extraordinary virtues. Some of the Negroes wear them to guard themselves against the bite of snakes or alligators; and on this occasion the saphie is commonly enclosed in a snake's or alligator's skin, and tied round the ancle [sic]. Others have recourse to them in time of war, to protect their persons against hostile weapons; but the common use to which these amulets are applied, is to prevent or cure bodily diseases; to preserve from hunger and

> thirst, and generally to conciliate the favour of superior powers under all the circumstances and occurrences of life.[49]

The misguided notion, according to Park's scheme, is taking literacy as tangential to the relation to the self, as merely independent from corporeality, as opposed to being able to supplant corporeality on occasions and with material dividends—precisely the feint of the letter of credit that not only represents him but also "Dr. John Laidley,"[50] who supplies it and the protocols of market exchange it harbors ideally.[51] What is not visible foremost in the value of the "saphies," despite the circuit of their own systems of exchange, is the market as the presiding paradigm, the ideally infinite arena of ideally infinite exchange securing human presence—the point of disqualification. The play of the imagination valuing the saphies does not coincide easily with the play of the imagination drawing modern subjectivity as the installation in the preeminence of market exchange through literacy. The discrepancy is as economic as it is anthropomorphic and racial, and the discrepancy provides the concluding point of the narrative. For, after failing to chart the entire course of the Niger River, Park leaves the African coast on "the ship Charles-Town, an American vessel, commanded by Mr. Charles Harris . . . intending to touch at Goree to fill up; and to proceed from thence to South Carolina."[52] The material conveyance that is taken by Olaudah Equiano as "a new refinement in cruelty" is,[53] above all, taken by Park as the means to greater security after "having been absent from England two years and seven months."[54]

The coordinates (both diachronic and synchronic) of the racialized autobiographical opposition might be schematized as follows:

"market/society"	"violence"	"market-society"
racial blackness (fetish: affective relations)		modernity as cultural peril
	Slave Ship	
racial whiteness (fetish: alphabetic script)		modernity as cultural safety
HUMAN CONDITION	MODERNITY	INDIVIDUAL CONDITON

That is, the significance of the genre exceeds its textuality insofar as the recorded phantasm of the individual appears rightly in the cultural situation brokered by post-Renaissance Europe: "The curiosity of the individual about himself . . . is thus tied to the Copernican Revolution: At the moment it enters history, humanity, which previously aligned its development to the great cosmic cycles, finds itself engaged in an autonomous adventure; soon mankind even brings the domain of the sciences into line with its own reckoning, organizing them, by means of technical expertise, according to its own desires."[55] In particular, the disposition of

African-derived populations in the European modernity and its permutations suggests that the "individual presence" groomed by the genre of autobiography as well as its sociotemporal context does not correspond to universal human presence.*

The complexity is representational, as the theoretical discourse on autobiography also acknowledges abundantly. The problem is that the subject of autobiography, despite the irresolvable inconsistencies it proposes, claims the appearance of untroubled veracity, not arbitration, the impossibility of the autobiographical figure being that it cannot overwhelm the complicated effort securing it. These textual issues receive the greatest attention in Gusdorf's "The Conditions and Limits of Autobiography," in which, following the description of the modern ethos of the autobiographical subject, Gusdorf rehearses extensively the representational allowances of the genre and its subject:

> The difficulty is insurmountable: No trick of presentation even when assisted can prevent the narrator from always knowing the outcome of the story he tells—he commences, in a manner of speaking, with the problem already solved. Moreover, the illusion begins from the moment that the narrative *confers a meaning* on the event which, when it actually occurred, no doubt had several meanings or perhaps none. This postulating of a meaning dictates the choice of the facts to be retained and of the details to bring out or to dismiss according to the demands of the preconceived intelligibility. It is here that the failures, the gaps, and the deformations of memory find their origin; they are not due to purely physical cause or chance, but on the contrary they are the result of an option of the writer who remembers and wants to gain acceptance for this or that revised and corrected version of his past, his private reality.[56]

With irresolvable inconsistencies, the phantasm of the individual, the subject of the autobiography, is the focal point of all sides of the autobiographical feint—in adamant hermeneutic circularity. The autobiographical figure, in the provision of

* The original manuscript contains here an introduction to a quote attributed to François Crouzet, from his book *A History of the European Economy, 1000–2000*:

> . . . demonstrates the point, as the economic historian François Crouzet, for example, in *A History of the European Economy, 1000–2000*, observes: This is to say emphatically, the "individual presence" groomed by the genre of autobiography as well as its socio-temporal context does not correspond to universal human presence.

A thorough search of this source, however, yielded no match. Based on the placement within the paragraph and the larger discussion, it is also possible that Barrett had meant to attribute the quotation to Gusdorf; here again, however, no quote was found to match. It appears that the actual supporting quotation is missing; further, the concluding line emphatically stating the non-universality of the individual presence of autobiography seems to be Barrett's own. To that end, the reference to Crouzet has been omitted and the assertion qualified somewhat by replacing "demonstrates" with "suggests."

the diegetic coherence, forms, in this way, one relay of the proliferating figures of individuality that characterizes the modern European societies and their permutations: the writer, the separate members of the reading audience, all of whom are more forthrightly the modern mobile agents of the civic infrastructure.

Atlantic Economies and the Self, Again

What the obverse features of autobiography signify, far more than the properties of narrative coherence, is the representational feint bolstering the disciplinary terms of modern economic and epistemic exchange, since the autobiographical subject, the phantasm of the individual, "a concern peculiar to modern man," proves to be the redoubling, ideally materializing gesture of the recuperative text defining the anthropomorphic semblances and the anthropomorphic displacements of the modern "systematic conquest" for and by means of which, as Gusdorf explains, the autobiographical subject remains the exemplary point of the discursive and cultural identity. The representational order of the autobiographical subject restates the representational order of the proliferating modern European cultural scheme. As much as it holds either rational or metaphorical rigor, the individual figure as construed by autobiography grants, or restates, the force of the civic and international protocols proceeding from the sixteenth century. The effective affinities, or synonymity, of the modern civic agent and the subject of autobiography rehearses, to follow the analysis of Weintraub, "a major component of [modern] man's self-conception: the belief that, whatever else he is, he is a unique individuality, whose life task is to be true to his very own personality.... [T]his conception of personality, this idea of the individualized person, is a part of the modern form of historical consciousness."[57] Literary critic James Chandler in the essay "The Emergence of Sentimental Probability" proposes analogously in relation to sentimental literature that the "'cultural revolution' in the literary public sphere for which [Adam] Smith was a primary theorist [in *The Theory of Moral Sentiments*] thus not only touches subsequent understandings of individual character, social cohesion, and political innovation but also the moral, social, and political practices that attend them."[58]

The point is confirmed by the open credit that the moral philosopher and incipient political economist Adam Smith grants in *An Inquiry into the Nature and Causes of the Wealth of Nations,* the boon of the extended European markets determined by the emergence of the Atlantic economies and their triangular trade routes. Smith remarks generally that "[t]he market of Europe has become gradually more and more extensive. Since the discovery of America, the greater part of Europe has been much improved. England, Holland, France, and Germany; even Sweden, Denmark, and Russia have all advanced considerably in agriculture and in manufactures."[59] He states more particularly the material and conceptual force the Atlantic economies hold for Europe in book 2, chapter 2, in which he outlines the commercial and internationalizing effects of the general introduction of paper money into European economies, an introduction risking inflation because it makes currency much less scarce a "commodity" but, more important, increases vastly the conceivable size of the market, ideally an infinite arena of infinite exchange. Smith explains:

> Let us suppose, for example, that the whole circulating money of some particular country amounted, at a particular time, to one million sterling, that sum being then sufficient for circulating the whole annual produce of their land and labour. Let us suppose, too, that some time thereafter, different banks and bankers issued promissory notes, payable to the bearer, to the extent of one million, reserving in the different coffers two hundred thousand pounds for answering occasional demands. There would remain, therefore, in circulation, eight hundred thousand pounds in gold and silver, and a million of bank notes, or eighteen hundred thousand pounds of paper and money together.[60]

The much greater number of commercial transactions that can be guaranteed by the same amount of gold and silver that once stabilized the smaller circuit of transactions becomes securely imaginable. The featured result of the extrapolation of the activity underwritten by gold and silver is the much greater availability of "currency" for disposal and investment beyond the confines of the nation, and this outcome holds Smith's greatest attention:

> But the annual produce of the land and labour of the country had before required only one million to circulate and distribute it to its proper consumers, and that annual produce cannot be immediately augmented by those operations of banking. One million, therefore, will be sufficient to circulate it after them. The goods to be bought and sold being precisely the same as before, the same quantity of money will be sufficient for buying and selling them. The channel of circulation, *if I may be allowed such an expression*, will remain precisely the same as before. One million we have supposed sufficient to fill that channel. Whatever, therefore, is poured into it beyond this sum cannot run in it, but must overflow. One million eight hundred thousand pounds are poured into it. Eight hundred thousand pounds, therefore, must overflow, that sum being over and above what can be employed in the circulation of the country. But though this sum cannot be employed at home, it is too valuable to allow to lie idle. It will, therefore, be sent abroad, in order to seek that profitable employment which it cannot find at home.[61]

In pursing and defining the modern dynamics of European markets, Smith rhetorically—if not logically—elides the international territories he glosses with the metaphor of the natural movement of water, "the channel of circulation," as if the American chain of islands only in the remotest way determines the economies of scale he outlines. As he acknowledges the growing importance of the intercontinental production and circulation of goods, Smith concomitantly attempts to make (what is from only one perspective) the abstracted system of trading appear more "natural" than the fertile landscapes and exotic demographies requisitioned for the commerce of Europe and its extensions. At the same time that he appreciates the intercontinental scope of the fiscal arrangements, he delineates the co-implication of the socioeconomic and subjectivizing imperatives of modern Western impulses, insofar as he codifies the emergent principles of capital accumulation as if the presence, condition, and labor conglomerated as racial blackness by the European husbanding of tropical agriculture can be accommodated in no reasonable or clarified way in the reckoning.

Literary critic Sidonie Smith, in order to theorize women's autobiographical practices more effectively, challenges in *Subjectivity, Identity, and the Body* the confidence in the unitary, anthropomorphic, essential self of the autobiographical gesture by highlighting these civic—as opposed to the mythic—contexts of the genre of autobiography:

> Politically, the enlightenment self is aggressive, individualistic in its desires, and liberal in its philosophical perspective. The French Revolution with its cry for liberty, equality, fraternity; the philosophical systems of Locke and Rousseau with their emphasis on empiricism and the experience of the individual's sense as originary loci of knowledge; the self-absorption of Romanticism and its preoccupation with subjective experience; the economic and political shift from aristocratic to bourgeois power; the progressive tendencies of Darwinism, particularly social Darwinism; the consolidation of Protestant ideology with its emphasis on all the accessibility of God to individual prayer and intercession: All these phenomena coalesced to privilege the self-determining individuality of desire and destiny.[62]

In the well-known collection of essays *On Autobiography*, Lejeune also enumerates the particularized cultural scheme of autobiography:

> Everyone is pretty much in agreement on one point: There exists a correlation between the development of autobiographical literature and the rise of a new dominant class, the middle-class, in the same way that the literary genre of memoires has been intimately linked to the development of the feudal system. Through autobiographical literature appears the conception of the person and the individualism characteristic of our societies; we would find nothing similar in ancient societies, or in so-called primitive societies, or even in other societies contemporaneous with our own, like the Chinese Communist society, where

> the individual is, as a matter of fact, prevented from looking at his personal life like private property that is capable of having exchange value.[63]

Whereas Smith outlines the march of European events validating and entrenching the phantasm of the individual as one of the most prized features of modern European cultures and societies, Lejeune remarks the subjectivizing discipline or "reality" that the phantasm of the individual holds for the purposes of commodity exchange, ultimately the most prized feature of modern European cultures and societies.

The "individual presence" groomed textually in European modernity is the key feature naturalizing the epistemological and social protocols of capital accumulation, the diachronic episode and synchronic formation marking as fully the break between classical and medieval Europe and modern Europe and its permutations. The limited, modern notion of "individual presence" extrapolated into the universal certainty effectively twins human experience—in the complex feint—with the relays of property, mobile forms of ownership, and the contractual, remunerative, and exploitative arrangements of the cash nexus, and ideally the proposition of the individual figure, the modern civic agent, the subject of autobiography, appears to precede and exceed the modern episode and formation from which that individual emerges, which is one ideological feint centrally considered by Macpherson in the study *The Political Theory of Possessive Individualism*. Macpherson, whose term "possessive individualism" captures the revolutionary premise that "individual presence" holds for the social, economic, and cultural reorganizations of Europe, describes the modern civic and epistemological reorganizations as follows:

> The individual, it was thought, is free inasmuch as he is proprietor of his person and capacities. The human essence is freedom from dependence on the wills of others, and freedom is a function of possession. Society becomes a lot of free equal individuals related to each other as proprietors of their own capacities and of what they have acquired by their exercise. Society consists of relations of exchange among proprietors. Political society becomes a calculated device for the protection of this property and for the maintenance of an orderly relation of exchange.[64]

In short, the emergence of the phantasm of the individual is powerfully overdetermined. The "individual presence" reported textually in the genre of autobiography and otherwise in its indigenous cultural context is an arbitrary and profitable, rather than inevitable, paradigm. Rather than revealing the form or veracities of the human "condition" (diachronically or synchronically), the posture of modern individuality obscures the force of its situation: concomitantly very specific and very general.

The role of literacy, the increased currency of scripted representations for the modern cultural reorganizations, is augmented overwhelmingly by the new protocols of sedimenting capitalist exchange, as a number of historians and theorists of the book and literacy emphasize. In the study *Men of Learning in Europe at the End of the Middle Ages* historian Jacques Verger underscores the esoteric quality of book culture particularly prior to the printing press technology of the fifteenth century, noting the rarity of general access to books due both to the expense of the parchment on which they were produced as well as to the taxing processes of the copyist who "worked slowly—about two and a half leaves a day, on average. In other words, in a year a good copyist produced barely five books of two hundred leaves; or to put it another way, to provide thousands books of this kind in one year, no less than two hundred copyists working full-time were required."[65] Verger enumerates the library holdings of medieval universities as ranging from several dozen volumes to several hundred, with only very few larger, exceptional holdings in Britain, France, or Italy. In the study *Writing and European Thought 1600–1830*, literary critic Nicholas Hudson writes that the "principal factors promoting literacy were Protestantism, which encouraged individual reading of the Bible, and the rise of the commercial middle class, a segment of society that prized literacy for its worldly advantages."[66] Social scientist Roger Chartier, examining the period between the end of the middle ages and the eighteenth century, notices the reassigned civic meanings attached to the book and literacy: "The legitimation of literary property was thus based on a new aesthetic perception designating the work as an original creation recognizable by the specificity of its expression."[67] Historian Henri-Jean Martin in *The History and Power of Writing* notes the extraliterary significance of literacy for European social organization: "The development of a market economy always favors writing. . . . [T]he circulation of men and goods, which increased connections and the exchange of information, generated progress in communication techniques (in the broad sense of the term). Indeed from time immemorial literacy developed along land, river, and sea routes and concentrated where routes intersected."[68]

Sociologist Adrian Johns in *The Nature of the Book* describes the communal, rather than individual, emphasis and dynamics of literate exchange in early modern Europe, particularly England. Johns details, for example, the courtly attachments of early literate culture and the way in which the internationally marked downfall of Galileo in the 1630s turns on the courtly sociality of print culture in which he is protected until the fall of his ally and patron in Rome, Ciampoli. Similarly, Johns details the communal processes of reading, certifying empirical and technical knowledge and experimentation, the ebullient communality of the production processes and the elaborate networks of regulatory structures supervised by London's Stationer's Hall. "The sources of print culture are therefore to be sought in civility as much as in technology, and in historical labors as much as in immediate cause and effect," he writes.[69] The characterization is of "reading itself as a skill, just as historically specific as the more obvious dexterity involved in experimentation. If reading has a history, then assuming that modern readers' responses to a printed page accurately reproduce those of the seventeenth century men and women becomes problematic."[70]

The epistemological and economic coincidence is that the "false witness" at the center of the vogue of autobiography develops in tandem with the earliest phases of capital accumulation, mercantile capitalism. Economist G. R. Steele explains that "[m]ercantilism originated during the transition from the feudal economy to merchant capitalism and international commerce, in the sixteenth and seventeenth centuries. A strong central authority was considered essential to the expansion of markets, and it was a mercantilist imperative that the power of the state should be enhanced by an accumulation of national wealth."[71] The mercantilist era, notorious for its opposition to free trade, is marked by measures such as the British Navigation Acts and French *exclusif*, measures aiming to ensure that the tropical products cocoa, coffee, indigo, rum, sugar, and tobacco (as well as gold and silver) extracted from American outposts are shipped exclusively on the vessels of their respective metropolitan centers, then refined and marketed in those metropolitan territories by its national agents and industries. The European annexation of the Americas, resulting in the opportunities to raise and traffic enormous quantities of goods in the new Atlantic economies, transforms the premodern axes of long-distance trade, the significance of the sea lanes of the Baltic trade, the Mediterranean Sea, the Indian Ocean, and the intercontinental arena of the silk roads; the annexation, inaugurating mercantilist policies and the enormous economic significance of the Caribbean basin, cannot be overemphasized in the modernizing progress of Europe and its permutations—economically and imaginatively. The emergence of modern subjectivity and the intrigue of mercantilist agendas constitute two registers of the social, economic, and cultural reorganizations of Europe and its extensions following the sixteenth century, the episode Gusdorf understands in terms of "modern man [and] . . . his systematic conquest of the universe."[72]

The complication, or obfuscation, is that the economic boon secured and resecured by Europe and some of its outposts at each node of the Atlantic economies, a boon radically augmenting European diets, shipping, markets, national formations, and social and cultural institutions, massively introduces sub-Saharan Africans and their descendants into the European "New World" or, differently put, into the newest mechanisms of European viability and, as forcefully, into individual and collective European imaginations. More simply stated, the revolutionary modern situation more and less forthrightly comprehends the circuit of goods premising modern forms of exchange, circuits and forms of exchange that describe the adamant force the intercontinental trade centrifugal to Europe and some of its outposts holds for the constitution of modern subjectivity.

European modernity and its permutations produce mutually reinforcing imaginative and material relays, one upshot being that the close association of alphabetic narrative with identity installs the subject not only in a self-knowing paradigm but, by exceedingly subtle effects, also as an ideally "integrated locus of productive activities within which the endless accumulation of capital . . . [is] the economic objective or 'law' . . . prevail[ing] in fundamental economic activity."[73] That the progress of European modernity and its permutations is at once imaginative and economic is the point historian Robin Blackburn underscores in a revealing allusion to European letters, particularly, the intrigue of Alexander Pope's *The Rape of the Lock*, which remains unimaginable without the revolutions in diet and habits secured by the mercantilist extraction of the labor resources along the West African coast, the tropical produce of the Caribbean basin, and the stark racial imperatives marking the Americas following the sixteenth century:

> In *The Rape of the Lock*, Alexander Pope showed how the drawing-room now commanded global resources to satisfy its whims and cravings. He observed that coffee was *par excellence* the beverage for those concerned with calculation, chocolate that of polite society; in both cases sugar would be added. The habit of smoking tobacco, using sugar and taking sweetened coffee, tea, and chocolate was spreading down through the social formation as urbanization proceeded, the professional and clerical classes grew, and waged or salaried labour became more important in both town and country.[74]

The reformation of collective behavior is profound. Economist Michael Perelman, considering in *The Invention of Capitalism* the coercive social policies of the inaugural laissez-faire economists such as Adam Smith, points out the arbitrariness and force of modernizing strategies of subjection when he details that "Smith was far more interested in changing human behavior than he was with matters of economic development."[75] Perelman states the broad economic context of Smith's theoretical interests and formulations as follows:

> At a time when self-provisioning was a serious barrier to the extension of the capitalist mode of production, classical political economy expressed an unremitting hostility toward conditions that would support the working class household's ability to provide for itself. Once political economy became confident that the household economy was sufficiently hobbled that its role as a producer would be subordinated to capitalist commodity production, economists seemed to lose all interest in the evolution of the social division of labor. Instead, they exhorted households to become more efficient producers of labor

> power. Finally, after problems of effective demand gained more prominence, economists treated the household as a locus of consumption. As a result, the role of the household as a site of production generally fell into oblivion.[76]

In the philosophically based investigation of *The Structural Transformation of the Public Sphere*, philosopher Jürgen Habermas outlines the phantasm of the individual (and its privacy) as the modern economic and legal apparatus allowing "property to become freely disposable for the exchange transactions of participants in the market; for the specification of its heirs to be left up to the free will of the owner; for the choice and exercise of a trade and the training of workers to become a matter of the entrepreneur's discretion; and for wages to be determined by a free contract between the employer and the employee."[77]

This is to say, if the genre of autobiography and its subject are diachronic novelties, they equally are synchronic entanglements. Since they aim to codify as their own textual *presence* other states of conscious presence belatedly confirmed in the reportage, the autobiographical statement is always already unsettling and its productive subject always already indiscernible or obscured. The one form of *presence* "embodies" itself in the aspect of completion and settlement (formalized as the text), which the other cannot. There is, accordingly, the beguiling misrecognition, or slippage, fundamental to the genre: "[w]hen it comes to autobiography, narrative and identity are so intimately linked that each constantly and properly gravitates into the conceptual field of the other."[78] The three morphemes of the term "autobiography" illustrate the close association between alphabetic narrative and the modern forms of identity sponsored by the genre: The self (*autos*) concomitantly discovers and produces the life (*bios*) within the conditions and limits of writing or textuality (*graphy*). Literary critic James Olney in the introduction to *Autobiography: Essays Theoretical and Critical* acknowledges "all three parts of the word" by asking: "What do we mean by the self, or himself [or herself] (*autos*)? What do we mean by life (*bios*)? What significance do we impute to the act of writing (*graphé*)—what is the significance and effect of transforming life, or *a* life, into a text?"[79] The puzzle is that, insofar as the phantasm of the individual, especially in its autobiographical form, ideally integrates the disparities, the resulting "individual presence" posits and pursues a position in which, in the words of literary critic Willis Buck, "[t]he mind, as it were, bears false witness against itself."[80] The perplexity (and its civic correlates) is not simply abstruse but—as already outlined—a profoundly historical formation. The autobiographical subject is, at once, the curiosity of synchronic investigation and the emphatic diachronic point of radically altered cultural relations—the modern. Thus, the autobiographical identification of the subject with the phantasm of the individual is not tied to narrative per se but to the disciplinary, technological, and contractual capacities of alphabetic script, the circumscriptions of textuality for the forms of social organization following the sixteenth century in Europe and its permutations.

Granted the preeminence of the phantasm of the individual, the significance of the dispositions of the two self-penned figures in *The Interesting Narrative of the Life of Olaudah Equiano, or Gustavus Vassa, the African, Written by Himself* and *Travels in the Interior Districts of Africa* is theoretically unintelligible as the material history that routinely disposes of human presence in more than individual ways, thus calling into question the veracity of the "individual presence" guaranteed (ontologically) in the figure of the reported autobiographical subject, (epistemologically) in the figure of the reporting autobiographical subject, (institutionally) in the "pact" through which these figures cohere. In other words, the referentiality of the autobiographical subject is not a riddled textual quandary simply, but registers the redefinitions of human presence following the sixteenth century. These redefinitions grant new significances in literacy, new significances that in the vogue of autobiography realize the terms of modern civic viability in the apparent equality of detailed disparate renditions of the immediate consciousness of emotion, perception, physicality, rational expression itself, sociality, temporality—that is, seemingly immediate renditions of consciousness itself. Hence, as indicated by the complex binomialism of Olaudah Equiano or Gustavus Vassa, all the more noteworthy, then, that the peculiar credibility of the autobiographical subject depends on a difficult figure of speech that at once supplants, negotiates, and implies the broader collective principles of the modern condition.

CHAPTER 3

Captivity, Desire, Trade

The Forging of National Form

"Abolition" seems, misleadingly, to mark a discrete episode in modern political development, an episode historically most peculiar to the nineteenth century, paradigmatically signaling the transformed mandate of the modern nation-state, reorienting the state purportedly to supply the condition of civic individuality as broadly and consistently as possible throughout its jurisdictions, and particularly across race or caste divisions. Abolition, as this type of discrete episode, seems to be the liminal point between the radically distinct legalities of slave regimes and regimes in which states of emancipation are presented as incontrovertible. However, as drawn recently and precisely, for example, by cultural critic Saidiya Hartman in *Scenes of Subjection: Terror, Slavery, and Self-Making in Nineteenth-Century America,* the analytical measure of the term exceeds this discrete episodic characterization. The historical and political transformations reveal instead the ways in which the "entanglements of bondage and liberty shaped the liberal imagination of freedom."[1] Abolition, Hartman details, yields the structural exposure of the state as the formal mechanism by which obligation is fashioned and refashioned, rather than the emancipatory mechanism for conceiving and realizing the end of the virulent subordination aimed at African diasporic people. To understand the upshot of discerning abolition in this way as a structural exposure, rather than simply a discrete historical event, amounts to recognizing that the state intensifies and extends its regulatory mechanism in the political redefinition signaled by abolition. The primary outcome of the redefinition does not annul the forceful calculation of the civic and social imperatives of the modern political state.

Recall that, even as alphabetic script would register for him autobiographical or even legal viability, the sub-Saharan protagonist of *The Interesting Narrative of the Life of Olaudah Equiano, or Gustavus Vassa, the African, Written by Himself* remains primarily unreadable in fully certain anthropomorphic terms. Insofar as he successfully draws racial blackness in autobiographical form, the narrator distresses the representational certainties of modern subjectivity. His experiences, from his abduction from West Africa to his consistently dangerous circuit of the Atlantic "New World" arena, press the representational certainties of Western modernity. As the primary textual sign of the violent impress of modernity, the narrator's autobiographical binomialism details the geographic, civic, and psychic distances insinuated in the composure of modern subjectivity. To follow the analysis of philosopher Charles Mills in *Blackness Visible: Essays on Philosophy and Race,* the reported violence categorically forecloses to Olaudah Equiano or Gustavus Vassa any identity other than that of a *subperson* who, rather than bearing modern awareness, categorically "[has] less mental capacity, with rights on a sliding scale from zero to a ceiling well below that of your white co-humans, a creature deemed to have no real history, who has made no global contribution to civilization, and who in general can be encroached upon with impunity."[2] Interrogating this status, Equiano's narrative restates the ratios of violence both proposing and soliciting this conceptual "unleashing of the inhuman," at once fundamental to Atlantic modernity and the proposition of racial blackness. That is to say, the narrator finds himself husbanded as an inhuman anthropomorphic figure who is, by nature, profoundly antithetical to "the dream of a totally 'enlightened' society, wholly transparent to the light of reason . . . a dream that can only be realized in a totalitarian universe in the form of an utterly administered society."[3]

These modern aspirations revise the clarity of anthropomorphic certainty so that, neither diegetically nor formally, nor phenotypically, nor socially, can Olaudah Equiano or Gustavus Vassa easily describe his own anthropomorphic certainty. The anthropomorphic figure of modern certainty is plainly economic and political, but, at the same time, it is the ineffable epistemological excess of these forms of consciousness that are codified through the transversal of the signifier. The figure entails the political and economic state of consciousness properly coordinated by alphabetic script and yet is incommensurate to this rendition, because it entails also the trace, or ideal, of agency irreducible to the transversal of the signifier. Rather, the experiences of Olaudah Equiano or Gustavus Vassa rehearse the violent, pervasive imperatives—economic, legal, and social—by which racial blackness overwhelmingly disappoints the modern resemblance of the human, signaling instead the "unleashing of the inhuman" that specifies the "human" population of the modern state.

In the philosophical tradition that Mills describes, G. W. F. Hegel refuses absolutely the humanity of the African populations dispersed, or overwhelmed, in the elaboration of Atlantic modernity, the refusal providing the fundamental ground of the theory of human civilization presented in *The Philosophy of History*. Detailing his concept of the geographical bases of world history, Hegel writes that the "Negro, as already observed, exhibits the natural man in his completely wild and untamed state. We must lay aside all thought of reverence and morality—all that we call feeling—if we would rightly comprehend him; there is nothing harmonious with humanity to be found in this type of character."[4] The African-derived person, the "subperson" in Mill's philosophical vocabulary, is in the Hegelian sense an enigmatic subject *without* History, a conceptual impossibility. For, the natural world and its inhabitants are inimical to History in the Hegelian scheme: being, rather, the point of negation anterior to the graduated, dialectical advance leading to modern temporality. The mediation of the natural world is constitutive of the self-consciousness as well as the instrumental mechanisms of the modernity recording the temporal and geographic movement of World Spirit away from "the Mediterranean Sea . . . the heart of the Old World" to the European arc of the Atlantic circumference.[5]

The annulment of racial blackness as human significance is a signal feature of the complex philosophical advance tracing this geographic movement. Initially, Hegel outlines several distinct historiographical enterprises: Original History resembles an act of reportage informed by the emotions of the events recorded as they transpire; Reflective History is a form of Universal History that attempts to grant a view of an entire country or the world; and Pragmatic History didactically coordinates past events with the intrigues of the present; Critical History examines historical narratives to gauge their truth and credibility; Philosophical History contemplates human temporality as the exercise of thought defined as Reason, a premise from which "the history of the world, therefore, presents us with a rational process" excessive to the simple aggregation of events. The constitutive principle of this final historiographical category is "that Reason governs and has governed the World,"[6] historical temporality being, accordingly, the unfolding of Reason, or more specifically still, the development and succession of the Idea of Freedom, the essence of Reason, as Hegel would have it. For, as the essential process of Reason, "[t]he History of the world is none other than the progress of the consciousness of Freedom."[7] This historiographical perspective, Hegel contends, eclipses fully sub-Saharan Africans, since temporality must be understood not simply as succession but, moreover, progression. Historical temporality, in the Hegelian scheme, as the progressively realized movement of Spirit, "the basis and substance of those other forms of a nation's consciousness [culture, morality, religion, political and secular existence],"[8] amounts to a graduated global advance discernible across the planet with the stark exception of sub-Saharan Africa and its inhabitants. He writes: "At this point we leave Africa, not to mention it again. For it is no historical part of the World; it has no movement or development to exhibit."[9]

The adamant movement of historical temporality, discernible everywhere beyond the limits of sub-Saharan Africa, is the "immersion of Spirit in Nature," followed by Spirit, "advancing to the consciousness of its freedom ... [in the] initial separation from Nature [that] is imperfect and partial," followed by Spirit proposing its independence from Nature indicating "the elevation of the soul from this still limited and special form of freedom to its pure universal form ... in which the spiritual essence attains the consciousness and feeling of itself."[10] The specification of the geographical and racial cognates of the advancement of Spirit comprises the greater project of *The Philosophy of History*. The gradations of temporal advance correspond in significant ways with geographic topographies that, more than contingent, remain "the natural connection that helps to produce the Spirit of a People ... the ground on which that Spirit plays its part ... an *essential* and *necessary* basis."[11] Largely in accordance with its topographical disposition, each nation more or less embodies the advancement of Universal Spirit toward the Idea of Freedom as the immanence of self-consciousness, for the "type and character of the people which is the offspring of such a soil ... [establishes] nothing more nor less than the mode and form in which nations make their appearance in History."[12]

The appearance of each nation on the stage of world history clarifies not only the historical trajectory but, as well, the possibilities and limitations of the three predominant topographical types—steppes or uplands, valleys, and coasts. Steppes are archetypically the location of the patriarchal political organization of nomadic herdsman, valleys the location of agriculture and the beginnings of legal relations defined beyond the political dynamics of the familial and, therefore, the location holding the origins of the State, and coasts are archetypically the location of commerce, long-distance trade, and the apotheosis of the regulative State and, therefore, also properly the location of the origins of History. The three continents encircling the Mediterranean Sea demonstrate these potentials and limitations, Hegel writes: "Africa has for its leading classical feature the Upland, Asia the contrast of river regions with the Upland, Europe the mingling of these several elements."[13] The continental topographies, as far as their capacities allow, generate waxing and waning forms of political organization that remain the materials tracing the linear advance of historical temporality, the development of Spirit resting on the "drawing back from the actual world,"[14] the contingencies of the natural, in order to reorient political organization.

Sub-Saharan Africa, however, seems inhabited by populations for whom the "standpoint of humanity ... is mere sensuous volition with energy of will" so that "the entire nature of this race is such as to preclude the existence of any such arrangement" designating the political.[15] The disqualification of sub-Saharan Africa and its populations organizes the linear progression of historical temporality: "The peculiarly African character is difficult to comprehend, for the very reason that, in reference to it, we must quite give up the principle which naturally accompanies all *our* ideas—the category of Universality. In Negro life the characteristic point is the fact that consciousness has not yet attained to the realization of any substantial objective existence—as for example, God, or Law—in which the interest of man's volition is involved and in which he realizes his own being."[16] Sub-Saharan Africa, classified primarily as steppes, holds populations purportedly existing in a state indistinguishable from the natural world and, accordingly, categorically without historical temporality, because neither political organization nor the self-acknowledgment on which political organization must be premised is possible in such a state.

Conversely, elsewhere, varieties of political organization are observable on all three topographies—steppes, valleys, coasts. "The first political form therefore which we observe in History, is *Despotism*, the second *Democracy* and *Aristocracy*, the third *Monarchy*."[17] These distinctions register the progressive advance of historical development that is annulled in Sub-Saharan Africa, given that the "History of the World is the discipline of the uncontrolled natural will, bringing it into obedience to a Universal principle and conferring subjective freedom."[18] Whereas steppes are the least conducive to this advancement, coasts are the most conducive, holding "that element of civilization which the sea supplies."[19] In this scheme, even if sub-Saharan Africa contained any possibility of historical temporality, its topographical classification as a steppe limits severely the possibilities of significant historical development. In sum, because Sub-Saharan Africa is purportedly void of temporality, it is also void of any form of anthropomorphic self-consciousness.

Neither Olaudah Equiano, Gustavus Vassa, nor the fraught coalescence of the two as a single autobiographical persona can be accounted for in this Hegelian scheme. The African-derived autobiographical performance would almost seem to void History itself. On this point, it is important to recognize that Hegelian temporality is not a continuum, its dialectical structure, rather, underscoring the historical impossibility represented by the African autobiographical figure. To quote *The Philosophy of History* at some length:

> Universal history—as already demonstrated—shows the development of the consciousness of Freedom on the part of Spirit, and of the consequent realization of that Freedom. This development implies a gradation—a series of increasingly adequate expressions or manifestations of Freedom, which result from its Idea. The logical, and—as still more prominent—the *dialectical* nature of the Idea in general, viz. that it is self-determined—that it assumes successive

> forms which it successively transcends; and, by this very process of transcending its earlier stages, gains an affirmative, and, in fact, a richer and more concrete shape;—this necessity of its nature, and the necessary series of pure abstract forms which the Idea successively assumes—is exhibited in the department of *Logic*. Here we need adopt only one of its results, viz. that every step in the process, as differing from any other, has its determinate peculiar principle. In history this principle is idiosyncrasy of Spirit—peculiar National Genius. It is within the limitations of this idiosyncrasy that the spirit of the nation, concretely manifested, expresses every aspect of its consciousness and will—the whole cycle of its realization.[20]

Each phase of historical development is categorically incommensurate to another, because each wholly reforms the self-consciousness of the immanent Idea of Freedom, as well as the political arrangements incrementally establishing the Idea of Freedom as the matter of civic individuation, for which sub-Saharan Africanity is only the negative condition of possibility.

Olaudah Equiano, Gustavus Vassa, and the autobiographical coherence of the two speak, then, emphatically and irretrievably out of sequence—Hegelian temporality being nothing if not adamantly sequential. The narrator negotiates the temporal and material designs of modernity, even as, conceptually, sub-Saharan Africanity is not open to the historical movement leading to modernity. The sub-Saharan autobiographical voice does not report Saturnian time, "a state of things antecedent to and beyond the limits of civil society and political combination."[21] It rehearses plainly the formal self-acknowledgment characterizing the vanguard of history, the Germanic European hegemony. This autobiographical posture cannot be reconciled with the unindividuated atemporality attributed to sub-Saharan Africa, from where Spirit retreats to begin positive historical development.

This historical movement bears elaboration: "with *China* and the *Mongols*—the realm of theocratic despotism—History begins," because both develop the patriarchal system of secular organization, in which the role of the civil state is approximated through the confusion of ordinances with moral law, "so that internal law—the knowledge on the part of the individual of the nature of his volition, as his own inmost self—even this is the subject of external statutory enactment."[22] That is, the structures of family piety that authorize social domination by tradition pre-date the civil order ideally provided by the modern State; they do not yield the conditions in which subjectivity can yet exist. The insufficiency is that "the reflection upon itself of the individual will in antithesis to the Substantial (as the power in which it is absorbed) or the recognition of this power *as one with its own essential being*, in which it knows itself *free*—is not found on this grade of development."[23]

Alternately, in India, "all that is rough, rigid, and contradictory is dissolved, and we have only the soul in a state of emotion—a soul, however, in which the death of the free self-reliant Spirit is perceptible."[24] Still, India offers the political differentiation of the civil sphere that China and the Mongols lack in their patriarchal regimes. The Indian caste system reorganizes civil power insofar as "individual members ramify from the unity of despotic power."[25] However, castes, insofar as they substantially retain the semblance of natural distinctions or qualities, betray an incomplete conceptual separation from the natural world, a flawed self-consciousness in which "internal subjectivity is not yet recognized as independent; and if distinctions obtrude themselves, their recognition is accompanied by the belief that the individual does not choose his particular position himself, but receives it from Nature."[26] In China and with the Mongols, inward freedom is repressed externally, while in India nature and Spirit are not yet disposed as polar opposites, with the result that self-consciousness is lost in the realm of the Imagination, governed too little, in "the most self-abandoned, helpless slavery;—a slavery, in which the abstract forms into which concrete human life is divided, have become stereotyped, and human rights and culture have been made absolutely dependent upon these distinctions."[27]

In Persia, "the beginning of World-History"[28] truly emerges, where uniform taxes stand as one index that "[h]uman will and activity here occupy the foreground, not Nature and its bounty."[29] Egyptian civilization, characterized by the tremendous cultural importance accorded the dead as evidenced by mummification and the Pyramids, "is the first to express the thought that the soul of man is *immortal*";[30] in other words, the express acknowledgment of the conceptual limits of the natural world. Greece, however, inaugurates the effectively modern, the transition from despotism to the regularization of social relations in which the individual, as the cognate of self-consciousness, develops. The individual, as the cognate of self-consciousness, achieves self-realization principally in three forms: the subjective work of art, or cultural production; the objective work of art, or the ordering of fundamental conceptual and belief structures, such as divinities or religion; and the political work of art, or the formation of civil peace among the aggregate of individuals. The individual is the transcendent reconciliation of subjectivity, objectivity, and the political, the political being those principles codifying the relations of the many individuals incarnated through the subject/object antithesis, the dynamic of the reasonable interiority contradistinct to the natural world. These relations coalesce as the State, the political work of art, "a living, universal Spirit, but which is at the same time the self-conscious Spirit of the individuals composing the community."[31] The historical advancement is corrupted, even as these forms of consciousness are developed—and because these forms of consciousness are developed. "The principle of subjective morality which was inevitably introduced, became the germ of corruption," because "[t]hought, therefore, appears here as the principle of decay—decay, viz., of Substantial [prescriptive] morality."[32] The objective construction of the anthropomorphic world cannot effect complete identification with the multiple perspectives it newly constitutes and, accordingly, subjective morality is intrinsically revolutionary.

As a result, when Roman hegemony succeeds Greek hegemony, the relations of collective sovereignty decline into the "*Aristocracy* of a rigid order, in a state of opposition to the people."[33] Nonetheless, the historical advance remains significant, "involv[ing] the expansion of undeveloped subjectivity—inward conviction of existence—to the visibility of the real world," specifically "the purification of inwardness to abstract personality, which gives itself reality in the existence of private property [at which point] the mutually repellent social units can then be held together only by despotic power."[34] As well, the Romans originate *positive law* that supplants the skewed jurisprudence of moral tradition and subjective judgment, disclosing instead "a principle of right, which is external—i.e., one not dependent on disposition and sentiment."[35] However, the shortcoming of these developments is that "[i]ndividual subjectivity thus entirely emancipated from control, has no inward life, no prospective nor retrospective emotions, no repentance, nor hope, nor fear—not even thought; for all these involve fixed conditions and aims, while here every condition is purely contingent."[36] There is, then, a partial lack of subjective interiority in the hegemony of Rome, the failure to rearticulate self-consciousness and civil choice as a collective principle as substantial as individuality, so that "[i]ndividuals are [not] thereby posited as atoms, but they are at the same time subject to the severe rule of the *One*, which as *monas monadum* is a power over private persons."[37]

The florescence of Christianity, the religious form in which "God is realized as a Subject, and as manifested Subjectivity is exclusively One Individual," transcends this spirit of political community, because "it is easy of comprehension by our consciousness in its outward aspect, while, at the same time, it summons us to penetrate deeper."[38] As the perpetuators of the Christian principle, the German world attains the apotheosis of historical temporality. Including the Visigothic kingdom, the Franks, the Ostrogoths, the Burgundians, the Angles, and the Saxons, the Germanic world transfigures the prepolitical possibilities of the Christian purification of subjectivity in collective service into the ideal terms of secular civility. Christianity, in this way, is posited as the precedent to rational political life. The practical effect is the advance from feudalism, functioning by outward force, to monarchy, functioning on intrinsic right, "for the supremacy implied in monarchy is essentially a power emanating from a political body."[39] The Lutheran Reformation, counterpoised to the mercantilism of the rest of Europe, codifies objective and subjective states for religious practice, insofar as it ensures that the "subjective feeling and the conviction of the individual is [*sic*] regarded as equally necessary with the objective side of Truth."[40] In sum: "The development and advance of

Spirit from the time of the Reformation onward consist in this, that Spirit, having now gained the consciousness of its Freedom, through that process of mediation which takes place between man and God—that is, in the full recognition of the objective process as the existence [the positive and definite manifestation] of the Divine essence—now takes it up and follows it out in building the edifice of secular relations."[41] Restated, the secular becomes an embodiment of Truth. This state of affairs remains particularly developed in Prussian Protestantism under the leadership of Frederick II at the opening of the nineteenth century, as exemplified by the Prussian municipal law. At this historical juncture, the "consciousness of the Spiritual is now the essential basis of the political fabric."[42]

Olaudah Equiano or Gustavus Vassa's disruption of this history is profound, then, and various. To begin, the self-composed African voice speaks inconceivably from the "coast," the topography symbolizing the potential for the most advanced historical developments premised on "connection with foreign nations."[43] Despite the almost interminable West African coastline, the "coast" accordingly cannot be the topography categorizing sub-Saharan Africa, its inhabitants, or the temporal disposition of the region. Olaudah Equiano or Gustavus Vassa, in addition to speaking through modern designs, impossibly participates in the exchanges and introspections of the commercialized, objectively coordinated relations privileging the "coasts" in the temporal scheme.

In the same way that it makes no sense for the autobiographical narrator to rehearse the civil networks of the progressive "coastal" typography, the narrator refutes the clarified motivation of history, the elaboration of cognizance and self-possession above the Sahara desert. The Hegelian paradigm cannot realize itself in the eventuality of Olaudah Equiano or Gustavus Vassa, because the proposed exorbitance of sub-Saharan Africa determines the substance of historical eventuality. Thus, the individual expressing reasonable interiority remains a racial concept, as Mills describes with the term "subperson." In the scheme, the positive condition of civic freedom holds a substantial form, as distinctly as the brute, negative condition excessive to civic freedom. Especially following the many successive processes of historical transcendence, these two seemingly anthropomorphic forms are fully incommensurate. The movement of history as the incremental reconciliation of the spiritual and the political through the apparatus of bureaucratic statecraft grants no meaning to Olaudah Equiano or Gustavus Vassa's experiences. For these experiences effectively exceed the condition of the repressed inward freedom assigned to China and the Mongolians inaugurating history, the hyperbolic imagination drawing Indian self-consciousness too closely to the natural world, the civic self-awareness signaled by the Persian taxation, the Egyptian powers of conception that transcend the natural world, the individuated self-posture of Greece, the civic acknowledgement of the principle of right made a point of self-conception in Rome, the Christian recasting of Spirituality in the light of individuated self-presence, as well as the Lutheran establishment of independent religious interiority. The perplexity is that, in order for the progressive dialectical scheme to work, the self-evidence of racial blackness must remain a civil, historical, and subjective nullity.

It is important to recognize the individual as the condition of subjectivity and sovereignty simultaneously—in other words, it remains the repository, the coincidence, of the introspection of thought, subjectivity, and the civic animation of intrinsic right, sovereignty. Whereas in feudal and earlier arrangements the civic expression of intrinsic right is not held generally, the Germanic ascendance realizes that "[s]overeign possession is not a peculium of the individual ruler, but is consigned to the dynastic family as a trust . . . of the body politic."[44] The historical transformation is that the civic sphere accommodates the expression of the introspective wills of the combination of subjects invested with the apparatus of personal right, particularly, introspective wills expressed through the privatization of property. Sovereignty entails the participation in the apparatus of personal right, while subjectivity does not entail the same necessarily, and the motivation of history is the unification or reconciliation of the two in the form of the individual. Nevertheless, the coalescence of sovereignty and subjectivity in the Hegelian scheme is the comprehension inveterately alien to sub-Saharan Africanity, so that the principle of individuality also remains the fundamental principle of racialization that discerns racial blackness as its negation.

In this way, Olaudah Equiano or Gustavus Vassa, uncertainly holding the posture of autobiographical individuation, seems to defy nature and temporality altogether. The material and substance of history is that "Reason governed and has governed the World," a progress formalizing Thought as the Idea of Freedom as immanent to self-consciousness, the certainty of self-consciousness.[45] The successive refinements of subjectivity yield Reason as temporality itself; however, Olaudah Equiano or Gustavus Vassa ideally must remain *without* the activity of Reason for the scheme to be sensible.

Needless to say, the set of Hegelian propositions that would have it seem this way are flawed. One measure of the flaw is that the metonymic and paradigmatic descriptions of the scheme do not coincide so that the scheme, rather than the sub-Saharan narrator, fails representational coherence. Hegel's paradigmatic rendition of historicity figures typography as the graduated materialization of Spirit that incrementally unifies subjectivity and sovereignty as the point of individuality, yet his metonymic formulation aligns typographical distinctions with the categorical differences that, to greater or lesser degrees, limit or do not allow this materialization of Spirit. The discrepancy in the formulations is that sub-Saharan Africa holds no coordinates in the paradigmatic rendition but does in the metonymic rendition. The metaphorical and metonymic renditions provide irreconcilable codifications of the fundamental design of temporality—the discrepancy being the figurability of sub-Saharan Africa.

If not the import of temporality, the profound conceptual force of racialization remains clear, philosophically speaking. The logical confusion, rather than logical clarification, traces (even as it elides) the historical role of sub-Saharan Africa, which must appear wholly illegible or insignificant to the design of the innovative apparatus of individuality and its politicizing infrastructures. In the words of Mills in *The Racial Contract*, "*white misunderstanding, misrepresentation, evasion, and self-deception on matters related to race* are among the most pervasive mental phenomena of the past few hundred years, a cognitive and moral economy psychically required for conquest, colonization, and enslavement."[46] Signaling the cognitive (if not representational) priority of racialization, the rhetorical quandary of the Hegelian scheme bears out this observation because, exceeding the rhetorical, the effect of the representational inconsistency is to recast the factual. For the substantive role of sub-Saharan Africa and its diaspora in the economic, epistemological, and political constitution of the European expansion beyond the landmass of Europe is indeterminate in this Hegelian confusion. Historian Robin Blackburn in *The Making of New World Slavery* notes:

> The acquisition of some twelve million captives on the coast of Africa between 1500 and 1870 helped to make possible the construction of one of the largest systems of slavery in human history. The Atlantic slave trade itself was to become remarkable for its businesslike methods as well as its scale and destructiveness. Over a million and a half captives died during the 'Middle Passage' between Africa and the New World; an unknown, but large, number died prior to embarkation; and once in the New World, between a tenth and a fifth of the slaves died within a year. Those who survived found their life drastically organized to secure from them as much labour as possible.[47]

The Hegelian historiography has virtually no record of, or any conceivable significance for, these developments, even as the Atlantic slave trade and New World slavery are fully coincident with the transition from feudalism to monarchy as well as the Reformation in Western Europe, the particular historical advances that set the Germanic world as the vanguard of history. Elided in the Hegelian rendition is the modernizing circum-Atlantic organization of violence, the systemization of violence against sub-Saharan Africans and their descendants that codifies the novel civic status of racial blackness from the epoch of the Spanish "Charles V [who] possesses enormous possibilities in point of outward appliances"[48] to the apparently propitious results in North America of the "industrious Europeans, who took themselves to agriculture, tobacco, and cotton-planting, etc."[49] The elision is the principal function of (violent) racialization in the revolutionary developments of statecraft that render, over this period, the interiorized position of self-identity, introspection "that Reason is the Sovereign of the World; that the history of the world, therefore, presents us with a rational process."[50]

Hegel's elision is also found in the articulation of incipient and acute mercantilist thought and policies across Europe that violently leverage the west coast of sub-Saharan Africa for the re-creation of Western Europe from the minor outpost of long-distance trade on the Eurasian landmass in the fourteenth century to the expanding commercial hegemon with diffuse, entrenched bureaucracies increasingly rationalizing, from the sixteenth century onward, its trade supremacy across the Atlantic, Indian, and Pacific Oceans. Whether marked by the year 1431, when the Portuguese begin to reach as far into the Atlantic Ocean as the Azores; 1492, when Christopher Columbus "makes landfall on the tiny island of Guanahini in the Bahamas";[51] or 1494, when the papal Treaty of Tordesillas grants Portugal the west African coast and Spain the "New World," one violently administered result is the global reach of this activity: "The slave trade was possibly the most international activity of the pre-industrial era. It required the assembling of goods from at least two continents (many different parts of Asia and Europe), the transporting of those goods to a third, and their exchange for forced labor that would be carried to yet another continent."[52] This generative vortex of European capitalism and the modern renewal of European cultural, material, and political infrastructures and their extension particularly to the "New World" certify the crucial historical and demographic significance of sub-Saharan Africa, a pivotal historical and demographic significance challenging the Hegelian assertion that when "the ultimate design of the World must be perceived . . . evil has not been able permanently to assert a competing position."[53] That is, whereas, according to Hegel, the linearity of historicity excludes, by nature, sub-Saharan Africa, the operations of the revised European market and civic structures following the sixteenth century demonstrate, on the contrary, the highly coordinated application of repeated force keenly directed toward sub-Saharan Africa, its polities, and their dispersed populations.

The matter of historical fact in the Hegelian scheme is, therefore, in question. David Northrup in *Africa's Discovery of Europe, 1450–1850*, for example, notes the diplomatic contacts of African and European states in the fifteenth century. The Papal Council of 1437–45, which convenes in response to the expanding Ottoman Empire that would capture Constantinople in 1453, includes Christian representatives of the Ethiopian emperor; in 1484 an official delegation from the Kingdom of Kongo reaches Portugal; in 1486 an embassy from the king of Benin also arrives in Portugal; in 1487 delegations from the Jolof kingdom came to Portugal; in 1488–90 another Kongolese embassy "helped make the monastery of Saint Eloy in Lisbon a second center of African studies in Europe, where Kongolese learned European religious and secular knowledge and where Portuguese missionaries were trained in Kongolese culture."[54] These fifteenth-century interactions challenge the reliability of the proposition that sub-Saharan Africa exists in its own peculiar atemporality.

Still more to the point, in "Hegel and Haiti," the political philosopher Susan Buck-Morss, by juxtaposing the historical and political intrigues of nineteenth-century statecraft to Hegelian formulations, directly undermines the fundamental dismissal of sub-Saharan Africa and its dispersed populations so necessary to Hegelian theory. Particularly concerned with the Hegelian "idea of the relation between lordship and bondage,"[55] Buck-Morss provides an immediate historical context in which African-derived persons prove primary political agents even as, notwithstanding, Hegel develops "the famous metaphor of the 'struggle to death' between the master and slave, which for Hegel provided the key to the unfolding of freedom in world history and which he first elaborated in *The Phenomenology of Mind*, written in Jena in 1805–6 (the first year of the Haitian nation's existence) and published in 1807 (the year of the British abolition of the slave trade)."[56] The new philosophical turn contemporaneous with these events acutely revises, Buck-Morss argues, the particularities of Hegelian thought, as well as philosophical discourse more broadly:

> Prior to writing *The Phenomenology of Mind*, Hegel had dealt with the theme of mutual recognition in terms of *Sittlichkeit*: criminals against society or the mutual relation of religious community or personal affection. But now this young lecturer, still only in his early thirties, made the audacious move to reject these earlier versions (more acceptable to the established philosophical discourse) and to inaugurate, as the central metaphor of his work, not slavery versus some mythical state of nature (as those from Hobbes to Rousseau had done earlier), but slaves versus masters, thus bringing into his text the present historical realities that surrounded it like invisible ink.[57]

The conceptual and material stakes of the Enlightenment coalesce plainly at the turn of events codified as the Haitian Revolution. For, insofar as, by the beginning of the nineteenth century, sub-Saharan Africanity articulates a national form within the exclusive market and political paradigms of Europe and its "New World" protensions, the treatment of race as the categorical principle of conceptual and material disposition must be restated. The restatement presents, accordingly, a considerable paradox:

> By the eighteenth century, slavery had become the root metaphor of Western political philosophy, connoting everything that was evil about power relations. Freedom, its conceptual antithesis, was considered by Enlightenment thinkers as

> the highest and universal political value. Yet this political metaphor began to take root at precisely the time that the economic practice of slavery—the systematic, highly sophisticated capitalist enslavement of non-Europeans as a labor force in the colonies—was increasing quantitatively and intensifying qualitatively to the point that by the mid-eighteenth century it came to underwrite the entire economic system of the West, paradoxically facilitating the global spread of the very Enlightenment ideals that were in such fundamental contradiction to it.[58]

The paradox does not reveal, foremost, as claimed in the Hegelian scheme, the co-implication of the state and Freedom, in which the state is, therefore, the historical materialization of Reason, the most manifest development of Reason. The state, rather, as drawn by the paradox, is an unreasonable, brutal apparatus ideally marking its brutality in terms of race. However, by the beginning of the nineteenth century the signal conceptual and material disruption is that "the black Jacobins of Saint-Domingue surpassed the metropole in actively realizing the Enlightenment [appeals to] human liberty."[59] To repeat the point then, the matter of historical fact places the Hegelian scheme profoundly in question. In relation to the metaphor of lordship and bondage, Buck-Morss reasons: "We are left with only two alternatives. Either Hegel was the blindest of philosophers of freedom in Enlightenment Europe, surpassing Locke and Rousseau by far in his ability to block out reality right in front of his nose (the print right in front of his nose at the breakfast table); or Hegel knew—knew about real slaves revolting successfully against real masters, and he elaborated his dialectic of lordship and bondage deliberately within this contemporary context."[60]

In either case, the ideal disposition of racial blackness is clear—if not reason as the categorical principle designed and diffused by the state. As argued in *The Philosophy of History*, the state and freedom are co-implicated fully, since "Freedom is nothing but the recognition and adoptions of such universal substantial objects as Right and Law, and the production of a reality that is accordant with them—the State."[61] The state, then, generates history, because it "first presents subject-matter that is not only *adapted* to the prose of History, but involves the production of such history in the very progress of its own being."[62] The mythological revolt of Jupiter against Chronos illustrates the principle allegorically in *The Philosophy of History*: "Thus, it was first Chronos—Time—that ruled; the Golden Age, without moral products; and what was produced—the offspring of that Chronos—was devoured by it. It was Jupiter—from whose head Minerva sprang, and to whose circle of divinities belong Apollo and the Muses—that first put a constraint upon Time, and set a bound to its principle of decadence. He is a Political god, who produced a moral work—the State."[63]

In contrast to the pure chaos of ungoverned time, the state overwhelms or transcends this chaos that is so immediate to the natural world and its cycles. By impersonal mechanisms, the state orders and realizes the collective social relation to the natural world that, accordingly, obscures the natural world as the basic contingency of consciousness. The evidence of this feat is Thought, the state and the individual being merely different substances of the extension of Thought. As a seemingly logical imperative, then, sub-Saharan Africa and its diasporas must remain "thoughtless," that is, beyond the representational limit of Thought, because the protracted violence of the European conscription of the people and resources along the African coastline cannot admit or represent, positively, the development of the Germanic state in Western Europe as "the Idea of Spirit in the external manifestation of human Will and its Freedom," or restated, "the Divine Idea as it exists on Earth."[64] Rather, the ideal agential coincidence of the state and the individual, the bureaucratic elaboration by which the natural world is supplanted, betrays along the West African coast that the modern state, with much greater historical effect, interpellates one in cruelty, despite the proposition in *The Philosophy of History* that this condition of consciousness defines the natural, sensuous world: "with a merely sensuous life—this being a form of consciousness which does not attain to general conceptions—cruelty is connected."[65]

The removal of sub-Saharan persons from the natural world of the West African coast, as formulated in *The Interesting Narrative of the Life of Olaudah Equiano, or Gustavus Vassa* is not a release from cruelty but, on the other hand, an abrupt disposal into the recurrent forms of cruelty designed by the incipient, impersonal networks of the modern state developing from Western European expansion. Not the cruel hostility of the natural world, but the vanguard state, within and without its borders, denies the narrator the idea of freedom as the immanence of self-consciousness, liberty of movement, as well as most opportunities for self-sustenance. In this instance, and as a matter of continued routine, the vanguard state does not complete a civic self-consciousness, mobilized through alphabetic script, but always incommensurate to this self-rendition, because insufficient to the epistemological terms of the subsumption irreducible to the transversal of the signifier, which is to say, the trace or ideal of transcendent agency. Very differently, the state openly coerces the narrator into the condition of the "subperson," to return to the term of Mills.

Even if these developments and their essential points of statecraft remain unreadable as historical eventualities, they plainly are readable as textual ones, even textual events in which the defining tensions rend the narratives more so than strictly resolve them. *The Interesting Narrative of the Life of Olaudah Equiano, or Gustavus Vassa* and other eighteenth-century slave narratives articulate, through one of the fundamental infrastructures of modern individuality, alphabetic script, the certainty that the comprehension of consciousness of being is never identical to "the selective recognition of humanity that undergirded the relations of chattel slavery."[66] The ontological negation of modernity that would be sub-Saharan Africanity does not sustain this premise of itself in the slave narratives, the self-reflexive formations of black "subpersons" that vividly disclose the structural mechanisms by which sub-Saharan Africans and modern civic presence are diametrically disposed. As the Hegelian scheme poses an ontological basis for the categorical difference of racial blackness, on the contrary, the self-descriptions of sub-Saharan Africans and their descendants strategically and repeatedly betray, as the basis of their narratives, the strictures and violences of sociality composing the force of racialization. The slave narratives pivot on depicting the substance of racialization as manifestly beyond—exorbitant and excessive to—the epidermal, or any matter of phenotype.

For example, as already argued, in rendering the scene of his manumission, Gustavus Vassa or Olaudah Equiano details the bureaucratic—therefore, closely administered—social exchanges regularized to instate and maintain racial blackness as a signal apparatus of the novel European management of long-distance trade—principles of trade profoundly altering quotidian relations across the Atlantic circumference. The scene of manumission, the most closely rendered of the narrative, presents the effective meaning of the narrator's body not as foremost phenotypical but, remarkably, as determined within the circuitous coherence of alphabetic script, monetary transactions, and the individual condition of "civility" chartered by modern statecraft. The sub-Saharan African body does not hold ontological singularity in the scene but obtains alphabetic and monetary renditions returning self-identity to the narrator by means of the bureaucratic infrastructures of the modern state. In the scene, the substance of racial blackness is not phenotypical, nor is it ontologically fixed, but it inhabits instead the formal structures of consciousness coalescing the state with the subjects composing the common relations of the state. The narrator embodies, in sum, not an ontological void but an anthropomorphic agent, the episode registering, in fact, this certainty: "When I got to the office and acquainted the Register with my errand he congratulated me on the occasion and told me he would draw up my manumission for half price, which was a guinea."[67] The force of racialization operates concurrently with the force of the modern state in the transaction that seems to return anthropomorphic certainty to the African body of the narrator, anthropomorphic certainty that the perspective of Olaudah Equiano otherwise represents from the opening of the text.

This later, indemnified anthropomorphic certainty, however, betrays no violence—merely the operations of exchange and contraction, which is to say, the functional self-consciousness of civic presence in the Atlantic arena, the passing of the "guinea" between the narrator and the Registrar succinctly depicting the confluent fiscal and social exchange. Thus, no particular body in the scene incorporates the ontology of racial blackness, immanent dehumanization—this position sustained only by those black bodies depicted on the "guinea," inert and commercially significant. Racial blackness, therefore, amounts not so much to corporeality or phenotype in the scene as, instead, the point of the calibration, regulation, and circulation of the resources superintended within the highly complex, innovative arrangements of the mercantilist political designs.

In effect, the scene turns on the dematerialization—or temporal re-materialization—of the narrator's sub-Saharan body, therefore oddly fixing the scene both within and without the bounds of reason, even as it draws the clarified location of reason, the interactions of exchange and contraction. The oddity is as follows: No catalogue of materiality is commensurate to the sub-Saharan African body in the economic calculations, imaginative grasp, or political jurisdictions of Atlantic modernity and, by privileging these fraught representational moments, African American slave narratives discern strictly the network of both organizational and social complexity maintaining the significance of race—as opposed to ontological states of being. The representational dilemma in proposing self-identity through the vexed artifact of the African-derived body is that, giving account of slavery and "themselves," ex-slave narrators, as an ineluctable task, must reproduce the experiences and trials of a "body"—their own—granted that sub-Saharan African bodies are understood in terms of a "fleshiness" that over-determines all other possible aspects of identity. Still, because the claims these narrators are making on the governments and cultures of the Atlantic arena are based on denunciations of an enforced and spurious confinement to a life merely of the body, to an existence as obdurate materiality, these narrators must not only recover their bodies within their narratives but also, more importantly, remove their bodies from the narratives. Paradoxically, the bodies ex-slave narrators are required to reproduce *through* language are the very marks of their remove *from* language, and the life of the mind, as well as the state.

The African-derived phenotype (the darknesses of our skins, the textures of our hair, the shapes of our noses, cheekbones, and buttocks) becomes the emblem through which notions of race are conflated with notions of sense and sensibility; our bodies become marks of our exclusion from a privileged presence of mind, a presence of mind diacritically opposed to "the most contracted of spaces, the small circle of living matter."[68] Nonetheless, the image of the exchange of the "guinea," the legal currency embossed with sub-Saharan African figures, illustrates vividly the strange insufficiencies of the circum-Atlantic "racist optics in which black flesh is itself identified as the source of opacity, the denial of black humanity, and the effacement of sentience integral to the wanton use of the captive body."[69] African American slave narratives repeatedly privilege the fraught representational moments that expose the contingencies of the racist optics.

On this point, it is important to recognize that *The Narrative of the Life of Olaudah Equiano, or Gustavus Vassa,* the most important eighteenth-century slave narrative, falls within the first of three rubrics: the preclassic narrative (prior to 1830), the classic (1830–1865), and the postbellum (appearing after 1865). The primary thematic distinction between the preclassic and classic slave narrative is that the second "transferred the stigma traditionally associated with slavery from the slave to the slaveholder,"[70] a thematic movement reinforcing the structural exposition integral to the slave narratives. Increasingly, the actions and conceptual universe of slaveholders structure the events of the narratives, rather than, for instance, the randomness of picaresque happenstance or the surreptitious workings of Providence; in effect, the slave narratives increasingly highlight that the determination of racial blackness, as a form of immanent dehumanization, realizes the covenant between slaveholding individuals and the state as the ordering principle of fiscal, legal, and personal commonality—as the image of the "guinea" exchanged between the narrator and the Registrar illustrates. The stigma of Atlantic slavery is not indicative of any condition of the natural world but, on the contrary, registers the deliberations of the state returning to individual consciousness as legislated social practice.

The primary distinction between the classic and the postbellum slave narrative is that the tone of the latter is more reconciliatory; whereas the classic narrative marks "the disappearance of the African-born freedman as narrator, the emergence of the Afro-American fugitive slave narrator, and the increasingly direct attack upon the entire slave institution,"[71] the postbellum narrative is informed by the prospect of the revised interracial democracy in the United States after 1865, often "designed to demonstrate" that "the course [the narrators] followed as slaves prepared them well to seize opportunity in freedom and turn it to honorable account both socially and economically."[72] The nominal end of legal enslavement secured in the United States by 1865 directly draws African-derived populations within the relation of state and citizen—as does the Haitian Revolution at the opening of the nineteenth century, and British Emancipation in the Caribbean in 1834—in ways that demand rescripting contact across the most quotidian practices of Atlantic modernity. The postbellum slave narratives record a form of existence for its narrators not so fully coded by manumission, so as to trouble in less dramatic but more diffuse ways the racializing concept that is the substance of the individual. Unlike Olaudah Equiano or Gustavus Vassa at the climactic moments of the eighteenth-century narrative, the protagonists of the postbellum narratives occupy already the legal presumption of individuality, the individual, national, and social possibilities of the presumption providing the basic thematic motives of the narratives.

The structural nature of the state-sponsored individuality granted across the Atlantic circumference remains the fundament of the thematic variations. In Hegelian temporality, the historical emergence of the state and the forms of consciousness it sponsors is equivalent to the transcendence of contingency, the radical condition of the natural world. The state essentially negotiates and maintains the broad efforts by which it becomes the intermediary between the natural world and the sustenance of those it overarches. Distancing itself and its subjects from the radical contingency of the natural world, ideally the state is an alternative principle of regulation affording greater guardianship than otherwise possible in contact with the natural world; however, African American slave narratives record the insistent, violent contingencies imposed on African-derived persons accounting for the coincident appearance of racial blackness and the activities of the modern state. The interests of the modern state, the narratives reveal, retain the interests of innumerable individuals in the imposition of the routinely violent contingencies of our African/American presence in historical modernity. These forms of agency structure Atlantic modernity.

Indeed, as literary critic Samira Kawash argues in *Dislocating the Color Line: Hybridity and Singularity in African-American Literature,* African American presence within the coordinations of the state, freedom, and individuality, particularly as recounted in the classic slave narratives, defies the categorical formalities of all three political and social ideals—the state, freedom, and individuality: "the system of property demands that one maintain an unambiguous relation to its law of division, wholly on one side or the other."[73] However, always bordering on and threatening "fugitivity," the anomalous African American presence in the "New World" confounds the very premises and coordinations of the state insofar as, "[i]f the fugitive is neither property nor subject, then the closed circuit of property and subject is momentarily interrupted or suspended in the disruptive figure of the fugitive."[74] The oxymoronic embodiment of the contingency of the state, the fugitive, "neither the property of another nor propertied in the self . . . is, from the perspective of the state, no place. Thus, the fugitive remains withdrawn, invisible, unrepresentable from the perspective of proper subjects and objects of property. Where the state provides a framework for assigning each individual an address, a localizable identity that ensures both addressability and responsibility, the fugitive has no address, cannot be addressed. The fugitive evades the regularized and regulated paths of circulation—of goods, of persons, of information."[75] In the chapter titled "Freedom and Fugitivity: The Subject of the Slave Narrative," Kawash is interested in the conceptual, legal, and subjective conditions of "fugitivity" incorporated in those once-enslaved African-derived persons who attain personal liberty, civic viability, or both. The manumission of Olaudah Equiano or Gustavus Vassa, despite its legality, connotes fugitivity in this sense, since the exchange of the "guinea" conceptually controverts the climactic issue of individuality. As the exchange of the coin denotes, the issue of individuality is alien to racial blackness, since the material imperative of the modern state remains to codify racial blackness for its systems of circulation.

The political articulation of the United States is exemplary. As already considered, the inaugural congressional compromises of 1790 depend in large part on racial intrigue.[76] The congressional compromises of 1790 vigorously empower the federal body through the allowance of taxation and, at once, conscript African-derived persons for the violent predations of Atlantic slavery. In this way the new national coherence was in large measure a racialized proposal in the form of the "functional relationship between slavery and economic measures."[77] Paradoxically, given the historical aspiration of the modern state, this functional relationship establishes in the interstices of the national configuration a population that the state aims to address foremost with violence, as a keystone of its viability, as much as the positive rights arrayed for the recognized individuals in its jurisdictions. African-derived persons, so as to configure the state, circulate only anomalously in the activities of the state. For Kawash, two particular points of interrogation arise: the material consequences of the fiat indicated in "the disposition of the fugitive's body, rather than simply the fugitive's narrative, [which] suggest[s] that . . . [s]lavery can bring enormous forces to bear [on that body] in order to restore the fugitive to his proper place, as property";[78] the subjective consequences of the fiat, which forebode "that the freedom of the politically recognized subject is a freedom conditioned and determined . . . is a socially achieved affect . . . [and therefore] cannot be the only possible freedom."[79]

In other words, the radically anomalous condition of racial blackness, the interstitial situation of racial blackness as a strict political determination in the "New World," ineluctably betrays the deliberate violence of the state, as well as the circumscribed purview of the state. And, in this sense, the state, constitutively, is wary of fugitivity, the point already manifest in the United States in the Northwest Ordinance of 1787. Having legal status even before the U.S. Constitution, this early compromise "barred slavery from a huge midwestern area, comprising the future states of Illinois, Indiana, Ohio, Michigan, and Wisconsin,"[80] while, as clearly, acknowledging fugitivity (abstracted through racial blackness) as a fundamental premise of the debated national cohesion: "There shall be neither slavery nor involuntary servitude in the said Territory. . . . Provided always, that any person escaping into the same, from whom labor or service is lawfully claimed in any one of the original States, such fugitive may be lawfully reclaimed and conveyed to the person claiming his or her labor or service as aforesaid."[81] The 1787 ordinance outlines the national jurisdiction both geographically and, as essentially, through the limitations it conceives on the subjectivity, the individuality—and their point of conflation, the sovereignty—of those designated by racial blackness.

The nationalizing terms of political community describe the figure of the fugitive requisite for the binding organization. Rather than fixing the basis of common consciousness as simply the social practice of positive rights, the state, to pinion the words of Hartman, immediately tempers "the tantalizing suggestion of the individual as potentate and sovereign . . . [with] the forms of repression and terror that accompanied the advent of freedom, the techniques of discipline that bind the individual through conscience, self-knowledge, responsibility, and duty . . . [to] the management of racialized bodies and populations effected through the racism of the state and civil society."[82] Hartman, in making this observation, refers specifically to the fortunes of the emancipated U.S. slave populations after 1865 who find their liberties curtailed abruptly by the varieties of "law attempt[ing] to accomplish what planters by themselves had failed to achieve: the complete separation of the freedmen from the means of production, the creation of a true agricultural proletariat."[83] Equally, however, her observation describes the crafting of general U.S. political consciousness from the incipient covenants of nationality.

The 1787 ordinance is followed in less than a decade by the passage of the 1793 Fugitive Slave Law but, what is more, the distinctions between the 1793 and 1850 Fugitive Slave Laws patently disclose the specter of African American fugitivity integral to the U.S. national paradigm, integral, in other words, to the political imagination specifying the common relations of the state. The 1793 law only outlines briefly the standards by which the fugitive is reprimanded before the law, limiting the length on the claims to fugitives to six months, stipulating that the expenses of the retrieval be borne by the state or territory making the request, as well as designating a $500 fine for anyone who impedes the retrieval of fugitives. As an adjacent point, the Missouri Compromise of 1820, even as it encumbers the expansion of slaveholding policies, reiterates fugitivity as integral to the composition of the state.

The extended revision of fugitive policy codified in the 1850 Fugitive Slave Act, however, rehearses the acute bureaucratic expansion of the state on this integral point, as well as the acute prescription of social consciousness and civic routine required by the legislation in its recomposition of the common relations of state-sponsored, individual sovereignty. This law empowers new commissioners, who exercise on this issue powers equivalent to any U.S. magistrate; requires federal, state, and territorial courts to enlarge their operations to facilitate enforcement; places financial liability for any escapes from custody on the marshals remanding the fugitives; commands "all good citizens . . . to aid and assist in the prompt and efficient execution of the law";[84] authorizes the seizure of the fugitive without due process, without representation before the law, as well as the disposition of all cases in "a summary manner."[85] The Fugitive Slave Act dictates, further, the use of "reasonable force and restraint as may be necessary"[86] in apprehension of the fugitive; imposes a fine limited to $1000 and imprisonment limited to six months for anyone who impedes the recovery of a fugitive in addition to making restitution of $1000 for each fugitive successfully assisted. More assiduously still, the Fugitive Slave Act regulates the range of payments for services to be made to the marshals; authorizes a ten-dollar fee to commissioners for each case resolved in a favor of the claim on the fugitive and a five-dollar fee for each case resolved by dismissal of the claim on the fugitive; stipulates that the costs of transporting the fugitive to the state or territory of the claimant be borne by the federal treasury; requisitions federal resources for the dissemination of claims made to fugitives; and, finally, also guarantees that claims made without the certifications prescribed by law might bindingly be adjudicated by commissioners, nevertheless, "upon satisfactory proof being made."[87]

Historian Don E. Fehrenbacher (with Ward M. McAfee) in *The Slaveholding Republic: An Account of the United States Government's Relations to Slavery* provides points of reference for understanding these political investments of the eighteenth- and nineteenth-century legislations. "In the case of the Northwest Ordinance, which Congress enacted not for the United States as a whole, but for a dependent area under its exclusive control, the [fugitive slave] clause was neither national in scope nor compulsive in its effect."[88] However, the 1793 law inscribes the anxiety more broadly and intensely, transforming the forms of participation that execute the common relations between individuals as statecraft, so as to press incrementally the constitutive mechanisms of the state. For instance, the "leading northern court decisions of the time consequently tended to counteract legislative trends [resisting the fugitive policy] by reaffirming the right of recaption, overturning provisions for jury trial, and upholding the supremacy of federal law over that of the states."[89] The reconstitution of the political import of fugitivity informs the fundamental exercises of the common relations unifying the polity. Thus, the 1850 law directly interrogates, even as it bindingly delineates, the imagination of the national compact, in effect lending "weight to the southern definition of what the federal government owed to slavery, while at the same time setting up an acid test of northern fidelity to the Constitution."[90] The antebellum provisions deepen profoundly the bureaucratic impress of fugitivity on the state, as well as incline radically toward fixing common self-understanding in the forms of "conscience, self-knowledge, responsibility, and duty" defined emphatically through "the management of racialized bodies and populations effected through the racism of the state and civil society."[91] The provisions outline the stark coincidence of bureaucratic and subjective routines that rightly would embody the state.

That is, the determination of national life resting on the conception and reconception of fugitivity embeds racial blackness in "the day-to-day exercise and acceptance (or rejection) of authority, as well as the relations between imperial powers—all of which are contingent on time, space, and human agency."[92] The conflation of racial blackness with the credibility, the conceivability, of the nation insinuates the political stakes of the nation, the acceptance or rejection of state authority, with the described character of racial blackness, the irksome point of political contention pressing the coherent relations of the nation to their critical limits repeatedly. For the disposition of African-derived persons haunts "the businesslike, matter-of-fact tone" outlining the legal safeguards for "selling people exactly . . . [like] selling barrels of wine or loads of wheat . . . [without] any sense of shame or moral ambivalence about [the] mission."[93] The modern patterns of long-distance trade, that is, not only grasp the West African coast and the two American continents, but as forcefully impress subjective paradigms, paradigms ideally also articulated in the fundamental arrangements of the state. The fractious point of government for the U.S. national cohesion reflects and extrapolates, then, the rudimentary design of the Atlantic trade relations, which "coordinated people, materials, and capital across market sectors and among geographically dispersed areas," in which the measure of success is "in bringing people and products together in flexible and novel ways."[94] In these eddies of circulation, the movement, the treatment, of African-derived persons is both a necessity and a threat.

In the United States, this point of statecraft, as a point of political contention, convolutes the meaning of the positive rights enacting the state. The consensus concerning the practice of individual liberties that consolidates the political union becomes more simply discord than consensus. Defining the increasing functional crisis for the state in the nineteenth century, this disintegration results in a series of judicial and legislative decisions, particularly after 1840, that place the effective meaning of racial blackness as the focus of national policy. "In the 1830s one did not know that a cataclysmic Civil War would come, but one did know that the apparently invincible institution of American slavery was an inescapable present reality."[95] In the 1840s the intrigue grows much more acute. The annexation of Texas in 1845, auguring the expansion of slaveholding territory and eventually slaveholding states, occurs at the same time as the intensifying negotiations with England over the possession of the Oregon Territory. These very separate national interests in the Western continent imply the application of the force of the state. By the mid-1840s, the Texans who settle in the northeastern territory of Mexico, initially welcomed by the Mexican government, consider strategies for U.S. statehood as well as the expansion of slavery across the south, ambitious strategies that the historian Bernard DeVoto in *The Year of Decision, 1846* summarizes as follows: "Texas threatened to form an alliance with France or Great Britain, and even to accept a protectorate under either. This was a threat to cotton and slave labor, and so would kill whatever opposition might exist in the South. It was also a threat to cotton manufacture and it meant the repudiation of the Monroe Doctrine; so it ought to force the North to accept Texas. If any opposition should remain in the North, however, it could be ended by coupling Texas with the acquisition of Oregon, which would gratify imperialists and pacify Abolitionists."[96] The controversial Wilmot Proviso of 1846 uncovers in the diplomatic calculations and the marshaling of the state as a military force the insistent measure of racial blackness integral to the national compact—as established by the congressional accords of 1790. "The newest slavery question emerged on August 8, 1846," writes historian William H. Freehling, "when President Polk asked Congress for a $2 million appropriation to conduct negotiations with Mexico. In response, a Northern Democrat, David Wilmot of Pennsylvania, moved that slavery be banned in any territory negotiated from Mexico. The House passed Polk's appropriation bill with Wilmot's Proviso attached, 85–79."[97] The Wilmot Proviso redacts the common relations of the state in a formula that, for the first time, aligns matters of diplomacy and state force with the paradigmatic disposition of racial blackness.

The convulsive vacillations of the state at this juncture dramatically alter the quotidian relations of the polity to the necessity and the threat of racial blackness, since the draconian Fugitive Slave Act of 1850 effectively nullifies the status quo attained "in [the] famous decision on *Prigg v. Pennsylvania* in 1842, [when] the United States Supreme court ruled that state and local officials need not supply police and judicial aid. Since the Constitution gives Congress exclusive power over fugitive slaves, the Court reasoned, state governments could proclaim themselves powerless to chase bondsmen. After the decision, many states passed so-called Personal Liberty laws, barring their officials from performing Washington's fugitive slave chores."[98] It is important to restate that this contentious point of the national compact directly and materially presses on "the day-to-day exercise and acceptance (or rejection) of authority, as well as the relations between imperial powers—all of which are contingent on time, space, and human agency."[99] This pressure tests and clarifies the full reach of federal force as, for instance, in the outcome of *Ableman v. Booth* of Wisconsin, in which "[t]he Supreme Court first denied the power of the state courts to reach the restraint of one held pursuant to federal process even through habeas corpus. Taken at its broadest, and there are no qualifications in the decision, the doctrine was a startling assertion of federal power. Only a year before, the leading treatise on habeas corpus had concluded that the state and federal courts had concurrent jurisdiction in habeas corpus with respect to prisoners held through federal process."[100] The consequential alignment of the disposition of racial blackness, state force, and diplomacy (or comity) incrementally marks the preeminent confusion of the national configuration.

The Kansas-Nebraska Act of 1854 exacerbates this confusion beyond the principles of bureaucratic order—within the immediate, quotidian relations of U.S.

territorial rule. The "measure . . . invite[s] American settlement into the underdeveloped part of the Louisiana Purchase above 36° 30'. In the process, the Missouri Compromise line barring slavery's northward advance [i]s repealed."[101] The unstated crux of the legislation is the anticipation of the drafting of a regional constitution and subsequent appeal for U.S. statehood in the territory—the slaveholding or non-slaveholding status of the anticipated state to be determined, then, by the majority sentiments of the influx of settlers. "In other words," observes Freehling of the Southern strategy, "Missouri slaveholders were perfectly free to spill over the border immediately and control an early territorial decision. If Yankees instead secured a territorial decree against slavery, Southerners were perfectly free to appeal the edict to the southern-dominated Supreme Court."[102] The resulting violence in the territory between slaveholding and non-slaveholding factions initiates the preamble to the Civil War, while in 1857 the Supreme Court ruling in *Dred Scott v. Sandford* provides the signal constitutional debate over the issue prior to Robert Anderson's moving Union troops from Fort Moultrie to Fort Sumter in Charleston harbor, South Carolina, thereby directly initiating the chain of violence that becomes the Civil War. The *Dred Scott* decision is delivered, then, when "popular sovereignty had degenerated into a mini–civil war in Kansas, known as 'Bleeding Kansas,' as southerners and northerners battled over the status of slavery in the territory."[103] The ruling establishes that African Americans hold none of the positive rights of membership in the national body that otherwise the state casts as inviolate, the explicit imperative being "to treat emancipation as legally meaningless and to mix free Negroes with slaves in one legal category based on race."[104]

The ruling equates with the phenotypical condition of racial blackness the absolute denial of civic status definitive of Atlantic slavery, hence aspiring to clarify the powers and character of the state in its expansion, as well as in administering the terms of quotidian interaction. The doctrinal specification of racial blackness as the limit of positive rights too fully exposes, nonetheless, the premises of state integrity acknowledged only more or less stridently in the controversies following the 1790 congressional compromise. Accordingly, by the final years of the 1850s, the "degree of Republican radicalism on slavery now mattered less than the degree of Republican militancy toward secession."[105]

The critical issue of positive rights, the animating principle of the state, appears as the gruesome, closing image of William Grimes's 1855 *The Life of William Grimes, The Runaway Slave*. The fugitive voice is intense with bitterness and rancor. After the narrator declares his hope that he is prepared for death, he writes: "If it were not for the stripes on my back which were made while I was a slave, I would leave my skin as a legacy to the government, desiring that it might be taken off and made into a parchment, and then bind the constitution of glorious, happy, and *free* America.

Let the skin of an American slave bind the charter of American liberty."[106] The series of images, even on the purely semantic level, are extremely complex and bear scrutiny. The two declarations confound one another. The first suggests that the scars of U.S. common relations lacerating his back renders his skin inadequate to serve as parchment fastening or holding together the most prized rhetoric of the American republic; just as his abused skin belies U.S. self-identification, its lacerated surface disqualifies his skin as an appropriate surface to touch and hold the physical printed word. Nevertheless, the second declaration calls abruptly for that incongruity or impossibility. There is no better parchment, William Grimes seems to say, than the lacerated skin of an American slave to gird the nation's prized but hyperbolically false self-declaration and self-knowledge. The "binding" pact of the United States is rendered ineluctably and profoundly unreadable when placed in proximity to the openly legible marks on his abused skin.

Suggesting the confusion of these sets of images, the multiple valences of the verb "bind" range provocatively across several meanings: to "hold together or . . . form . . . into a single mass"; to "bandage," "cover a wound with dressings and bandages," or "make fast (anyone) with bonds or fetters; to deprive of personal liberty, make a captive or prisoner," and so on (*Oxford English Dictionary*). As much as national coherence, "bind" connotes the social wounds and disunion in fact characterizing the nation and its extensions, social wounds literally legible on his skin and juxtaposed to the ideal of quotidian cohesion represented by the "constitution" that is the grammatical object of the verb. William Grimes's declarations both uphold and collapse the distinction between parchment (a vessel or apparatus of literacy) and the African-derived body. The peroration turns on confusing the distinctions between literacy, technologies of literacy, and their hyperbolic corporeal opposite—African-derived bodies. The narrator places his African-derived body within the most consequential operations of literacy in the United States, and the mind/body distinction superintending modern race relations falters here, as the verb "to bind" vacillates under the pressures of its deployment. According to the passage, the African American body bears important, even nationally devastating, knowledge. For there is inscribed in William Grimes's text and skin alike the knowledge that the impact of literacy, or "sets of techniques for communications and for decoding and reproducing written or printed materials[,] . . . is determined by the manner in which human agency exploits it in a specific setting."[107] In the antebellum United States literacy functions, Grimes emphasizes, in an atmosphere strictly, contentiously, politically crafted in the service of racial domination and mythologizing, for which African-derived persons prove violently indispensable.

From the mid-1830s, the classic slave narrative regularly pronounces this paradigmatic contradiction of the design of "New World" democracy. The classic slave narrative, emphasizing the activities and conceptual interests of slaveholders, troubles subjectivity as an ineluctable historical development (in the Hegelian sense), as well as the seemingly ineluctable premise of the modern state, particularly as a mechanism of force, remaining equivalent to positive rights. The classic slave narrative delineates the modern interiority of consciousness—subjectivity—as holding and expressing, self-perplexingly by its own formula, immediately violent imperatives as cognates of the immanent idea of Freedom individuated by the power of the state. It is in this sense that the classic slave narrative "transfer[s] the stigma traditionally associated with slavery from the slave to the slaveholder," in the words of Marion Wilson Starling, author of the first book-length study of slave narratives.[108] The classic slave narrative presents racial blackness as a political determination indicated, with violent enforcement, in the corporeality of African-derived persons in order to maintain closely calculated systems of exchange and affiliation. The condition of fugitivity, so central to the elaboration of the United States from its inception, is the allowance for this enforcement.

Historian Lance Banning, in *Citizens of the World: London Merchants and the Integration of the British Atlantic Community, 1735–1785*, notes of the mercantile commerce rendering the material conditions of Atlantic modernity that a "single act, such as the exchange of East Indian cloth for West African slaves, required years of preparation and coordination in the markets of India, England, Holland, France, Africa, and the Americas."[109] This system of exchange newly requisitions statecraft—the United States being the paramount Enlightenment example—as well as the foremost conceptual energies of innumerable people to maintain itself, however, at grave human costs, the classic slave narrative insists. The scene of manumission of Olaudah Equiano or Gustavus Vassa captures the incommensurability of racial blackness to the Atlantic commercial and social networks perpetually "combining goods and people from many points around the world, and then managing multiple activities simultaneously."[110] The classic slave narrative more completely renders, however, the wayward relations of the settled terms of community under these conditions, betraying above all the quotidian violence sustaining the community, the supervised conditions of trade, as well as, finally, the national composure of the United States, illustrated, for instance, by the gruesome images of William Grimes penned in ironic panegyric to the state.

The hostile, often violent, terms of sociality emphasized by the classic slave narrative exposes the abstract, market organization of the Atlantic modernity depending on "the small gestures of everyday life," the broadly coordinated market and its dedicated adherents "reenact[ing] and sustain[ing] a vision of the world that made mass extermination ordinary, and perhaps possible,"[111] in the words of historian Thomas Holt. The exposure, as already suggested, articulates the

African-derived body in structures of captivity that belie the most fully advertised political announcements of the "New World" but, moreover, the classic slave narrative, as intently, removes the prized African-derived body from the detail of the narrative in order to delineate the questionable forms of consciousness, the more or less general compact, ideally effacing African-derived populations except as figures of bodily capacities and vulnerabilities. Restated, the classic slave narrative "transfer[s] the stigma traditionally associated with slavery from the slave to the slaveholder" by drawing the stigma in the visceral specificity of the African-derived body, the key detail in the network of social animosities and conflicts (rather than simply ordered relations) finally "mak[ing] possible a global structure of imperialist politics and labor relations that racialize consumption as well as production."[112]

James Bradley's very brief narrative account of enslavement, published March 7, 1835, in the "New Hampshire abolitionist paper"[113] the *Herald of Freedom*, exemplifies very briefly the structural emphasis of the classic slave narrative on the normative violence sustaining the articulation of community, the sanctioned conditions of trade and, foremost, the national composure of the United States. Bradley, enslaved as a field hand in South Carolina and Arkansas, but born in Africa, states immediately, "I always longed and prayed for liberty and . . . [would] try to study some way to earn money enough to buy myself, by working in the nighttime."[114] He then recounts his abuses at the hands of his master, before relating the labor allowing him to save seven hundred dollars to purchase himself, his movement to Ohio, where he is admitted into Lane Seminary, and his education. The climactic reiteration is that "I do not believe there ever was a slave, who did not long for liberty."[115] The brief narrative does not privilege uniquely the moment of manumission. The framing of the narrative, as notably, insists on the common African diasporic aspirations to freedom. The narrative hesitates once, however, in another register, in its most graphic portrayals, which set the emotional priority of the narrative beyond the formality of emancipation. James Bradley recounts being the subject of unmotivated violence: "I was tormented with kicks and knocks more than I can tell. My master often knocked me down, when I was young. Once, when I was a boy, about nine years old, he struck me so hard that I fell down and lost my senses."[116] He reports, in addition to his injuries, his bodily exposure, apparently as unmotivated as the violence directed toward him: "I have said that I had food enough. I wish I could say as much concerning my clothing. But I let that subject alone, because I cannot think of any suitable words to use in telling you."[117] Words fail the report, because the governing sensibility of the encounter, rather than self-evident rationality, determines trauma as the principal contingency of social proximity and identity.

The narrative, to this end, represents the stigma of slavery in images of various African diasporic injuries, suggestively rendering the sensibilities of the specter-like slaveholder, the principal agent of the mise-en-scène, though only the oblique point of scrutiny. At the emphatic point of the slave narrative, the slaveholder, the sanctioned figure of the state, defies reasonable expression, open only to the oblique representation rather than easy, ready codification whether civilizer or patriarch—as usual. That is, while the aspirations of African diasporic populations to liberty do not appear confused and disturbed, random and traumatic, as James Bradley rehearses them, the enfranchised forms of self-consciousness that cast the common relations of the state readily appear confused and disturbed, random and traumatizing. Bradley draws his bodily injury and exposure as the point of his emphatic self-identification when recalling enslavement; however, he is unable to describe the sensibilities governing and demanding the gratuitous violence and exposure. In short, as rendered in the brief passage, the condition of the African-derived body delineates the questionable character of Atlantic modernity, rather than the subhumanity of the dispersed populations of sub-Saharan Africa.

This typicality of the classic slave narrative profoundly revises the discourses that previously entangled race and enslavement in the United States. For instance, the anti- and proslavery exchange between Samuel Sewall and John Saffin in Boston almost a century and a half before the advent of the classic slave narrative presents arguments that turn, above all, on the question of African American agency or the ontological condition of racial blackness, displacing even the oblique—nonetheless direct—interrogation of the condition of the slaveholder, who embodies the condition of the subject cum individual exercising the modern impress of racial categorization to its extreme.

Samuel Sewall's abolitionist statement, "The Selling of Joseph: A Memorial" (1700), turns foremost on biblical references, acknowledging the original equality of all the children of Adam and Eve as well as the illegality of the selling of Joseph by his brethren, questions the longevity of Noah's cursing of Ham—if African-derived persons are to be understood as the posterity of Canaan—and also questions the status of African-derived persons as captives of war, if this is to be understood as the grounds of U.S. enslavement. Although the argument is primarily biblical, it is important to note that it begins with the recognition of African American agency: "The Numerousness of Slaves at this day in the Province, and the Uneasiness of them under their Slavery, hath put many upon thinking whether the Foundation of it be firmly and well laid."[118] The argument's reference to slaveholders is brief, and it incompletely anticipates the signal disruption of James Bradley's brief narrative, the sexual license insinuated in the economic and social arrangement: "[I]t is too well known what Temptations Masters are under, to connive at the Fornication of their Slaves; lest they should be obligated to find them Wives, or pay their Fines."[119]

John Saffin's pro-slavery response, "A Brief, Candid Answer to a Late Printed Sheet, Entitled, The Selling of Joseph," concedes that slavery may not be original to, but is legal nevertheless as prescribed by, Abraham, reiterating as well the argument on the legality of slavery for captives of war. Saffin emphasizes, above all, the ontological condition of racial blackness as the entirely negative condition of social being: "cowardly," "cruel," "libidinous," "deceitful," "false," "rude," all of which demonstrates, contrary to the governing analogy of Samuel Sewall, the uncertainty of any parallel between African-derived persons and the biblical Joseph.[120]

In *The First Emancipation: The Abolition of Slavery in the North*, historian Arthur Zilversmit analyzes the Quaker context of Samuel Sewall's abolitionist statements, noting further that following Sewall, other Quakers, "like William Southeby, attempted to persuade non-Quakers to give up slavery,"[121] and that by the mid-eighteenth century, disturbed by a trip to the South, John Woolman "did not submit his *Considerations on the Keeping of Negroes* to the Quaker meeting for approval until eight years after he wrote it, but in 1754 the Society of Friends not only approved the work, but published it and gave it a wide distribution through the network of Quaker meetings."[122] John Woolman rejects the notion that "Favours are peculiar to one Nation, and exclude others," introduces the language of rights and equity to the abolitionist debate, acknowledges racial division as a practice of sociality, revisits the question of captives of war, and fully privileges the notion that slavery amounts to the moral undermining of community—another significant preface to the intrigue of the classic slave narrative. Ultimately, the Quaker example is not merely discursive, but practical: "In 1773 the New England Quakers took the final step; they agreed that members should free all their Negroes, regardless of age or capacity" and "[i]n 1783 New England Quakers went even further and initiated a policy of compensating their former slaves for their past services."[123] Pennsylvania Quakers emancipated their slaves in 1776 and New York Quakers in 1777.

Beginning in 1759, Anthony Benezet, a Quaker schoolmaster in Philadelphia, intensely criticizes the slave trade, arguing "Africa was a fertile continent with civilized natives who wanted only to be left in peace in their homeland," rather than "prisoners of war who would have been executed by their captors if they had not been rescued by the slave traders."[124] While the slave trade would not be made illegal for some fifty years, until 1808, the revolutionary political crisis yielding the independence of the thirteen mainland colonies exacerbates the hypocrisy of slaveholding in a political configuration ostensibly dedicated to the rights of liberty and, accordingly, the first attempt at cessation of the slave trade as well as immediate abolition occurs in Rhode Island in 1774. Still, gradual abolition begins in Connecticut in 1774, in Rhode Island in 1784, in Pennsylvania in 1779 (causing an electoral backlash in 1780), in New York in 1799 (after initial defeat in the 1780s), in New Jersey in 1804. Zilversmit summarizes, as follows, the national import of these abolitionist successes, particularly in New Jersey and New York: "The immediate effects of the gradual abolition laws adopted by New York and New Jersey were slight. No Negroes would be emancipated until twenty years after the enactment of the laws that promised them freedom. But in the long run these laws marked the beginnings of a new system of race relations and labor in the North. And even beyond this, the triumph of gradual abolition in New York and New Jersey marked the point at which the sections began to tread diverging paths, the point at which the nation became a house divided against itself."[125] At the conclusion of the eighteenth century and beginning of the nineteenth century, in addition to the subjects of the classic slave narratives, a new generation of participants in the abolitionist/pro-slavery debate is born, including David Christy, Thomas Roderick Dew, E. N. Elliot, George Fitzhugh, Alexander McCaine, Edmund Ruffin, Thornton Stringfellow (proslavery); James Freeman Clarke, Ralph Waldo Emerson, Alexander McLeod, John Greenleaf Whittier, James Russell Lowell, Henry David Thoreau, Harriet Beecher Stowe, Walt Whitman (antislavery).

The signal abolitionist event of the 1820s was the publication and dissemination of David Walker's forthright text, *Appeal to the Colored Citizens of the World, but in Particular, and Very Expressly to Those of the United States of America*, a pamphlet offering the unprecedented formulation of the issue of abolition as a matter of direct and exclusive consideration for African diasporic persons in the United States, its opening address being, "My dearly beloved Brethren and Fellow Citizens."[126] The compound salutation immediately conflates the status of racial blackness and the state-sponsored rights of civil existence, already implying Walker's national vision that exceeds the question of the legal or political validity of the perpetual enslavement of African-derived persons. The argument, divided into four articles, is wide ranging, sharing some of the features central to the intensification of the pro- and antislavery debate from the 1830s to the Civil War: the question of Christianity and social conduct; the economic principles of enslavement; the imagined consequences of a diverse, free black population; the ironic appropriation of U.S. national discourse yielding symbolic as well as social analysis. Further, the pamphlet challenges directly the Enlightenment thought of Thomas Jefferson, acknowledges the origins of the intercontinental Atlantic world in some detail by alluding to the roles of Spain's Charles V and Bartolomé de las Casas, engages in a forthright analysis of racial whiteness, also gauges the role of the market in the disposition of racial antipathy, and concludes with an extended rejection of the colonization schemes to remove African-derived persons to Africa. In these years prior to the beginning of the intensification of the debate around 1830, the national imagination of civil society in relation to racial blackness turns unsuccessfully to the question of the expulsion of African-derived persons from the national landscape: "From the organizational meeting of the American Colonization Society in 1816 until the end of [Robert] Finley's oversight of the institution in 1825, the society remained an innocuous body. But it did excite the imagination of missionary-minded Protestants; win the confidence of most slaveholders, and gain the support of an impressive array of social and political leaders."[127]

Most noteworthy because of the social and political effect, Walker's *Appeal* calls for African American emancipation by violent means if necessary, so that "in Georgia, Virginia, North Carolina, Louisiana and South Carolina anyone—slave, free-blacks and whites[—]caught with the pamphlet were tried and usually found guilty of inciting insurrection."[128] Political scientist Hasan Crockett in "The Incendiary Pamphlet: David Walker's *Appeal* in Georgia" observes that although "[b]y 1827, a few years before Walker's *Appeal* appeared in Georgia, there were literally thousands of state, county, and local laws controlling the behavior of enslaved and free blacks,"[129] the appearance of the document elicited direct governmental response. Mayor of Savannah, William T. Williams, writes to Harrison Gray Otis, mayor of Boston, "demand[ing] the arrest and punishment of the author."[130] Even as he refused the request Harrison Otis sent a representative to question Walker, as well as advised southern-bound captains and crews to beware of importing the document. In Georgia, the passage of Senate Bill no. 18 required all ships docking in the state to quarantine its black employees and passengers as well as barred black residents of the state from contact with the docked ships; section eleven of the legislation forbade the teaching of literacy to African Americans. "The legislators reasoned that if blacks are kept away from all written material the probability of them acquiring or understanding seditious material is lessened."[131] Yet the political stakes of the response to the *Appeal*, as Crockett describes, are broader still: "The reality that a seditious pamphlet was circulating in the south, written by a black man who was being protected by northern laws propelled Georgians' anti-*Appeal* mania. How dare a black person write such provocative words, how dare it be distributed in our state, and how dare northern sympathizers thumb their noses at us?"[132]

The reenergized abolition movement proceeding from the 1830s—particularly under the leadership of William Lloyd Garrison—largely reiterates and amplifies, then, the new, volatile directness of David Walker's discourse. Undertaking his unremittingly strident version of abolitionist protest in the *Liberator* beginning in January 1831, William Lloyd Garrison ultimately proclaims the U.S. Constitution a proslavery compact, as well as displays prescient public reconciliation to the disjunction of the northern and southern states. The historians Richard Ellis and Aaron Wildavsky, in "A Cultural Analysis of the Role of Abolitionists in the Coming of the Civil War," emphasize the strategic limitations of this Garrisonian sectionalism as an ironically flawed abolitionist imperative, observing that "[t]he Garrisonian's adoption of the doctrine of disunionism . . . reveals the fallacy in this argument. 'No Union with Slaveholders' meant that the North could cleanse its hands of sin while leaving slavery untouched in the South."[133] Garrison, in other words, leads a reenergized abolitionist crusade as foremost a moral rather than political opportunity, a point of distinction leading to the early schism of the movement by 1840. In "William Lloyd Garrison and the 'Pro-Slavery Priesthood': The Changing Beliefs of An Evangelical Reformer, 1830–1840," historian William L. Van Deburg outlines the moral insistence of Garrison by documenting his contentious relation to religious orthodoxies, a defining aspect of his abolitionist leadership: "[I]n their campaign to eradicate the national sin of slavery, as they termed it, the Garrisonians censured the actions of all those who would not bear unqualified testimony against the evils of the southern labor system. By doing so, they not only alienated a large segment of the nation's clergy, but also challenged the moral leadership of that influential body as a whole."[134] By the middle of the decade the short-lived American Union for the Relief and Improvement of the Colored Race, an organizational challenge to Garrison's abolitionist leadership, attests to the rivalry between Garrison and the "American clergy . . . forced into taking a stand on the issues Garrison and his supporters had so glaringly illuminated."[135] Van Deburg observes further: "The fact that many churchmen were opposed to Garrison's immediatism served to deepen his suspicion that they were apologists for the slave system. It was this suspicion which most tellingly influenced Garrison to disregard all counsel, both temporal and spiritual, emanating from those clergymen who refused to take an active part in the campaign to liberate the nation's oppressed bondsmen."[136]

Reiterating the uncompromising demand to end the several slave regimes in the United States, Garrison presents the issue as the preeminent measure of civic, personal, or religious virtue, and he is instrumental in insinuating this polemic into the widest currencies of public consciousness. Rather than finally civic, economic, or political, his abolitionist reform describes, instead, the terms of self-consciousness animating antebellum social relations as insidious and destructive.

In "Abolition at the Ballot-Box," published June 28, 1839, in the *Liberator*, William Lloyd Garrison clarifies his moral critique:

> Once more, I beg not to be misapprehended. I have always expected, I still expect, to see abolition at the ballot-box, renovating the political action of the country—dispelling the sorcery influences of party—breaking asunder the

> fetters of political servitude—stirring up the torpid consciences of voters—substituting anti-slavery for pro-slavery representatives in every legislative assembly—modifying and rescinding all laws which sanction slavery. But this political reformation is to be effected solely by a change in the moral vision of the people—not by attempting to prove that it is the duty of every abolitionist to be a voter, but that it is the duty of every voter to be an abolitionist. By converting electors to the doctrine that slavery ought to be immediately abolished, a rectified political action is the natural consequence: For where this doctrine is received into the soul, the soul-carrier may be trusted anywhere, that he will not betray the cause of bleeding humanity.[137]

In this statement the civic, the economic, and the political are epiphenomenal, wayward expressions of the corrupted forms of self-awareness determining national coherence as well as the most proximate intercourse. Garrison's arguments aim at forms of self-conception and address the institutional mechanisms implied by the civic, the economic, and the political. The open appeals to affect and sentiment consistently characterizing his writings pinion the abolitionist position to address the fundamental emotional awareness—individual and collective—that is profoundly thwarted by the rudiments of U. S. national life. His abolitionist stance calls into question directly the routines of self-expression holding both social sensibility and social policy.

Historian James Brewer Stewart, in the articles "The Emergence of Racial Modernity and the Rise of the White North, 1790–1840" and "Modernizing 'Difference': The Political Meanings of Color in the Free States, 1776–1840," proposes the primary significance of Garrison as an abolitionist to be his iconic role in promoting the racial "amalgamation" increasingly viable, in the 1830s, as "respectable" manifestations of Northern urban thought and intercourse. Stewart recognizes the fully antithetical position of Garrison's social criticism: "To Garrison and his supporters, only a comprehensive espousal of women's rights, religious perfectionism, and nonresistance—the moral antipodes of mobs and mass parties—could inspire the transformation of 'corrupted' majority values."[138] The point is, nonetheless, that the spectacularly novel social terms of Garrison's abolitionist imperative appear deeply provocative in a moment of regressive racial relations:

> [I]n light of the increasingly volatile, gender-focused racial contentiousness of the late 1820s, compounded now by nullifiers and insurrectionists, it is impossible to imagine any event more disruptive than the sudden appearance of a biracial abolitionist movement that included women as well as men. Never before had struggles over racial boundaries and the masculine attributes of "respectability" carried such potential for violence as they did in 1831, when white Garrisonians invited people of all skin colors and both

> genders to crusade to "uplift" the free black community in the North and hasten the end of southern slavery.[139]

The social intercourse of Garrisonian abolition augurs an entirely altered economy of respectable social exchange—as abolitionist success would more dramatically still. Fully apparent in the figure of Garrison is the certainty that the stakes of the abolitionist debate insinuate themselves into the most routine postures of self-consciousness. Differently put, if colonization is the iconic referent for the abolitionist discussion of the 1820s, then Garrison, as the iconic referent for the abolitionist discussion in the 1830s, dramatically marks the movement of the debate from the ready imagination of geographical and phenotypical differences to the direct recognition of the spectacular proximities of modern racial subjects and "subpersons."

The violent social atmosphere of the urban North in the 1830s reflects the tense circumstance, Stewart contends, that the "abolitionists' first struggles to secure racial equality had instead spawned an unprecedented upheaval among the vast majority of whites in the free states that solidified into an unmovable political consensus of highly ordered white supremacy."[140] Particularly as insinuated with abolitionist designs, the aspirations of free African American communities in the North to the terms of social respectability keenly troubles the political, class, and ethnic policies of public recognition, in short, the certainty of who might "claim parity with all other citizens."[141] The galvanizing political campaign of white supremacy is civically, culturally, as well as physically violent—encompassing legislative restrictions on African American voting rights, the dissemination of racial caricatures in the press, the popular psychological vortex of minstrelsy, as well as recurrent mob violence. The aim is to impose social chaos on African American communities: "On every social level then, from barrooms to church meeting halls, the continuing efforts of African Americans to put themselves forward as equals provoked deepening racial resistance from whites preoccupied with their own pursuits of 'manliness' and 'respectability' . . . . Consequently, white harassment increasingly marred Sabbath observances and school-day activities, and the buildings themselves became the targets of the earliest race riots that first erupted in the early and mid-1820s in Boston, New Haven, Providence, Pittsburgh, and Philadelphia."[142] Throughout the 1830s, William Lloyd Garrison appears the arbiter of the profound turbulence by which "northern social relations underwent extraordinary transformations involving people of every station and rank."[143] In this decade, racial advocacy becomes one steadfast component of public identity.

By 1840, the national conversation becomes so ideologically intense that it even fractures the abolitionist movement. The fracture in the abolitionist ranks involves leaders such as William Henry Furness, Henry Stanton, Arthur Tappan,

Theodore Weld, and John Greenleaf Whittier distancing themselves from William Lloyd Garrison's strategies of moral reform in order to champion political agitation and pressure as the means to national success. In 1832, Garrison's "New Abolitionists" re-organize as the New England Anti-Slavery Society and in 1833, by his resolution, the American Anti-Slavery Society forms as a national, rather than regional, initiative. By 1834 the Massachusetts Anti-slavery Society emerges from these transformations, Maine, New Hampshire, and Vermont fashioning local organizations also. Abolition in Massachusetts, with Garrison at the lead, "meant to the Society not only freedom but the eradication of all the incidents and results of slavery, including all the laws, discriminations, social customs, and practices which bore against the Negro race."[144] Nonetheless, as early as 1835 political action much less embroiled in the ethics of racial socialization and self-constitution proves to be dramatic and effective. Arthur Tappan, president of the American Anti-Slavery Society, and his merchant associates, "suspect[ing] that Garrison, the Boston firebrand, was earning more enemies for the cause than friends," execute the scheme devised by Lewis Tappan, in which "the New York leaders decided to flood the country with antislavery literature. The postal effort and the uproar it caused quickened the antislavery pace and aroused the nation to the slavery question."[145] When at "the end of July some one hundred and seventy-five thousand copies of four periodicals passed through the New York Post Office,"[146] the result is that in Charleston, South Carolina, mailbags are stolen from the steamship *Columbia* and burned before the effigies of abolitionists leaders and, by August, the anti-abolitionist rallies protest the dissemination of the pamphlets throughout the southern states. One irony is that Arthur Tappan, even as for "a time in early 1835 [his] dissatisfaction with the Garrisonians nearly caused him to leave the movement,"[147] earns a type of infamy synonymous with Garrison, since in "the summer of 1835 that symbol in the Southern minds [of the abolitionist enemy] was Arthur Tappan, President of the Antislavery Society," which in the proslavery defensiveness "was a position Garrison usually filled."[148]

Garrison's conviction that abolition primarily describes moral reform alienates the clergy as well. During the 1830s, Garrison revises his initial disappointment with organized religious support for immediate abolition to open critique of the clergy and unreflective religious practice, points of criticism that he articulates more strongly still in the 1840s. "Separated from his eminently orthodox Baptist roots," in the words of Van Deburg, "he found it increasingly easy to reject those elements of his evangelical heritage which seemed to do little for man and nothing for the suffering slave."[149] At the opening of the 1840s, William Lloyd Garrison finds himself greeted with alarm rather than support from Lyman Beecher, and he faces unfruitful searches for sites to hold abolitionist gatherings, having ultimately to advertise in the *Boston Courier*. Nonetheless, by the middle of the decade, "abolitionist agitation had progressed to the point where the American clergy was forced into taking a stand on the issues which Garrison and his supporters had so glaringly illuminated."[150] The clergy rebuffs, rather than joins, the ranks of immediate abolition. In 1834 the Baptist Board of Foreign Missions reiterates its Christian brotherhood with southern slaveholders; in 1836 the Presbyterian Synod of Philadelphia deems radical abolition an impediment to universal emancipation; the Methodist Episcopal Church in 1836 openly condemns Garrisonian doctrines. Additionally, in 1834 and 1835 a group of ministers, "in order to combat his influence,"[151] form the American Union for the Relief and Improvement of the Colored Race, representing more moderate abolitionist protest, and by 1839 the challenges to Garrison's leadership of the Massachusetts Anti-Slavery Society include plans to replace the *Liberator* with a new anti-slavery newspaper, a tumult from which "the Garrisonian ranks did not emerge unscathed," because "[a]t least two dozen dissidents chose to separate themselves from the society following the meetings."[152]

The public disarray at the opening of the 1840s, then, is acute. At the annual meeting of the American Antislavery Society in New York in May 1840, the tensions heighten between those abolitionist leaders whose "success with petitions, personal lobbying, and pressure politics to elect sympathetic state legislators and congressmen had convinced them of the need for a new political party dedicated to the abolition of slavery," and William Lloyd Garrison, who diminished "political action and favored disunion rather than working within the framework of the 'proslavery' constitution," advocating, furthermore, "women's rights, nonresistance, temperance, and anti-clericism."[153] At the meeting, Garrison asserts his control within the society by managing to nominate to the business committee Abby Kelley, "a popular Abolitionist speaker and espouser of woman's rights,"[154] with the result that the nomination elicits objections to a woman's serving on the committee and, ultimately, the resignation of Arthur Tappan from the presidency of the American Anti-Slavery Society, as well as "its executive committee and over three hundred delegates from eleven states."[155] This group reassembles as the American and Foreign Anti-Slavery Society, oriented toward "political action and back[ing] the newly organized Liberty party."[156]

The international articulation of abolitionist forces at the World's Anti-Slavery Convention, held in London in June 1840, extrapolates some of the tensions of the Garrisonian and anti-Garrisonian polarity defining the U.S. movement even as the convention also signals—in the estimation of historian Douglas H. Maynard—a watershed, "the beginning of the sustained movement toward international organization which has led to today's extensive network of world conferences and international agencies."[157] The English Quaker abolitionist Joseph Sturge, most remembered for his "famous fact-finding trip to the West Indies in 1837, a trip which led to immediate emancipation of British colonial slaves in place of the gradual apprenticeship system,"[158] is the central organizing force of the event. The outgrowth of the formation of the British and Foreign Anti-Slavery Society in 1839, the convention draws over four hundred delegates from Britain, France, the British West Indies, and the United States. Garrison, having delayed his departure for London until after the May meeting of the American Anti-Slavery Society, arrives on the fifth day of the convention, resolving not to enter the convention, but to watch the proceedings from the visitors' gallery, where the women delegates were barred from direct participation in the proceedings. Indeed, the controversy develops with the very planning for the convention: "Some of the conservative antislavery leaders in America, who opposed 'Garrisonianism' and its tendency to associate various radical reforms with the abolition movement, wrote to London of their apprehensions, and Sturge, disturbed by the controversy in the United States, feared that it would disrupt the London meeting. He and his colleagues were also opposed to the active participation of women in reform efforts, and supplementary statements were issued by the London Committee, making it clear that only male delegates were expected."[159] At stake in the political moment, which is to say, Garrison's fundamental insistence, is the question of the circumscription and the tenor of public agency, seldom recognized as the ineffable confusion of public intercourse with the structures of the imagination, moral and otherwise.

In the 1840s, the disruptive force of interrogating slaveholding nationality overwhelms more than the terms of civilian protocols and public debate. It, more ominously, also begins to trouble the regular exercise of federal relations, the premise of which is comity, the appeal of one state to "the law of another state for the content of its rule of decision."[160] In particular, the 1842 Supreme Court decision *Prigg v. Pennsylvania* registers and exacerbates the dilemma. The decision upholds the rights of slaveholders to return African Americans to slaveholding territory notwithstanding the developing systems of jurisprudence in the North antagonistic to slaveholding. In the case, the Supreme Court adjudicates the competing claims made in 1832 across the border of Maryland and Pennsylvania by, on one side, Margaret Morgan, a colored woman living in virtual freedom, who moves north with her husband and, on the other side, by Edward Prigg, the attorney representing the heiress of the original owner of Margaret Morgan's parents. The dispute becomes "the most famous fugitive slave case before the Supreme Court prior to the Fugitive Slave Act of 1850 and one which highlighted the controversy over the states'-rights vs. central Government's powers current in pre–Civil War America."[161]

The dispute raises three national issues in particular, questions confusing, rather than clarifying, the legal powers of the separate but theoretically allied governmental entities coordinated as the United States; whether the Constitution and the Fugitive Slave Act of 1793 forecloses a trial by jury for any alleged fugitive, the degree to which state legislation might supplement federal legislation and, therefore, also the extent of the powers of Congress to set legislation on the issue of slavery. The issue of a trial by jury discloses the greater interest of the dispute beyond the jurisprudential questions, since "[t]he controversial aspect of this legal possibility was whether the trial would be in the state from which the fugitive fled or the state to which he fled. The Southern contention was that the fugitive should be tried (if at all) in the territory in which the owner would best be able to prove his claim."[162]

The greater interest of the case, this is to say, reaches to the immediate hold of the slaveholder on the mechanisms of public management and, as the Fugitive Slave Act of 1850 soon dictates, public deportment and obligations. The ruling affirms the right of Congress to legislate on slavery in this way, denying the right of the subordinate government bodies to legislate on the issue of fugitive slavery, the consequential nuance being, however, that the subordinate governments hold entirely the right to determine whether or not their officials aid in the execution of the federal act: "*Prigg v. Pennsylvania,* written by Justice Story in 1842, invalidated Pennsylvania legislation that prohibited a master from reclaiming his slave without a warrant from a magistrate as inconsistent with the Constitution's fugitive slave clause and Congressional statutes enforcing the clause. *Prigg* established the supremacy of explicit constitutional protections of slavery over inconsistent state regulation."[163]

Simply put, the competing interests of the various, interlocking agencies in regard to the federated national state intensify. The series of Northern legislation known as the "Personal Liberty Laws," first emerging in the 1820s but proliferating rapidly after the 1842 ruling, document this effect of *Prigg vs. Pennsylvania,* insofar as the "decision precluded the opportunity for a trial by jury for fugitives, antislavery men seized upon the principle of the same decision that state magistrates could be withheld from executing the fugitive act."[164]

In other words, the "Personal Liberty Laws," notwithstanding that they were distinct legislative acts of disparate jurisdictions, all sought to resist the direct hold of the slaveholder on the mechanisms and routines of government, especially in non-slaveholding states. These laws are passed, for example, in Indiana (1824), Connecticut (1838, 1844), New York (1840), Vermont (1840, 1858), Massachusetts (1843), New Hampshire (1846), Pennsylvania (1847), and Rhode Island (1848). The array of measures legislated to retard slaveholding influence in these Northern jurisdictions include provisions for appeals against seizure (to be adjudicated by trial by jury) or, further still, the uniform extension to all fugitives of the right to a trial by jury as well as the right to state-appointed defense, the restricting of state officers from performing the duties necessary to the observance of the 1793 Fugitive Slave Law, banning the use of state facilities to support the federal statute, as well as the stipulation of severe punishments for the seizure of free persons to traffic as slaves. Restated, the measures contest the mechanisms of public management that, as increasingly becomes evident throughout the 1840s, have the reach of defining and scripting both the most random individual contact as well as the most officious individual actions.

In other words still, the federal protection of the interests of the U.S. slaveholding regime yields the tense circumstances in which "it was made apparent that the defense of slavery included abrogation of civil liberty, including civil liberties of citizens of the free states [with the upshot that in these states] the opinion opposed to the 'slave power' began to grow."[165] From 1836 to 1844 these circumstances already overwhelm the routines of the U.S. Congress in what is known as the "gag-rule controversy." Historian William Lee Miller notes that in accordance with "House rules, the first thirty days of a congressional session were all petition days. Each day's proceedings started off, after an interlude, with the people's representatives hearing what the people wanted to intercede and remonstrate about."[166] However, after the 1835 postal campaign of Arthur Tappan and the American Anti-Slavery Society, and in particular the reading of an abolitionist petition by Massachusetts Congressman George Briggs in 1835, "that winter, while the House was coping with the first of the season's petitions, the Senate was discussing alternative methods—Jackson's and Calhoun's—of coping with the 'unconstitutional and wicked' circulation of abolitionist publications, with their odious prints."[167] The result is protracted and raucous, escalating to both verbal and physical assaults among members of Congress.

It is important to acknowledge that, whereas the "gag-rule controversy" disrupts and revises the procedures and execution of the federal agency, *Prigg vs. Pennsylvania* followed by the Northern retort of the "Personal Liberty Laws" dispute, in the significance of public actions, the ability and the reach of the federal consensus to describe strictly the quotidian actions of public life. Most particularly, they dispute, in the significance of public actions, the extent to which unequal access to personal security marks the viability of the nation as a project of racialization, the systematic elaboration of "essentialist representations of race and social structures of domination," in the words of social scientists Michael Omi and Howard Winant.[168] The controversy concerns which attitudes, postures, and actions remain available in the public sphere, available in the name of the "nation," in the lawfulness of the federal and local state, or in the scripting of civilian formalities, rather than simply federal procedures and execution. These entangled legal and extralegal tensions rivet finally public bodies and perceptions, tensions disclosing, to the distress of modern political exemplarity, that the civil society, "the institutional infrastructure for political mediation and public exchange" that defines the U.S. federal territory since 1790,[169] demands fundamentally and acutely the assignation of African diasporic persons as populations whose needs will not be met by the prevailing system of governance.

The pronounced caution with which Ralph Waldo Emerson enters the burgeoning national discord at the close of the 1830s and the opening of the 1840s "only with great reluctance" and primarily in "defense of the principle of free speech, which was then threatened by a nearly universal repression of abolition oratory"[170] underscores the caustic atmosphere [dis]allowing personal identity, political expression, and collectivity. At this moment, "in the late thirties and early forties a number of respectable citizens, including some prominent Unitarians, were declaring their allegiance to the organized efforts of abolition. Among these were Theodore Parker, Ellis Gray Loring, Edmund Quincy, Wendell Phillips, and, most important, Emerson's lifelong friend William Henry Furness."[171] Like these other Unitarians, Emerson also begins to reassess and relinquish the view that, "[r]egarding a social problem such as slavery[,] . . . any reform movement which sought to impose a solution through coercive legislation or some other outside force was doomed to failure since such action would do nothing to change the hearts of the individuals most affected, in this case the slaves and the slaveholders, and thus would limit itself to dealing with mere symptoms rather than the causes of the evil."[172] The ideological differences between his 1838 "Divinity School Address" and his 1844 speech concerning emancipation in the British West Indies signal Emerson's emergence as a proponent of abolition. The first speech ignites "perhaps the most significant public controversy of his entire career,"[173] and the second offers the "conclusion of [racial] equality . . . [which] cannot be over-emphasized in its importance to his decision to actively speak out against slavery at this time."[174] In sum, the ideological change, as both moral quotient and political action, involves the plain reassessment of the possibilities of the social presence of racial blackness; yet equally to the point in the transformation is his patent admission of the unsatisfactory common ground of modern social life, which is to say, the unsettling vortex of the market exchange of capitalist relations of production.

In the essay "Self-Reliance," his most famous iconoclastic pronouncement of social being, reflecting Unitarian as well as Transcendentalist tenets, Emerson states archly, as though modern society is the antithesis—rather than the apotheosis—of the human: "Society everywhere is in conspiracy against the manhood of every one of its members. Society is a joint-stock company, in which the members agree, for the better securing of his bread to each shareholder, to surrender the liberty and culture of the eater."[175] The volatility of this arrangement gainsays any ideal of civil society as the collective manifestation of a "civilizing process," realizing, rather, the discouraging perpetuity in which "[w]e are afraid of truth, afraid of fortune, afraid of death, and afraid of each other."[176] This popular generation of hostility and trepidation yields merely inadequate social bonds that, therefore, must be supplemented, in contradistinction, by the philosophical conviction of self-reliance, the self-recognition extending even to the certainty that "the reliance on Property, including the reliance on governments which protect it, is the want of self-reliance."[177] Given that this social paradigm belies the stated imperative of civil society, the intransigent, indeed structural, moral deficit facing the subject of modernity appears overwhelming, precisely the disquieting awareness urging Emerson to the associational activism of abolitionist reform—notwithstanding his Unitarian and Transcendentalist views. Indeed, for literary critic John Carlos Rowe, this equivocation forms the irreconcilable schism always fracturing the work of Ralph Waldo Emerson from 1844 to 1863:

> Yet herein lies the fundamental problem with Emerson's political writings from 1844 to 1863—the period of his most active commitment to the cause of abolition as well as the period of his 1855 lecture, "Woman": Emerson either must abandon the fundamentals of transcendentalism or the principles of political activism. Transcendentalism reveals itself to be at fundamental odds with the social reforms regarding slavery and women's rights. This conflict is at the heart of what can be viewed in no other way than as the intellectual schizophrenia of Emerson in these writings in this period. When he endorses a liberal political position, he must abandon transcendentalist principles; when he embraces transcendentalism, his politics are patronizing and impractical as the formula for 'reform' in *Nature* and his other early writings. In short, Emersonian transcendentalism and political activism in the mid-nineteenth-century America were inherently incompatible.[178]

In the essay "Abolition, the Emersons, and 1837," Len Gougeon outlines additionally the variety of endorsements within the Emerson family of abolitionist advocacy, all of which precede the conversion of Ralph Waldo Emerson to the reform movement. His sister, Mary Moody Emerson, and his stepfather, Reverend Ezra Ripley, "were prominently involved in the antislavery agitation of the 1830s and 1840s."[179] Charles Emerson, Ralph Waldo Emerson's younger brother, delivers in Concord a lecture on slavery as early as 1835, a lecture based on the milestone of West Indian emancipation, which he deploys as the call to immediate emancipation in the United States. Lidian Emerson, Ralph Waldo Emerson's wife, is from the outset a member of the Women's Anti-Slavery Society, established also in 1835. Literary critic Susan Belasco, in "'The Animating Influences of Discord': Margaret Fuller in 1844," analogously, compares the critical preoccupations of Margaret Fuller and Ralph Waldo Emerson, who both appear in the December

20, 1844, edition of the *New York Tribune*, however, "Fuller, publicly working on developing American culture and taste, and . . . Emerson, publicly supporting organized protest."[180] Belasco is interested in explaining, then, the discrepancy between the two intellectual comrades, who share a long acquaintance beginning in 1836, the philosophical convictions of Transcendentalism, as well as ties to the alternative social experiment, Brooke Farm, led by George and Sophia Ripley. In other words, the antislavery and proslavery disparity, in addition to developing the bureaucratic, judicial, and legislative paroxysms of the United States, supplies what becomes among the most easily recognizable and verifiable terms of social identity, civil and social interaction. The disparity, formulated as a conversation over or dismissal of racial blackness, comes to measure patterns of sociality, in addition to political practice—testing finally which dispositions to racial blackness are tenable in the name, the articulation, of the nation.

The unmistakable clarity by the 1840s is that, beyond official procedures, this point of articulation disturbs the ideally elegant task of civil society, the diffuse management of agreement and disagreement in the inevitable "coming together of private individuals, in a sphere that is neither the family nor state,"[181] the interactive trace of agreement and disagreement that putatively forecloses extreme, various forms of violence. Sociologist Krishan Kumar, in noting the Hegelian innovation of the term, writes: "Civil society, as a moment in the progress of the Spirit towards the universality of the state . . . is a part of ethical life, the part that provides the middle term between the family and the state. It therefore partakes of that unity of 'abstract right' and 'subjective morality' that is the formal principle of ethical life. It goes, that is, beyond individuals and the relations between individuals to encompass the life of the community as a whole. Civil society is a process of mediation."[182] By these alternative means, civil society provides the law of order that is much more delicate and extensive than the immediately coercive reach of the state—these contradictory principles determining, in their conflict, the terrain of the political. Still, even as this tension plots the putatively "universal" compass of the political, the economic subsumption and racial imperative on which both civil society and the state rest belies this apparent universality. Rather, civil society, the state, and the political remain deeply ingrained in the "extremes of extravagance and poverty, with the permanent possibility of a large number of people falling below a certain standard of living, losing any feeling of right, integrity and honor; in effect becoming a 'rabble.'"[183] These modern forms premise their collectivity, in other words, on strategic exclusion, exclusion calculated and enforced with the reckless lawlessness they purport, in their modernity, to annul but, in fact, strategically determine, given "precisely the capitalist nature of civil society and all that it entails."[184] The disconcerting exposure, the paradoxical excess of the "universal," delineates the perpetual force by which civil society, the state and their convergent designation of the political, obtain the random, violent sway otherwise disavowed. The historical predicament—that is, the wayward political progress—amounts to the keen lawlessness by which civil society perpetually secures itself, keen lawlessness that, curiously, proves the absolute law of civil society. The questionable disposal of African American communities through forms of select aggression and carnage provides, to this end, the routine of the U.S. bureaucratic and social cohesion, equally defining, nonetheless, the abolitionist point of agitation.

Restated, the civil society, derived from the independence of the original seaboard colonies, stipulates economic, political, and social abjections securing race as the ideal point of application. However, the abjection constitutive of the federal state ironically overwhelms the civil fortification of racial whiteness that the federal state attempts to mandate. The confusion is, at least, threefold: U.S. national policy becomes logically self-riddled once it becomes designed patently to circumscribe and foreclose the broad freedoms of white men since, from its founding, the modern Atlantic democratic experiment of the United States sanctions "chattel slavery, race-based immigration and naturalization restrictions, U.S. ineligibility of women and the foreign-born for the highest political offices, segregation, or many of the other forms of civic hierarchy"[185] so as to inscribe and enforce white masculinity as the adamant concern of civil society. Historian Rogers Smith describes the intensity with which the national agency pursues the adamant placement of white masculinity at the center of the U.S. civic arrangement, as follows: "[W]hen restrictions on voting rights, naturalization, and immigration are taken into account, it turns out that for over 80 percent of U.S. history, American laws declared most people in the world legally ineligible to become full U.S. citizens solely because of their race, original nationality, or gender. For at least two-thirds of American history, the majority of the domestic adult population was also ineligible for full citizenship for the same reasons."[186] One further irony, then, is that the burgeoning national discord, notwithstanding the ontological denigration (and, thus, the routine enslavement or persecution) of African-derived persons, increasingly confronts the recognition (and denouncement) of the lawlessness of white men. The irony is that white men, at once, remain the fully exemplary figures of civic animation within the advance of modern political community.

The contradiction enmeshed in the complexity and the rhetoric of the dispute by the 1840s exposes the white male figure of political modernity in terrifying terms, the unreserved architect of emotional, ideological, legislative, sexual, and social persecution while, at once, the premise of modern political agency. Beyond the disputed legislative and national agendas, this acute cultural and political paradox registers the quotidian state of affairs in which hostility pervades like oxygen, igniting the agencies of government, feeding the sibilance of public discourse and derision, agitating the reasonableness of trivial exchanges and encounters, corroding the address of sentiment, fitfully inflaming the caustic turn to self-consciousness and expression. The diffuse, fomenting hostility—disclosed with particular intimacy by African American slave narratives—belies, paradigmatically, the advertised order of the burgeoning federal experiment and, moreover, the still grander modern apotheosis.

To restate the point, the collective condition in which hostility functions essentially as if it were oxygen discounts the ideal of "civil society," the sociopolitical boon of the modern advance, the intractably peaceful and rational coordination of demographic conflicts. Yielding the coherent social relations responsible foremost to the mechanisms of the state, civil society aims to recast "the natural human systems of needs and particular self-interests, puts them in relation with each other through the capitalist social institutions of production and exchange and, thus, on the basis of the mediation and subsumption of the particular, poses a terrain on which the State can realize the universal interest of society."[187] However, civil society—the political alibi of modern social formations administering the imperatives of Atlantic modernity—indicates a strictly riddled ideal, because the concept advertises the "civilizing process contained in market exchange and capitalist relations of production,"[188] even as the market exchange of capitalist relations of production credits and extends elaborate new systems of coercion, control, or violence as the priority of governance.

Racial blackness remains the (inter)national trace of this fundamental exposure for, given the historical formation of the market exchange of capitalist relations of production, the odd self-annulment of the concept of civil society is emphatically and profitably the point of racialization at which enslaved or persecuted African-derived persons are rendered within the premises of the modern state. Consider again that the 1790 legislative fiat, on which the new guarantor of U.S. national viability (federal taxation) depends, designates racial blackness as the political, if not human, point betraying the inconsistent and violent ideological premises of modern political community. In effect, the modern civic proposition of self-coherence, holding national identity as its most hyperbolic form, proceeds from the conscription of sub-Saharan Africans and their descendants into the severest routines of the Atlantic commercial cycles, as well as the severest routines of individual and administrative European imaginations. The phenotypes consolidated "as" racial blackness mark the allowance, political and otherwise, for the irredeemable prurience, the predatory acquisitiveness, or the ready sweeping violence of the Atlantic market exchange and its primary sanctioned agents. These ineluctable, productive forms of hostility establish, from the fifteenth century on and throughout the Atlantic arena, the means by which "the economic medium of civil society can be said to fill the role of nature [and, thus, seemingly yield in modernizing contrast] the rational order of the political realm."[189]

At its basis, this rational order of the political realm sweepingly licenses the sway of the white male agents of modernity, elaborating, at once, adamant (inter)national systems of constraint as the condition of this possibility, systems of constraint that set the conceptual and material priorities of governance to be the management of the economic and psychic environment sustained by hostility, as if it were oxygen—and notwithstanding the effective premise of civil society. For aligned (but not identical) with the state, the terrain of civil society holds in common with it, as its historical point of possibility, the routinization of hostility. Rather than a "civilizing process," the abstract management of the financial and social capital of the political community, which entangles civil society and the state, derives from the dire practices of primitive accumulation that civil society, even more than the state, disavows and neglects.

Animating the social relation to the state, civil society does not reflect, then, "universal interest" so much as it would prescribe it, in order to align "universal interest" with the disavowal of the always already inadequate reach of the violence securing the market exchange of capitalist relations of production. As Michael Hardt observes, the recognition of this entanglement of civil society and the state forms the oblique point of convergence between the disparate, unlikely theoretical projects of Hegel and Foucault: "The educative social processes that Hegel casts in terms of abstraction and organization, Foucault recognizes in terms of training, discipline, and management. The channels or striate in which these processes function, recognized as social institutions by Hegel, are characterized by Foucault in terms of deployments (*disposifs*) and enclosures (*enfermements*)."[190] The constraints of the political formation, pervading the conceptual and the material, define the positive registers of sociality.

This exposure, with the publication in 1845 of Frederick Douglass's *Narrative of the Life of Frederick Douglass*, gains especially popular notice. Douglass's autobiographical assault on slaveholding and its supports, with striking rhetorical effect, protests the lawlessness of antebellum civil society concentrated as the exceptional racialization of African-derived persons. The narrative protests that the result is, foremost, the moral vortex defined violently through the predilections of the unchecked white masculinity shaping "society as a cycle of conflict, riven by power struggles between different racial and ethnic groups, all of whom seem inexorably bound to the Ixion wheel of domination and subordination."[191] Douglass stresses that the federal association licenses "the meanest as well as the most wicked of men,"[192] rather than the preeminence of civil order—exposures that he achieves through detailing the intimacies of the immediate social contact ascertaining racialization and subtending the system of enslavement. Substantially, the striking effect of the narrative is due to its crafting, as literary critic Robert Stepto points out: "What marks Douglass's narration and control of his tale is his extraordinary ability to pursue several types of writing with ease and with a degree of simultaneity. The principal types of writing we discover in the tale are syncretic phrasing, introspective analysis, internalized documentation, and participant-observation."[193] The rhetorical control of the text, Stepto argues, remains patently with Douglass, despite the rhetorical limits of the new genre in which the narrators remain, literary critic James Olney discerns, "in an irresolvably tight bind as a result of the very intention and premise of [the] narrative, which is to give a picture of slavery 'as it really is'"[194] in order to enhance, above all, the abolitionist moral and political agenda. The narrators, in this way, never simply undertake the self-reflexive act of self-representation—the practice of autobiography.

The striking rhetorical effect of *Narrative of the Life of Frederick Douglass*, however, is the entanglement of both. The narrator locates at the center of the portrait of "slavery as it really is," not foremost the beleaguered body most emblematic of enslavement, or the tremendous trauma, but the impressions of his prescient mind, managing to interrogate, in the circumstances of ferocious persecution, "selfhood and the community of historical precedents, social identifications, and literary-cultural traditions that constitute it."[195] The narrator's opening gambit, for example, is pensive inquiry: "I have no accurate knowledge of my age, never having seen any authentic record containing it."[196] The confusion becomes, at once, an introspective concern and the sociopolitical arrangement: "By far the larger part of the slaves know as little of their age as horses know of theirs, and it is the wish of most masters within my knowledge to keep their slaves thus ignorant. I do not remember to have ever met a slave who could tell of his birthday."[197] The opening of the narrative performs a peculiar self-nullification, betraying, in addition to the distress of the enslaved condition, the political agreement—the engagement of civil society and the state—promoting and regulating the confounding treatment. To be in the narrator's confusion is to be, by calculation, in a routine of systematic subordination: "The white children could tell their ages. I could not tell why I ought to be deprived of the same privilege."[198] The narrator's initial demonstration is the fully abstracted set of ideals he insistently contemplates, as closely as he rehearses the material constraints of legal bondage.

But, almost as immediately as he assumes the posture, the opening pensiveness cedes to the dire social exchanges drawing the narrator to understand his position in the categorical hierarchy that is more and more widely administered as the narrative progresses. The pensiveness dissipates before the first social exchange rehearsed in the narrative "rhetorical exposure of the black woman's suffering body . . . disclosing," in the words of literary critic Jenny Franchot, "the sins of the white fathers by turning slavery's hidden interiors into the publicized exterior of prose."[199] The horror and sentimental structure of this first closely drawn scene depend on the violent unruliness of the only member of the political community of the state present in the scene, the narrator's "owner" (and perhaps father) Captain Anthony, who is "not considered a rich slaveholder . . . own[ing] two or three farms, and about thirty slaves" and employing as his overseer Mr. Plummer, "a miserable drunkard, a profane swearer, and a savage monster."[200]

Captain Anthony's outrage at the narrator's Aunt Hester's disobeying him—spurning Captain Anthony's desires, the narrator implies—generates the mayhem in which, "after rolling up his sleeves, he commenced to lay on the heavy cowskin, and soon the warm, red-blood (amid heart-rending shrieks from her, and horrid oaths from him) came dripping to the floor."[201] Three positions mark the scene: Aunt Hester, whose emotional and physical persecutions represent "the blood-stained gate, the entrance to the hell of slavery";[202] the narrator, who cowers before "the bloody transaction . . . expect[ing] it would be my turn next,"[203] and Captain Anthony, embodying by political agreement the "social order of citizenship, one where men (rarely women) regulated their relationships and settled their disputes according to a system of laws; where 'civility' reigns, and citizens take an active part in public life."[204] Captain Anthony embodies, in the Hegelian specification of the term "civil society," "a moment in the progress of the Spirit towards the universality of the state . . . [as] a part of ethical life, the part that provides the middle term between the family and the state."[205] Even Captain Anthony's paroxysm does not diminish this standing but rather, by political agreement, registers it as well as, by political agreement, the designated ethical life sponsored by the state. In other words, not despite but because of the coalescent presence of the figure and law of the state, the scene emits terrifying energy as the opening, structural dilemma of the narrative as well as, culturally, by redacting the Garrisonian moral denouncements of slaveholding.

The urgent moral issue in the scene, regarding the nationalizing concept of civility, is that—by national design—terror supplants civility absolutely but does not supplant the agency of the state. Of the principle characters in the scene, Aunt Hester has much more to fear from Captain Anthony and his actions, authorized by myriad material and political networks, than he has in any way to fear from Aunt Hester, "her hands tied to the hook."[206] Terror, because it is the magnification and solicitation of fear, has its source in the position of Captain Anthony with the open sanction of the bureaucratic, legislative, and policing practices of the state. Thus, from his third position in the scene, the narrator fails to confirm anywhere, as proposed by modernity, the seemingly boundless reasonableness of "the self-seeking economic actor"[207] whose equanimity indicates the equal boundlessness of civil society, the effective composure of the state. In the scene, already perplexed by the adamant rules and regulations of the Atlantic market paradigm that denies him basic forms of self-orientation, the narrator witnesses further the cultural and political design providing legal credit to virtually any form of violence that might sustain (racially defined) extreme subordination. In sum, the three positions in the scene cannot analogize any formulation of civil society—as a modern, a state, or a universal condition, which is to say, the fundamental condition of agency establishing "the hallmark of the modern world."[208]

Rather, the drama of the scene is raucous, and moral as well, more directly indicating, in the words of cultural critic Hortense Spillers, "a distinction in this case between 'body' and 'flesh' . . . impos[ing] that distinction as the central one between captive and liberated subject-positions."[209] According to Spillers, the "flesh," which precedes the "body," is "that zero-degree of social conceptualization that does not escape concealment under the brush of discourse or the reflexes of iconography."[210] The "flesh" is "a primary narrative" that records the historically constitutive violence of modernity seeking "the person of African females and males [who] registered the wounding."[211] This complex moral and political palimpsest is the exposure of the scene, the exposure of the mayhem and terror Captain Anthony generates as the crux, at once, of his civilian, libidinal, masculine, and proprietary identities. If the "body"—"a private and particular space, at which point biological, sexual, social cultural, linguistic, ritualistic, and psychological fortunes converge"—is available beyond the condition of the "flesh,"[212] then it is available as the violent repudiation of racial blackness coordinated with the representation, if not composition, of identity and power as a modern phenomenon.

Literary critic Deborah McDowell, in her essay "In the First Place: Making Frederick Douglass and the Afro-American Tradition," reads this structural transaction in the scene through the nuances of gender, observing that "Douglass's repetition of the sexualized scene of whipping projects him into a voyeuristic relation to the violence against slave women, which he watches, and thus he enters into a symbolic complicity with the sexual crime he witnesses."[213] McDowell is interested in the curiosity that, although "the whippings of women are not the only ones of which Douglass's *Narrative* gives account, they predominate by far in the text's economy as Douglass looks on."[214] Both feminist analyses are interested in the cultural materiality of the transaction, the open determination of social and representational positions consolidated by the mayhem of the scene. Order remains from Aunt Hester's bruised silence, whether the seeming order of civic license, civic communication, or literary genealogy.

The disturbance—representational and otherwise—insofar as it materializes a structural exposure, cannot be recuperated simply as the fiat of civil society, the nationalizing proposition foremost promoting the "fetishism involved in bourgeois relations, in which the social bond is exchange value and where the social character of activity . . . results in social relations assuming 'the fantastic form of a relation between things.'"[215] The particular terror of the scene is that it clearly does not depict a relation between things but, instead, the disposition of the corporeal that only can be construed as lawless yet on which, nonetheless, the national proposition depends. Jenny Franchot, in "The Punishment of Esther: Frederick Douglass and the Construction of the Feminine," plots along the coordinates of gender, as do McDowell and Spillers, this relation between corporeality and civic abstraction. Franchot argues: "Th[e] shift from often impassioned descriptions of women in slavery to virtual silence about them in the comparative freedom of the North testifies to the repression of the feminine required by the middle-class virility that Douglass emulated."[216] This trajectory already is evident by the conclusion of the first chapter, in which "Douglass's narrative construction of Esther's punishment fixes upon her body, which in all its stark and damaged materiality . . . stands as a condemnatory sign of an otherwise elusive patriarchy."[217] Even as he would protest it, the narrator constructs his identity in ways that rearticulate the *constitutive* force of the violence that the scene decries.

Literary critic Jeannine DeLombard, in "'Eye-Witness to the Cruelty': Southern Violence and Northern Testimony in Frederick Douglass's 1845 *Narrative*," articulates this difference between the violated corporeal and viable civic abstraction, not in terms of gender but within the premises of Ralph Waldo Emerson's Transcendentalist discourse: "If in *Nature* the organ of sight is inviolate to the point of oxymoronic incorporeality, in the *Narrative* it is as vulnerable as the rest of the slave's brutalized body. For this reason, I suggest, Douglass, in a series of witnessing scenes, gradually shifts the metonym of authorship from the vulnerable, corporeal eyeball to the unassailable, immaterial voice, a shift that corresponds with the text's overall progression from slavery to freedom and from South to North."[218] The position that Frederick Douglass abandons as abolitionist and narrator is the stance in which "it is through his or her embodied self that the shared experience of enslavement is articulated."[219] Insofar as it defines the trajectories of the narrative, the abstraction of civilian address and being (hyperbolic in Transcendentalist discourse) fails to deem adequately those injuries and the scenes of injury tethered politically to civil confidence and consciousness: "Emerson's 'transparent eyeball,' then, with its attendant association of universal subjectivity and transcendent poetic vision, provides a stark contrast to the embodied subjectivity and traumatized eyewitness perspective represented by Douglass's 'burst' eyeball."[220] The contradistinction between these positions, emphasized by the rhetorical (mis)alignment between Ralph Waldo Emerson's "transparent eyeball" and Frederick Douglass's "burst eyeball" is structural, so that, despite all attempts to fix these positions essentially, Douglass negotiates the transposition, approximating alarmingly "the full humanity and universal subjectivity" taken for the civil condition, the condition excessive of injury.

Literary critic Christopher Castiglia, in "Abolition's Racial Interiors and the Making of White Civic Depth," understands similarly the distinction between embodiment and the abstraction of civilian commonality, "the central [distinction] between captive and liberated subject-positions" in the argument of Spillers.[221] Castiglia contends that the distinction produces the "locations where subjectivity and state interest blend into affective hybrids that create the possibilities for independent critique and forms of self-management that limit both possibilities."[222] As already suggested, the scene of Aunt Hester's injury draws the entanglement of "subjectivity and state interest" in chaotic, startling terms—conceptually as well as rhetorically. The interests of the state might be questionable, given the direct implication of those interests in the chaos. However, to pursue Castiglia's analysis, the abolitionist agenda that disputes the dichotomy of embodiment and civic abstraction central to the scene refuses "to define citizenship by placing blacks outside the borders of the nation . . . therefore to define the national interior as white," as in the earlier strategy of the American Colonization Society. The abolitionist agenda proposes, instead, "citizenship in relation to the individual characters of citizens."[223] This revision, to quote Castiglia, turns on "affect, which characterizes white Americans as fully feeling subjects, and civic abstraction, which becomes the possession of black Americans":

> If slavery, as critics have argued, forced black Americans to bear the burden of embodiments spared white Americans who, in contrast, could identify with national abstractions such as virtue and liberty (abstractions that, as Toni Morrison argues, take on meaning only in visible contrast to enslaved black bodies), reformist abolition invested blacks with the burden of abstract civility, now viewed as defining their interior "characters." Racial difference persists, then, not on the physical body as an index of inferior character (as proslavery advocates claimed), but as differentiated interior states requiring different relationships to nationalism and social agency: By imagining African-American interiority as comprised of (the desire for) civic abstraction, white abolitionists saw black Americans as static emblems of a national "character" that sympathetic affect entitled white abolitionists to challenge and change. At the same time, sympathy as an affective state particular to liberal whites allowed an identificational mobility within the nation symbolic only for the already-enfranchised white subject. White reformers took on blackness, not on the surface of the skin, but as a suffering interior, a civic "depth." With an inner experience of

> black suffering, white reformers claimed a public authority that differentiated them from other whites, even while it maintained an affective difference from persecuted blacks.[224]

The Garrisonian, reformist scheme skews the coordinates of self-consciousness, so much so that racial whiteness seems the point of embodied appraisal and racial blackness the cipher of the immaterial ideal by which nationality becomes discernible.

The dramatized persecution of Aunt Hester, written by a narrator for whom the violent chaos largely predicts his own future, renders the fraught national paradigm as a tragic experience that fully disrupts the routine terms of self-identification. The narrator highlights the profound disruption—and its potential political analogue—for his readership. The disruption is that the (historically) appropriate impersonation of the human—modern civic animation—cannot be located, as Castiglia points out, in racial whiteness, its presumed coordinates. The disruption, equally, is that the ascertaining of racial blackness does not seem impertinent to the articulation of national civility.

The persecution does not depict the national landscape suffused with "the possibilities for independent critique and forms of self-management,"[225] the political proposal of the modern civilian universe. It depicts, instead, the sinister political viability brooking neither "independent critique," which Aunt Hester's actions offer, nor any "forms of self-management" beyond the extent of her torture, her torso lacerated and bleeding. The cultural effects of this type of disturbing speculation prove widespread as, for instance, the separately evolving social consciousnesses of Ralph Waldo Emerson, his family, and his friend Margaret Fuller indicate. The avid readership of *The Narrative of the Life of Frederick Douglass*, which sells seven editions by 1849,[226] indicates the same. The pensive crisis is that the national substance, the imagination of political collectivity, seems imperiled by the extreme powers and status it might confer; rather than civility and reason, the advent seems the dismay, the pandemonium, of unruly, excessive authority.

Even as the interactions legalized within the federal compact fail to accumulate as national civility, the extreme abstraction of the national representation accrues, nonetheless, even more decisive political force. That is, "Manifest Destiny," the 1845 slogan penned by John O'Sullivan in *The New York Morning News*, restates the national consolidation in transcendent terms as, concomitantly, African American testimony more and more vividly enumerates the civilian violations sponsored by the national arrangement:

> A large number of the separately printed [slave] narratives were issued in pamphlet form, cheaply printed, bound with paper covers and sold for about twenty-five cents. The more lengthy and better bound ones could be had for

> a dollar or a dollar and a half. *The Interesting Narrative of the Life of Olaudah Equiano, or Gustavus Vassa, the African, Written by Himself* (1789) went into at least ten editions by 1837; a Dutch and a German edition are extant. At least six editions of Charles Ball's *Slavery in the United States* were issued between 1836 and 1859. By 1856 *The Narrative of Moses Roper's Adventures and Escape from American Slavery,* first published in 1837, had reached ten editions and had been translated into Celtic. Even so trivial a volume as *The Life of James Mars* (1865) saw eleven editions by 1872. Josiah Henson's narrative reached its six thousandth copy in 1852, having been published in England, as well as here in America. By May 28, 1858 advance orders for the "Stowe edition" of Henson's book alone totaled 5,000 copies. In the 1878 edition it is claimed that 100,000 copies of the book had been sold. Indeed a Dutch translation appeared in 1877 and a French edition in the following year. Within two years after its publication in 1853, *Twelve Years a Slave: The Narrative of Solomon Northup* had sold 27,000 copies. *The Narrative of William Wells Brown* sold 8,000 copies (four editions) by 1849. Needless to say, *The Narrative of the Life of Frederick Douglass* and *My Bondage and My Freedom* (1855) were widely read.[227]

But, at once, the abstract basis of the national consolidation becomes more pronounced. The longstanding controversy concerning the annexation of Texas demands innovative speculation on the national consensus for its resolution. The articulation of "manifest destiny" as the materialization of national life, in the "sustained propaganda blitz that continued until the declaration of war [with Mexico] on May 13, 1846,"[228] profoundly abstracts even further, almost beyond the issues of corporeality, the meaning of the federal association. For the innovative federal coordinates disregard the substance of locality and community and, indeed, the immediacy of the quotidian temporality—nonetheless the corporeal sway—of national being, in order to provide "a *theologized* image of the nation that was far more reassuring to anxious Americans than the secular conception of society that opponents of annexation had been forcefully articulating since 1836."[229]

The annexation of Texas, entangled with the question of the enslavement of African Americans, adamantly forecloses as the national configuration "a free, multiracial citizenry living in republican harmony."[230] Literary critic Lyon Rathburn, in "The Debate over Annexing Texas and the Emergence of Manifest Destiny," rehearses that the controversy begins with the territorial uneasiness pervading the historical moment of the Missouri Compromise. The 1817 Adams-Onis Trancontinental Treaty stipulates that "American claims on the Columbia River and Pacific Coast would be safeguarded and American neutrality in the Spanish colonial conflict would remain intact . . . [and also that] the United States would surrender all claims west of the Sabine River [Texas] while Spain would surrender all claims east of the Mississippi [Florida]";[231] however, the treaty is "a measure that deeply threatened many Southerners," yielding, along with the restrictions of the Missouri Compromise, "a pronounced sense of entrapment."[232] Three years later, Henry Clay, then congressman from Kentucky, essays legislation that annuls the treaty, with the results that "some [national leaders] continued using the language of providential destiny in calling for the acquisition of Texas, [while] others had begun echoing the civic vocabulary of classical republicanism in expressing their fears of social disintegration." Rathburn, in this way, observes further that the "emerging division over slavery had given new saliency to the old Montesquieuian warning that diverging interests within an expansive republic made its dissolution inevitable."[233]

Andrew Jackson, not succeeding at attempting to purchase Texas during the first seven years of his expansionist presidency, yet trepid of the rising political opposition against him, demonstrates executive restraint when Texas secures its independence from Mexico in 1836. Still, the controversy intensifies earnestly. Benjamin Lundy's *The War in Texas,* "a primary source for the Whig and abolitionist opposition to the annexation,"[234] expressing the Montesquieuian republican fears, remains the cornerstone of John Quincy Adams's successful congressional opposition to the annexation that responded to "Northern anxieties that acquiring Texas would give the South disproportionate political strength in the federal government."[235] Assuming the presidency in 1841, John Tyler displays growing interest in Texas, certain that the expansion of markets and territories would offer recovery from the economic downturn of the late 1830s. Early in 1844, the treaty of annexation "that Secretary of State John Calhoun had completed secretly with Texan officials"[236] is submitted to the Senate then shortly published by the *New York Evening Post.* In June Congress rejects the treaty—the paramount victory of the opposition led by John Quincy Adams. The immediate election mandate of James Polk, however, is the annexation of Texas, in alignment with the "Jacksonian ideologues [who] saturated the culture with the transcendent tenets of manifest destiny between 1844 and 1846 as a way of tranquilizing the apprehension . . . that annexing Texas would undermine the vulnerable foundation of the republic."[237] When Mexican armed forces cross the Rio Grande in May 1846, "manifest destiny" becomes imperative.

The severity of abstraction of "manifest destiny" poses the nation as a form of transcendent, not merely political, administration. In short, the nation is in no way necessarily a corpus. The fully abstracted measures (far beyond congressional votes, declarations of war, presidential mandates, or treaties) necessary for the monumental national redefinition receive subtle codification, then, in the neologism "manifest destiny," in which, as the principle of government, the nation *embodies* aspirations to acquisition and subordination—not understood foremost within the material relations harboring the family, the state, and the construction of the quotidian world intermediate to the two, but confirming foremost the vision of remote conquest as the geographic ubiquity uniting in purpose "an uncontrollable landmass without community or organic ties."[238] The nation is known, most correctly, in the reformulation as an impulse, managed bureaucratically—management in which civil society might be always already in the offing. Championing a novel point of national imagination that, in effect, redoubles the antithesis between corporeality and civic abstraction, the neologism functions to precipitate finally an astonishing geopolitical transformation:

> It is startling to learn from D. W. Meining's great historical geography that in 1824 the United States of Mexico, as the former Spanish colony then named itself, and the United States of America were not dissimilar in size and population: The southern nation spanning 1.7 million square miles with a bit more than 6 million people, the northern comprising 1.8 million square miles and 9.6 million people. By 1853, more than half of Mexico, a million square miles, more than the Louisiana Purchase, had been transferred to the United States. The discrepancy in population had increased exponentially, 23 million Americans compared to 7.5 or 8 million Mexicans. Geopolitical realities had, to understate the case, undergone a fundamental change.[239]

"Manifest Destiny," in a phrase, makes an entirely new nation of the United States.

Nevertheless, the fomenting political quagmire—despite the exponential population and territorial transformations—remains, increasingly, in the northern states. The disgruntling effect is that the extrapolation of the national consolidation results in the direct contraction, not the expansion, of civilian license, the immediate autonomies of quotidian exchange. "Annexation," Freehling writes, "probably ensured a physical war with Mexico and a resulting verbal confrontation over slavery,"[240] given that the Wilmot Proviso, attached to the $2 million presidential appropriation requested in 1846 "to conduct negotiations with Mexico," stipulates "slavery be banned in any territory negotiated from Mexico."[241] In other words, the new ubiquitous nation, even if transcendentally determined, immediately raises the question of the ubiquity of policy—moreover, with the sectional responses to this issue leading to the monumental crisis of the Compromise of 1850, the recalculation of the Fugitive Slave Law of 1793.

The political junction is monumental, because the five principle issues to be resolved in the legislation contend over the systemic, rather than the merely prophetic, shape of the nation, including additional territorial expansion, internal geopolitical templates, international boundaries, the municipal character of the federal capital and, ultimately, the arrangements of comity determining the extent of the rights of property permitted over African American persons. More particularly stated, these points of contention are the admission of California to the union (and the future status of Oregon), the territorial organization of Utah and New Mexico as federal jurisdictions, the still open question of the boundary between Texas and Mexico, the status of slavery in Washington D.C. and, ultimately, the zeal with which Southern proprietors might press, in the non-slaveholding states, their claims of property in African American persons. Senator Henry Clay, "in enumerating these questions counted them off upon his fingers and called them the five bleeding wounds of the republic."[242] Even as the prophetic rendition of the nationality does not comprehend corporeality, the systemic rendition does so abundantly, the very thought of the systemic reach of the nation educing corporeality.

The legislative wrangling on these five points, counted out by Senator Clay on his fingers, lasts most of 1850, from January to September, the impasse exacerbating the sectional discord being that "California had formed a free state constitution and was applying for admission to the Union. The North felt that she was entitled to immediate admission. The South proposed to withhold admission in order to prevent the prohibition of slavery in the territories of Utah and New Mexico."[243] Three legislative proposals open the congressional conflict: Mississippi Senator Henry Foote introduces an unconsidered resolution and bill for the organization of the territory appropriated from Mexico; Virginia Senator James Mason introduces a revised fugitive slave law; and Senator Thomas Benton of Missouri introduces a bill to finalize the state jurisdiction of Texas. At the end of January, Senator Clay offers a set of resolutions intending to draw together the separate matters as a single legislative package that proposes, specifically, the admission of California, the organization of Utah and New Mexico without the prohibition of slavery since these territories are non-slaveholding under Mexican law, the compensated reduction of the size of Texas restoring territory ceded from New Mexico east of the Rio Grande River, the drafting of a stringent fugitive slave policy, and the proscription of the slave trade—but not slavery—in the District of Columbia. Wisconsin Senator James Doty, toward the conclusion of February, in the middle of six weeks of debate on the legislative package, introduces a resolution effectively calling the question on the admission of California; it is defeated, however, by a filibuster. The response to this burgeoning impasse is the formation of the Committee of Thirteen, chaired by Senator Clay, which by the beginning of May submits a report, in effect foregoing the force of Mexican anti-slavery law in the southwest, and proposes three bills, which "President [Zachary] Taylor called the omnibus."[244] The legislative proposal restates two bills introduced in early April by Senator Stephen Douglas, who chairs the Senate Committee on Territories, with an additional bill prohibiting the slave trade—but not slavery—in the federal capital. The first bill admits California to the union, organizes the territories of Utah and New Mexico along the lines of what becomes known as "popular sovereignty" on the question of slavery; the second refines Senator James Mason's fugitive slave law; the third addresses the status of slavery in the federal capital.

By the middle of May debate begins, and within two months the omnibus proposal disintegrates over the issue of the Texas boundary. The bills are separated. The organization of the Utah territory is passed first at the beginning of August, given that the organization of New Mexico is entangled with the controversy over the borders of Texas. By mid-August, the bill admitting California to the union is passed, as well as a separate bill organizing New Mexico as a federal territory (and compensating Texas $10 million for the land east of the Rio Grande River). Senator James Mason's fugitive slave provisions, revised further, pass eight days later. The ban on the slave trade in the District of Columbia passes in mid-September, with unanimous Southern opposition in the Senate. The uniform reach of the federal administration is tested, as fully as established, by these governmental maneuvers coordinating (and re-coordinating) the meeting of geographic abstraction and the national, visionary abstraction. The paradox, to repeat the point, is that the political coordination and territorial expansion structures the quotidian more closely. If the consequence of the legislative confrontations is the prophetic expansion of the national geographic space, equally it seems the emphatic constriction of "social space" in the name of civil and political composure, especially in the North given the intensified might of the provisions for capturing and returning fugitive slaves to the south. The new terrain of the nation—encompassing California, the New Mexico territory, Texas, the Utah territory, as well as the re-imagined District of Columbia—demands the buttressing in the Northern states of the mass conviction that African-derived persons remain antithetical, inexorably, to the national terrain. The acquisition and political certification of the new landmasses for the federation turn on the disposition of African-derived persons in the new jurisdictions, just as the new bearing of the Northern states in the conglomeration stipulates the reconsidered disposition of African-derived persons in the North. The legal quagmire at the center of the revised fugitive slave provisions forebodes the circumstances of a broader, civilian quagmire in the Northern states. The "conflict still remained concerning the extent to which the federal rules should reflect the Northern states' belief that any Black brought before a court in the North should enjoy the presumption that she was free until proven otherwise, and the Southern belief that proceedings in the North were little more than summary extradition hearings, where the presumption was reversed, and that any alleged slave could get a full and fair hearing once they were returned to the state of their alleged master."[245]

In this way, the sectional incongruity produces, rather than the equanimity of comity, the crises of individual consciousness and action more and more confounding the judiciary of the Northern states, the legislative self-rule of the

Northern states, as well as ultimately the sociality of the Northern states. The judicial development, as stated by legal scholar Anthony Sebok, is that "[u]ntil 1850, federal judges (if they ever heard a runaway case) applied the procedure of the state in which they sat. . . . Under the pre-1850 scheme, as conceptions of due process changed in a Northern state, the federal procedure, which relied on state procedure, thus changed accordingly [specifically in relation to the 'Personal Liberty' laws]."[246] That is, the recalibrated, expansive form of the federal compact, following 1850, bestows "slave catchers with guaranteed access to Southern slave law in every fugitive slave case: Upon seizing a black in the North, they then would need only to invoke a shred of federal procedure in order legitimately to introduce Southern law."[247] Sebok's analysis reconsiders the analyses of Robert Cover in *Justice Accused: Antislavery and the Judicial Process*, in which Cover codifies the judicial problem as "the moral-formal dilemma," the circumstance as a result of which "[t]he legal actor did not choose between liberty and slavery. He had to choose between liberty and consistent limits on the judicial function; between liberty and fidelity to public trust; between liberty and adherence to the public corporate undertakings of nationhood; or, as some of the judges would have it, between liberty and the viability of the social compact."[248] In brief, the reiterated principle of nationality, the Compromise of 1850, ironically highlights the corporeal basis of the burgeoning federal abstraction and its obligations, the disposition of African Americans. Insofar as the reemphasized standard of civic presence demands the active, critical appreciation of human chattel, the reemphasized corporeal determination of the federal abstraction and its obligations confounds general interactions.

By 1854, the social effect of the demand is clarified repeatedly. Dramatic tests of the new federal policy concerning the apprehension of fugitive slaves occur in February and April of 1851—the Shadrach and Sims cases in Boston. In the first instance Shadrach is rescued, the political controversy having, on the one side, the position of "the Garrisonian abolitionists [who] redoubled the vigor of their attacks on constitutional obligation" and, on the other, the position of "Benjamin Robbins Curtis, soon to sit on the Supreme Court, [who] defended the [revised policy] and upbraided those who would prefer the liberty of a mere black to the unity and security of a white man's country."[249] In the second instance, Sims, "[b]y dint of military might,"[250] is returned to the South, causing a furor. In this way, in late May 1854, when Anthony Burns is apprehended and imprisoned under the terms of the revised Fugitive Slave law, the resulting mayhem is far-reaching.

During a speech by Wendell Phillips in Faneuil Hall two days after the arrest of Anthony Burns, one member of the audience announces "that a group of Negroes was attacking the Court House"[251] where, imprisoned, Burns awaits extradition.

The immediate rush to the Court House draws Thomas Wentworth Higginson, who several years later would lead the "First South Carolina Volunteers,—the first slave regiment mustered into the service of the United States during the late civil war,"[252] to the front of the group of men charging the courthouse with a battering ram. Inside the building, fifty or so deputies are taken by surprise but manage to repulse Higginson and one other protester, who briefly make their way into the building. As the deputies expel the two, a gunshot is fired from the protesters, killing one of the deputies. Nonetheless, the fate of Anthony Burns remains unchanged for, "on June 2, while church bells tolled, Burns, guarded by a thousand-man escort, was marched to Long Wharf through Boston streets, where some fifty thousand spectators, draped in mourning emblems, booed, hissed, cursed, and cried, 'Kidnappers, Kidnappers.'"[253] To repeat an important point, these acute and escalating tensions describe a collective condition, a quotidian state of affairs, in which hostility functions essentially as if it were oxygen, discounting the ideal of "civil society," the sociopolitical boon of the modern advance.

In "From Civil Society to the Social" political scientist Mark Neocleous draws the distinction between Hegelian and Marxist examinations of civil society, so as to specify the social, following Karl Marx, "not as a descriptive category, but as a fundamentally critical one, pointing as it does to the alienated nature of human relations within bourgeois society." That is, "[r]ather than replace idealism with materialism in a Feuerbachian manner [Marx] criticizes both idealism and materialism by developing the concept of 'human sensuous activity, practice', 'human society or socialized humanity,' a materialist idea of social humanity which he makes a point of distinguishing from the 'old materialist' standpoint of civil society."[254] In other words still, the social is not an abstraction of collectivity—national or otherwise—as is civil society, the paradigm of the seemingly boundless reasonableness of "the self-seeking economic actor."[255] The social, rather, is the affective and sensuous immediacy of collectivity that critiques the civil society.

In this regard, the case of Anthony Burns dramatizes the escalating social cost of the sectional division, as well as its renewed federal compromise. For the hostile, apprehensive proximity between the military escort necessary to remove Burns from Boston and the fifty thousand spectators witnessing the removal illustrates, hyperbolically, the devastation of the sensuous terms of private and public existence functioning finally in deference to the agency of the national state, the point of oversight of civil society. Accordingly, it is important to recognize that civil society is not opposed to the social but compounded by it in ways that fully overburden the social, as the aftermath of the attempted rescue bears out: "The 'revolution of public opinion' in Massachusetts was indicated by State Street support of the petition for the immediate repeal of the Fugitive Slave Law which was signed by three thousand Bostonians, including members of the mercantile community,"[256] and as the "fate of the 'Court House rioters' also indicates the state of Massachusetts antislavery sentiment."[257]

The efforts to convict the rioters and particularly those who fired revolvers, although pursued ardently by U.S. District Attorney B. F. Hallett, do not come to fruition. In fact, Asa O. Butman, assistant to the district attorney, warns one of the suspected murderers to escape. Still, Justice Benjamin Robbins Curtis convenes a grand jury at the beginning of June that by mid-July dismisses the murder indictment, returning instead against eight defendants indictments for riot. When the U.S. district attorney summons another grand jury in September, sending his assistant to Worcester to gather evidence, Butman must "depend on [Thomas Wentworth] Higginson to save him from a threatening mob."[258] Nonetheless, B. F. Hallett in October secures a five-count indictment against six of the rioters (including Higginson) as well as Theodore Parker and Wendell Phillips, speakers at Faneuil Hall, all of them charged with the obstruction of a federal marshal. Beginning in April of the next year, the trial, based on the earlier statute rather than the 1850 law, ends without indictment, given that the earlier provision does not speak to the specifics of the case; moreover, all the subsequent efforts by the U.S. district attorney to pursue the case further fail, the larger upshot remaining that Anthony Burns is "the last fugitive slave returned from Boston."[259]

All of this is to say that the agency of the state becomes, in a variety of ways, terrific: "It cost an estimated $100,000 for a brigade of Massachusetts militia, a phalanx of policemen, a United States infantry company, and a detachment of artillery to return a solitary slave to Virginia."[260] In this way, the violence enmeshed with the civic management and operations of the state more and more accredits the abolitionist conviction that, as put by literary critic John Stauffer, the "essence of sin and slavery was a denial of self-sovereignty, a negation of will and the idea of freedom,"[261] thus forming "a world of American desperation best understood by slaves."[262]

Particularly after 1850, the idioms of common exchange, the sensuous terms of human proximities and consideration, uncannily reflect the violent disorder that Frederick Douglass describes at the conclusion of the opening chapter of his narrative. The social imperative calculated to support the renewed civic abstraction and to define civic propriety is the pervasive, uniform aggression given an ideally specified, unabated reign. The effect remains, for those not holding fully this immediate predisposition, the "denial of self-sovereignty, a negation of will and the idea of freedom." As the case of Anthony Burns and the "Personal Liberty Laws" demonstrate in the Northern states, this legislated aggression is not as easily quarantined as it is strictly or expeditiously imagined.

The resulting turmoil is not restricted only to the Northern states; virtually coincident with the Anthony Burns case, the passage of the Kansas-Nebraska Act in early 1854—attempting to articulate further the national geography—illustrates the insidious reach of the unrest. The act aims to diffuse the sectional animosities by revisiting one of the central provisions of the Compromise of 1850, the principle of "popular sovereignty" that "referred the determination of the status of slavery in the territories during the territorial period to the local courts."[263]

Translated into the terms of the Kansas-Nebraska Act four years later, "popular sovereignty" designates that a numerical majority of either proslavery or antislavery settlers, rather than congressional decree, would determine the statutory fate of the region and its subsequent statehood. The immediate outcome is the rising civic disorder that entwines the extension of U.S. civil society with the violent disintegration of the social landscape: "After several years of peopling the territory, Yankee settlers would have likely been numerically overwhelming. Neighboring [slaveholding] Missourians' best shot at capturing Kansas was to cross the border first, secure slavery in an early territorial decision, and then to cling to the fait accompli until the statehood vote."[264] By 1856, the violence in the territory between these two camps becomes legendary. Stauffer portrays the historical moment in some detail:

> Kansas had erupted into full-scale guerilla warfare before the Pottawatomie massacre, and there were numerous reports of murder, rape, and plunder. On Wednesday, May 21, 1856, three days before Brown's Pottawatomie raid, proslavery settlers burned and pillaged the nearby town of Lawrence, Kansas. The very next day, Preston Brooks bludgeoned Charles Sumner in the nation's capital. Abolitionists and free-soilers of the North felt they were living under a "regime of terror": "Violence reigns in the streets of Washington," wrote William Cullen Bryant, editor of the *New York Evening Post*, following the attack on Sumner. "Violence has now found its way into the Senate chamber. Violence overhangs the frontiers of [Kansas] Territory like a storm cloud charged with hail and lightning. . . . In short, violence is the order of the day." Bryant warned that "this plot" of the Slave Power "will succeed if the people of the free States are as apathetic as the slaveholders are insolent."[265]

Simply put, the historical, political advance, understood as the generation of civil society, devastates the social world that it would manage. The application of law in the interest of the federal uniformity is indistinguishable from acrimony.

The geographic transformation that corresponds to the federal transformation is that the Kansas territory, once stretching upward across the Midwest to the U.S. border with Canada, is severed so that most of the vast tract of land becomes the Nebraska territory. The Kansas-Nebraska Act, introduced in Congress in

January 1854 by the Illinois Senator and presidential aspirant Stephen Douglas, makes this concession so as to divide (possible) states between the North and South, reiterating the basic terms of the Missouri Compromise. In short, "two territories were created instead of one, one west of a slave state and the other west of a free state."[266] The measure fails the year before in 1853 and, with political turmoil virtually foreshadowing the hostile social terms of the Kansas territory in 1856, the dominant political parties find themselves in strained realignment as the bill passes at the end of January: "The rising tide of indignation in the North was frightening to many Democrats who would have to face angry voters, indignant at contrivers or supporters of this measure. Furthermore, the nature of the Democratic majority in the House provided the problem. On paper it was so huge, 159 to 75, that there might seem to have been no conceivable trouble. But the difficult hurdle was that 92 of the 159 Democrats, by far the greater part, came from northern constituencies."[267] The impending congressional elections exacerbate the confusion, and Northern Democrats "felt they would have a chance in the coming election if they were fighting a positive battle to extend democracy, whereas if they were forced on the defensive by charges of destroying the Missouri Compromise they were in grave danger."[268] The party divisions among the nonslaveholding states are various: "Of the thirteen delegations which the northern Democrats 'controlled,' only Pennsylvania, Illinois, and California showed any real loyalty. New England, New York, and New Jersey failed utterly. Even Michigan and Indiana, bailiwicks of Cass and Bright, fell away. Ohio and Wisconsin would have little of the measure."[269]

Coincident, then, with the violent confusion of the Anthony Burns case, the broad disorder of federal authority, legislative processes, and social immediacy in the passage of the Kansas Nebraska Act exposes the beleaguered imperative of the social. Beleaguered because increasingly distressed by the expanding imposition of the abstract national scheme of civil society, as in the Anthony Burns case, the confusion abrogates the controversial obligation grounding the federal abstraction, the critical appreciation of human chattel as the foremost determination of racial blackness, violently secured. The extremity of the measure, however, produces political and social paradoxes that undermine the idioms of immediate exchange and undermine in particular the distinctions of corporealization mediating the aggression demanded by the federal compact. The extremity of the measure, its compromising of the social, enacts variously the condition of seeming, pervasive lawlessness, both black and white bodies falling to the violence that, by law, is stipulated as the primary political feature of racial blackness.

Although in 1857 the decision of the U.S. Supreme Court in the *Dred Scott v. Sandford* case attempts to clarify the rule of law paradoxically obscured in the national turmoil, the decision exacerbates the turmoil, proving to be the most controversial rendered by the U.S. Supreme Court. The ruling, given by Chief Justice Roger B. Taney on March 6 and 7, intends to resolve the escalating abolitionist and proslavery tensions taking on not simply discursive formations but, increasingly, militarized formations in the United States and the organizing territories. It aims to excise African American populations definitively from the civil imagination of national coherence. The conviction of the chief justice that most famously codifies the ruling declaims African Americans "were not intended to be included under the word 'citizens' in the Constitution, and can therefore claim none of the rights and privileges which that instrument provides for and secures to citizens of the United States."[270] The ruling poses racial blackness as a "nationalizing" political effect, ultimately irrespective of the meager distinctions in social status between enslaved and free African American populations, or the differing political status of the states and the territories. The national configuration, in other words, disposes African American populations to be juridical nonentities, even if fully conceivable in terms of social presence—a form of exclusion from the terms of civic nationality that suggests the heights of the abstraction of that civic nationality.

Extremity of abstraction, however, is not necessarily commensurate with the logical, as the deeply questionable reasoning of the pronouncement details. In the decision, the court is faced with resolving a palimpsest of national inconsistencies, since "[f]ugitive-slave cases required judges to assign responsibilities and rights in the working of American federalism in ways that the framers had chosen to evade; they had political repercussions that courts were ill-equipped to cope with; and they juxtaposed conflicting demands of legality and morality."[271] *Dred Scott v. Sandford* exhibits all of these quandaries, as a brief rehearsal of the twenty-seven years of intrigue culminating in the ruling bears out: Dred Scott arrives in Missouri in 1830, as chattel personnel of Peter Blow, who sells Scott to Dr. John Emerson. In the eleven-year period between his arrival in Missouri in 1832 and his death in 1843, Emerson travels with Scott to territories designated as non-slaveholding by the 1820 Missouri Compromise, particularly Illinois and Minnesota. Upon Emerson's death in 1843, Scott is transferred to Emerson's sister, Eliza Irene Sandford, whose husband, John Sandford, is immortalized in the court ruling. In 1846, Scott's suit for freedom, based on his sojourn in the territories, begins moving through the Missouri judiciary system, reaching the Supreme Court ten years later, for he "won a brief victory in the Circuit Court of St. Louis, only to be reversed by the Missouri Supreme Court, which refused to be bound by the law of other states or federal laws applicable only to territories."[272] The Blow family amply supports Scott as the case proceeds through its several phases, powerful evidence of the life-long friendship that Scott maintains with his initial slaveholders, especially with Taylor Blow, the son of Peter Blow, Scott's contemporary and friend from childhood. In May 1857, two months after the ruling denying Dred Scott's plea for emancipation, Sandford dies in an insane asylum.

In response to this intrigue entwining the reach of federal and state powers with familial rivalries, national geography, personal attachments, psychological turmoil, positive law, and property rights, "Chief Justice Taney... crafted a long, fifty-six-page opinion that began by denying blacks the right to sue in federal court. He asserted that at the time of the adoption of the Constitution blacks were not citizens of the United States, and he argued that since 1787 blacks had not acquired any additional rights to the Constitution's privileges."[273] Altogether—although logically inconsistent given this dictum—there are five primary judgments to the ruling, to follow the analysis of Don E. Fehrenbacher, author of the most comprehensive scholarly study of the case, *The Dred Scott Case: Its Significance in American Law and Politics*: the ruling of the lower federal circuit court is subject to review by the Supreme Court; African Americans are not national citizens and, thus, have no right to bring suit in federal courts, the reasoning being that the lower federal circuit court should not have aspired to jurisdiction over the case; Scott did not become free as a result of his sojourn in Fort Snelling, Minnesota; Scott did not become free by his sojourn in Illinois, because his status is determined by the state to which he returns; finally, the plea in abatement, for these reasons, must be returned to the circuit court to be dismissed for want of jurisdiction.

The glaring inconsistency of the ruling is that "[i]f the court decided that the plea in abatement was not properly before it, then the question of whether Negroes could be citizens for federal purposes could not have arisen."[274] Needless to say, this logical inconsistency is profound, presenting an overwhelming quandary for the history of the Supreme Court and legal scholarship. Fehrenbacher elaborates: "The most obvious flaw in the whole argument is that it proves self-destructive and leads ultimately to an absurdity. If, because of their stand on the Negro citizenship or jurisdiction question, three of the six justices invalidating the Missouri Compromise restriction actually had no right to consider the other major substantive issue—that is, the effect of Missouri law upon Scott's status after his return from Illinois,"[275] paradoxically, the Supreme Court makes juridical pronouncements despite its own declaration that federal courts have no jurisdictional power relevant to the case: The contours of logic—nonetheless the exercise of national sovereignty—become virtually illegible. The failure is compound, the failure of reason and the failure of comity.

Still, notwithstanding these failures, the instruction of the court on this matter resolutely announces racial blackness as the idealized corporeal limit of the idioms of common exchange, the "human sensuous activity" recognized and superintended by the uniform national conventions of civil society. The instruction, in other words, poses racial blackness as the idealized national form for the disintegration of the social. In short, in 1857 the condition of seeming, pervasive lawlessness requires the re-articulation of the fundament of law to grant the contrary appearance of a peaceable conception of civil society.

In other words, the violence made available by the force of the national configuration to conceive of and apprehend the fugitive slave, the essential corporeal figure of racial blackness in the sectional dispute, states the ideal focus of the aggression free to civil combination. The urgent confusion remains that the intensifying national violence abrogates this simplicity, the broadening acrimony and injury accruing too randomly across the corporeal distinctions that are reemphasized by "[Roger] Taney's deliberate choice to elaborate the nature of citizenship along a black-white axis."[276] The ruling reiterates, to state again the insight of Spillers, the distinction between the "flesh" and the "body," "the central one between captive and liberated subject-positions."[277] The re-clarified point of law—always ironically approaching lawlessness—envisions "high crimes against the flesh, as the person of African females and males registering the wounding.[278] As the Anthony Burns case and "bleeding" Kansas demonstrate, however, the historical, legal, and national distinction overestimates the strict divisibility of the "flesh" and the "body," never disassociated fully by the arbitrary fiat of citizenship or racialization.

The untenable exposure, rather than the easy clarity of citizenship or race, is the closely defined, violent aggression yielding, both diachronically and synchronically, the integrity of the nation. There are several immediate paradoxes. The historical paradox is the confounding of the Hegelian scheme, the obscurity of modernity as the watershed of resolute, progressive order; the national paradox is the pervasive configuration of force that can never be entirely sufficiently managed; the legal paradox is the enforcement of the recognition of the extreme limits (racial) and motives (economic) of civil combination and the violence it stipulates. Racial blackness, at the center of this economic, imaginative, and social compress, bears and refracts these paradoxes, revealing the politics of modern subjectivity to be foremost defined and swayed in relation, not to positive inalienable rights, but to the aggressive deprivation of ineffable rights—the adamant and questionable select agenda of civil society.

CHAPTER 4

The Intimate Civic

The Disturbance of the Quotidian

The political unrest of the antebellum United States—the advance toward the mass aggression and violence of war—encompasses, in turn: the federal abstraction, geographic expansion, bureaucratic complementarity, and public sociality. Public sociality, the final and most circumscribing modality of the unrest, elicits the corporeal most directly. The most immediate features of corporeality become the indices for either the application of aggression and violence within the ideal of U.S. civil society or, appositely, the (in)controvertible suspension of the severe traumas sustaining U.S. civil society. The terms of the civil combination register the corporeal foremost in relation to degrees of peril, the situation drawn in detail, for example, by ex-slave narrators, whose lives span the divergent societies of the antebellum sectional divide. The slave narratives record closely the cultural circumstances in the United States determining that the African American body remains a vexed artifact, the crucial sign underwriting the social realities of both free and enslaved African American populations, the sign of the obdurate fleshliness that overdetermines all other possible aspects of identity. Thus, a central textual dilemma for the narrators becomes that, in providing the account of slavery and "themselves," the paramount task of the ex-slave narrators is to reproduce the experiences and trials of a "body"—their own.

The difficulty is that, in order to authenticate themselves as African Americans, these narrators must highlight the hegemonic terms by which African American identity is construed, the body and the life of the body; however, because the claims they are making on the government and culture of the United States are based on denunciations of an enforced and spurious confinement to a life merely of the body, an existence as obdurate materiality, these narrators must not only recover their bodies within their narratives but, more important, also remove their bodies from these narratives. There seem four principle ways in which ex-slave narrators undertake this task, four principle patterns by which bodies are represented in slave narratives: the body as intensive and extensive object, the body in its relation to self-authorization, the body as a form of knowledge, and finally, figurations of the master's body.

Of these four categories, the first, the body as intensive and extensive object, most fully reflects the legislation and enforcement of a mind/body split as the discrepancy between racial blackness and racial whiteness. In this mode of representation in slave narratives, the body is an entity imposed upon, and in its tortured or injured state, tellingly juxtaposed to the voice and language. The African American body is voided of language, while the adversarial, torturing or injuring slaveholder or overseer is most fully vocal. The African American body (and individual) is defined by spectacular physical pain, a circumstance that, as a matter of course, "bring[s] about an immediate reversion to a state anterior to language, to the sounds and cries a human being makes before language is learned."[1] African Americans, at these moments in the narratives, appear most fully confined within the limits of their bodies, bodies transformed into entirely self-referential, unbearably discrete and intense artifacts, violently denied the possibility of extending into the world the consciousnesses, voices, the language, co-implicated with discrete corporeality. Cultural critic Elaine Scarry explains that physical pain "does not simply resist language but actively destroys it,"[2] with the result that pain has vast political consequences insofar as "the relative ease or difficulty with which any given phenomenon can be *verbally represented* also influences the ease or difficulty with which that phenomenon can be *politically represented*."[3] In the coordinated application of pain—whether torture or war—the highly contestable abstractions of a cultural or political regime is substantiated or verified by the "incontestable reality" of selected physical bodies, the certainty of the pain experienced by the victim or combatant seeming to confer its quality of "incontestable reality" on that power bringing the pain into being. Nevertheless, Scarry notes, it is precisely because "the reality of that power is so highly contestable, the regime so unstable,"[4] that it is necessary to inflict the pain in the first place. Narrative representations of the tortured or the injured African American body, the sensuous excess of civil society, are virtually ubiquitous in the texts of ex-slave narrators.

The second category, the body in its relation to self-authorization, draws the narrators' achieved will or self-authority through the depiction of her or his own body. The ex-slave narrator draws the movement of a scene that either diminishes or enhances her or his social being by emphasizing or repudiating the depiction of her or his body. In *Narrative of the Life of Frederick Douglass,* Frederick Douglass, in a highly dramatic rhetorical reversal, narrates his escape by withholding all information about the episode; his body is at issue only insofar as it remains the primarily absent focus of concern, the absence comprehended by the self-authorizing presumptions of modern subjectivity. As his body is obscured increasingly in or removed from the narrative, Douglass's self-authorization is rendered more and more manifest. In *Incidents in the Life of a Slave Girl,* Linda Brent offers her most graphically recounted bodily distress when narrating her seven-year tenure in the garret of her grandmother's house; nonetheless, she includes in the episode triumphant maneuvers of self-authorization, her most effective manipulation of her adversaries. From her garret, she writes letters to her master that are carried north then mailed back to North Carolina to convince him she is no longer in the vicinity. She watches her duped master from her garret, with great satisfaction, these self-assertive actions directly juxtaposed to her emphasized corporeality.

The third pattern, the body as a form of knowledge, illustrates the African American body, above all, as significant, and the drama and dynamics of determining this significance holds the foreground of a pivotal scene or the narrative as a whole: How does one, or an institutional authority, go about reading, and what can be read as the significance of, an African American body (or an African American life)? Simply put, more than brutalized, the African American body is meaningful in this mode of representation, so as to be outlined primarily through the attempts, whether positive or negative, to make sense of the African American body, rather than apparently to remove this body from sense (as in scenes of brutalization). As already illustrated, William Grimes's 1855 *Life of William Grimes, the Runaway Slave* draws its final image precisely in this way. Lucy Delaney structures her postbellum narrative *From the Darkness Cometh the Light* (c. 1891) entirely in this way, its climax being the courtroom scene in which her status as a free or enslaved person is rendered authoritatively. The legal issue involves establishing the biological relationship between Delaney and her mother (who was legally free but wrongfully enslaved at the time of Delaney's birth), so that insofar as African American bodies remain paramount to the narrative, they remain so as the bearers of meaning and, in particular, legally ascertainable meaning.

As might be expected, the delineation of the master's body remains the least prevalent of the corporeal representations in the slave narratives. In this instance, the attention drawn to racially white bodies overshadows the narrative appearance of African American bodies. The delineation of the white body, generally the master's body, becomes the fulcrum of a dramatic crisis or of the narrative as a whole. Either the episodic burden or the narrative burden of corporeality rests, with alarming effect, on the quintessential modern and national figure whose universal subject-position reportedly "lies elsewhere in a discrete core, abstracted from society."[5] Mary Prince's brief *The History of Mary Prince, a West Indian Slave* presents her pivotal point of rebellion along these lines. The crisis that precipitates her leaving her master's house in open defiance of her legal condition arises from her master's demands that she bathe him, the act of persecution that she reports as more irksome than the many physical assaults she endures. Besides the sexual persecution implicit in the episode, the act of viewing and washing the master's body rehearses with patent effect the extremes of subjugation and degradation definitive of New World slavery. William Craft's *Running a Thousand Miles for Freedom* provides the most extended version of this mode of representation. The master's body is crucial to the narrative, but also entirely counterfeited, since William and Ellen Craft escape from Georgia to Pennsylvania by train once Ellen disguises herself as an ailing Southern gentleman, and William shadows her/him as the faithful body servant. Ironically highlighting the white body, the masquerade of the husband and wife destabilizes, recasts, and subverts the semiotics of mindfulness and mindlessness that would draw the modern and national contradistinction between the two conditions, racial blackness and racial whiteness. Unlike most slave narratives, the master's body provides the primary agency of the abolitionist advocacy.

These several modes of representation, of course, are not arbitrary. They remark the rancorous public sociality in which, to borrow the observation of the historian Leon Litwack, the "inherent cruelty and violence of southern slavery requires no further demonstration, but this does not prove northern humanity."[6] The strategies remark, then, African American ingenuity in response to the readily hostile, if not violent, codes of civil society assigned to organize the informalities of corporeality. That is, from the position or vantage of civil society, the detection of corporeal blackness signals the apparently absolute limit of public sociality and public space, the absolute limit shaping, not simply the routine individualizing effect of civic consciousness, but moreover the ruling political fiat. On this point, historian Patrick Rael observes, "[n]othing intrinsic to their natures united the millions of Africans who had been brutally torn from their cultures and their descendants into a solidified political whole, [even as] somehow Americans both black and white came to understand reality and predicate policy on just this basis."[7] The basis, as the slave narratives document, stipulates that the strictures and forces of public sociality, determining the normative effects of racialization, regulate a failure of identification, which is signaled corporeally and is, thus, urgent in the most immediate of proximities. The slave narratives engage and record this basis of civic reality and political policy, aiming to recast the U. S. programmatic identifications by portraying relentlessly the violent social costs they entail.

James C. Pennington's 1849 *The Fugitive Blacksmith,* for example, offers narrative and rhetorical points of emphasis that confound the uncomplicated expectations defining the conceptualizations of racial blackness and whiteness. Pennington's reflections on the decisive moments in his personal quest for freedom reverse routinely assumed premises of U.S. antebellum racialization. One peculiar moment of direct address to his readers is precipitated by Pennington's witnessing, as a young man, the beating of his father: "Being a tradesman, and just at that time getting my breakfast, I was near enough to hear the insolent words that were spoken to my father, and to hear, see, and even count the savage stripes inflicted upon him."[8] Witnessing this event causes Pennington to repudiate his condition as a slave and to resolve to escape. "Although it was some time after this event before I took the decisive step, yet in my mind and spirit, I never was a *Slave* after it."[9] At this heightened moment of his narrative, Pennington makes an unexpected and unusual racial appeal. The incident is recorded in a way that calls attention to more than the pronounced physical violence he witnesses and its disturbing emotional effect on him and the rest of his family. Pennington justifies his determination to no longer be a slave with a rhetorical question: "Let me ask anyone of Anglo-Saxon blood and spirit, how you would expect a son to feel at such a sleight?"[10]

The appeal is not to the feelings, judgments, or experiences of African Americans, as one might anticipate, but to the sensibilities and self-assurance of those most emphatically understood as white in the imagination of the United States. Rather than ask his readers to comprehend experiences and matters entirely foreign to them, James Pennington asks that they consider what is most familiar to their own attitudes and self-understanding. He asks that, in order to understand his experiences, they draw on their own. He offers them no alien authenticity but rather a proclamation of shared sensibilities, a shared sense of an appropriate response to witnessing the injury and humiliation of a would-be patriarch. Moreover, Pennington not only poses the question but also implies that he understands "Anglo-Saxon blood and spirit" and that he does so with no taxing or unusual effort. Even more, he insinuates that his rejection of slavery and his eventual escape from the United States slave regime is a justified, if not obvious, response to his trauma. He presents his readers with a critical reading of his situation forestalling the imagination of stark, impenetrable divisions between the consciousness as well as the social relations of racial blackness and racial whiteness. The injured African American body triggers this critical understanding.

The crisis—rather than polarized racial positions—clarifies familial, masculinist, and social imperatives that designate a common discourse and common experiences insinuated in the episode. Much is common across the gulf of race,

Pennington assumes, and the apparent effortlessness of the assumption must complicate the reader's notions of the experiences documented in the slave narratives as well as the experience of reading the texts themselves. A large portion of what Pennington shares with his readers, in other words, are comprehensions they already possess. In documenting United States slavery, he offers a vision of an exorbitant "chattel principle"[11] exceeding individual suffering or terror and disturbing widely esteemed institutions, such as the family and the sentiments the family fosters.

It is also worthwhile to recognize that Pennington's conception of the shared cultural sensibilities across the U.S. racial apartheid underscores the apprehensions and insights of the black feminist critique so influential in reforming the literary critical reception of slave narratives. Key to Pennington's trauma is the diminished entitlements of a "son" realized through the demonstration of the belittled circumstances of a "father." Pennington's recollection centers the drama of enslavement, repudiation, and escape in the postures assumed by men and the cultural commerce among men. However, for those not as fully invested in such prerogatives promoted across racial lines, such as African American women, this rendition of the travails and triumphs of enslavement is glaringly inadequate. The central figure of the slave presented by Pennington conforms, in this way, to Frances Foster's estimation of the typical figure to appear in slave narratives:

> The Heroic Slave narrates a success story. He has endured the most inhumane environment imaginable and, without stooping to revenge, has escaped with his life and his integrity. He is Everyslave, innocent, ignorant, and abused but a human being who needs only free soil in which to blossom into an industrious, literate, and totally moral citizen. . . . His is decidedly a temporal and essentially parochial theme—liberation in this life of those physically enslaved in the southern United States.
>
> The Heroic Slave struggles not only against physical brutality and oppression but also against the subjugation of his human spirit. . . . He knows only that he lives within an institution that denies his humanity and threatens his very survival and that he is willing to risk his life to save himself.[12]

The transversal of the racial dichotomy of U.S. sensibilities formulated by Pennington's rhetorical appeal occludes other exigencies of social existence fostered by the profligate license of the slaveholder.

Pennington's rhetorical question conceives together the familial and the national, the immediate and mediate forms of social organization that civil society, by definition, conjoins. The point to notice is that his query appreciates the decorous terrain of civil society, even as it fully appreciates his expulsion from that terrain. Thus, in his portrayal there is no failed representational gesture accompanying the report of the trauma of social being enforced by the U.S. racial policy of slaveholding. Ultimately, the injured African American body invokes a posture beyond injury (the civil), this modern posture of publicity co-implicating the familial, civil society, and the national. Articulated through the tripartite template of this scheme, the posture rehearses the prescriptions and contingencies of U.S. social proximity and identity with no representational failure, no matter how deeply traumatic the prescriptions and contingencies prove.

Pennington, as it were, places the spectacularized African American body within the terms of civility in ways in which, for instance, James Bradley's brief 1835 account does not, the difference imputing a libidinal issue. Bradley, recall, writes: "I have said that I had food enough. I wish I could say as much concerning my clothing. But I let that subject alone, because I cannot think of any suitable words to use in telling you."[13] The failed representational gesture of the account provides the graphic point of affect. Yet Bradley's bewildered acknowledgment of the prurience of the legalized relations of the slave regime is not the paramount feature. Obtaining only oblique representation rather than easy codification, the slaveholder, the sanctioned figure of the state, defies reasonable expression in the scene. This rehearsal of the contingencies of U.S. social proximity and identity highlights the U.S. federal compact granting statutory force to the prurient arrangement of the scene beyond rational calculation. The affective state of the white masculine figure substantiated by the statutory force of the federal compact defines Bradley's dilemma in the scene. The description of statutory order in the scene is the description of white male affect plainly irreducible to the rational calculation urgently reported of modern consciousness and modern statecraft, as well as the arrangements of civility extending between them.

The eccentric, unruly libidinal principle of the scene advertises one of the most striking points of ideological unrest in the antebellum debate over the legitimacy of the U.S. slaveholding regime, the "generalized sense that the South was a society in which man's sexual nature had no checks upon it,"[14] a point of critical interest most fully pronounced in the renewed abolitionist strategies of the 1830s, according to historian Ronald Walters. In Bradley's depiction, the depiction of the routine and racialized corporeal proximities so crucial to the imagination of interstate comity and national being, the representational (as well as the federal) aporia remains the appearance that wayward libidinal impulses attain full social agency in the conflated private and public spheres of the slaveholder. In the depiction, the reign of the state seems to sanction and turn on conditions of affect as much as, if not more than, the overwhelming condition of rationality normatively attributed to the modern state and its investments in civility. Rather, imperatives that foreclose the open mechanisms of affect as simply the reliable dynamic of the public sphere advertise the state and its investments in civility. As theorized, for example, by John Locke in *Two Treatises of Government,* modern political formations safeguard liberal consensus, liberal fraternal license, through the translation of the libidinal design of the heteronormative family into structural, rather than affective, significance. In chapter seven of *The Second Treatise*—"Of Political or Civil Society"—Locke writes:

> The *first Society* was between Man and Wife, which gave beginning to that between Parents and Children; to which, in time, that between Master and Servant came to be added: And though all these might, and commonly did meet together, and make up but one Family, wherein the Master or Mistress of it had some sort of Rule proper to a Family; each of these, or all together came short of *Political Society,* as we shall see, if we consider the different Ends, Types, and Bounds of each of these.[15]

In the concept of the state, then, there seems nothing exorbitant to the libidinal design of heteronormativity except, unreasonably and unacknowledged, the force of the libidinal itself. The "implausibility" troubled in Bradley's portrayal, therefore, is that the state never might appear, in its comprehensive reasonableness, in any way an immediate rendition of (white male) affect, wayward or unruly affect especially, even as the modern state ideally establishes white male fraternal license as its priority—its raison d'être. Simply put, the libidinal rudiment of modern political identity is defined, by "the bourgeois universe of signification," by "the bourgeois control of the means of socialization,"[16] by which the statutory rightly or virtually amounts to the formalization of interaction.

If there is confusion on this point, however, the racial blackness of the narrator accounts for this issue, "the Symbolic Object constituting the Lack, the Void of these qualities that have been postulated as the absolute sign of the certainty of being human. That a man or almost a man can exist, lacking these [statutory determinations], sets into play the terror that these [modern] attributes can be lost."[17] In the scene, the truly modern disorientation, the ideological unrest, the troubling representational failure, appears to be the axiological groundlessness of the modern advertisement of the human, in fact, always already the vertiginous trace of its disintegration. The human, as a modern coordination, is threatened, in other words, by its adamant precariousness. The particular incivility of the scene, beyond the disregard of the familial, masculinist, and social imperatives that James Pennington recognizes in his narration, is that the recollection "present[s] white men, not black men, as sexual aggressors,"[18] as statutory agents codifying aggression or violence in the most immediate terms of corporeal proximity.

As significantly, beyond these most immediate terms of corporeal proximity, the state seems not so simply the mechanism of comprehensive reasonableness but, on the contrary, the diffuse constituency of white male affect. The structural exposure, countenanced at the situation of the African American body, is that the human, as the modern coordination, insinuates a statutory presence animating the terror of licensed violence into the diverse exchanges of immediately proximate bodies and populations. This terror defines the human, and antithetically the inhuman, attaining the principal point of aleatory social coordination—rather than the orderly anthropomorphic ideal advertised as modernity. This perplexity of the human exposes the violence that promotes the human, the exposure of the rudimentary political terror severely compromising modernity as an institutional premise—not at all, in this way, the historical epoch uniquely able to manage the Idea of Freedom as immanent to self-consciousness, the institutional measure of sovereignty and subjectivity. The libidinal character of Bradley's depiction sets prurience within the statutory compass of the state, a strategic point of abolitionist concern, to follow again Walters:

> In its libidinousness the South could only be compared to other examples of utter depravity and dissolution. Thomas informed an audience of attentive young ladies that "THE SOUTHERN STATES ARE ONE GREAT SODOM" and his account was seconded by another abolitionist who had lived in Virginia and Maryland. "The sixteen slave States constitute one vast brothel," the *Liberator* declared in 1858. Twenty years earlier the *Pennsylvania Freeman* spoke of the "great moral lazarhous of Southern slavery. . . ." Thomas Wentworth Higginson decided that, compared to the South, "a Turkish harem is a cradle of virgin purity." Henry C. Wright preferred comparison with New York's notorious Five Points district, much to its advantage, of course. Like Sodom, brothels or a harem, the South appeared to be a place in which men could indulge their erotic impulses with impunity.[19]

This point of abolitionist strategy presumes that white male affect definitively cannot make sense in the political formulations of Western modernity.

Bradley's depiction presents white male affect as the paramount, wayward contingency of the political modernity assigned to the U.S. federal jurisdiction, illustrating particularly the civic presence drawn by white masculinity refusing the doctrinal imperative of modern psychic and political consciousness, the "channeling [of] all libidinal energy to a productive finality."[20] For the modern state proposes its far-flung order as the transposition of the authority ordering the proximities and the affective attachments of nuclear domesticity—premises its order, that is, on redoubling this libidinal arrangement as the foremost conceptual paradigm for the aggregate, anonymous relations within its jurisdiction. The modern state, as the extrapolation and refinement of the heteronormative model, aspires to the bureaucratization of a libidinal economy exercised as procreative domesticity, a bureaucratization establishing anthropomorphic modernity according to the template of the nuclear family. For the state to retain, then, its statutory coherence in the figure of sovereign subjectivity patently exceeding the heteronormative charter of desire and authority, the reportedly certain platform of the statutory imagination, amounts to abrogating the presuppositions on which the state rests—the disintegration of its statutory announcement.

The perplexity is that the statutory power of the slaveholder, as Bradley's narrative appreciates, strays regularly to prurience at the very least, drawing the compass of white male affect well beyond the presumptive heteronormative animation of the modern state and its civil designations. The quandary culturally defines the African American body, detailing, to borrow the words of philosopher Paul C. Taylor, that "blacks in the USA occup[y] a strangely paradoxical position, as social and political outcasts, who were integral, in large numbers, to the economic and, in the South at least, the private life of the nation."[21] Given first-person rendition by the classic slave narrative, these polemical depictions, interrogations, and insinuations, escalating the "perception of the slaveholder as an enemy of justice, immoral, and criminal,"[22] receive the fullest attention in the accounts rendered of or by enslaved African American women. Harriet Jacobs's *Incidents in the Life of a Slave Girl* remains the preeminent example, meticulously "deliver[ing] to Northern readers the sensational exposé of sexual transgression under Southern slavery requisite for their proper understanding of, and political action against, the peculiar institution of the South."[23] The narrative draws the jurisdiction of the state in libidinal terms irreducible to the charter of heteronomativity posed as the opposite extreme of civil society, complementary to and definitive of the state.

The central intrigue of *Incidents in the Life of a Slave Girl* refutes promptly the seeming clarity of the nuclear domesticity influencing political agency and intermediate civic agency. The narrative details, beyond the prurience of the slaveholder, the aleatory libidinal compass of the controversial chattel relationship. Literary critic Jennifer Rae Greeson notes, in the article "The 'Mysteries and Miseries' of North Carolina, New York City, Urban Gothic Fiction, and *Incidents in the Life of a Slave Girl*," the various aberrations of the libidinal design of heteronormativity catalogued throughout the plot, "including the forced and observed copulation of field hands (I, 49), breast torture (I, 13, 22), the selling of mulatta women into prostitution (I, 23, 85, 105), the implied homosexual rape of a male slave chained to his master's couch (I, 192), as well as abortion, infanticide, and lingering death in illegitimate childbirth (I, 13–14, 52, 58, 122)."[24] The catalogue underscores the situation of the African American body beyond civility, in the violated position of sensuous human practice—paradigmatically, the material location, the coerced sign, of the hostile social relations advancing the nationality and, moreover, modernity. It is important to notice, particularly, that the routine aberrations of the libidinal design of heteronormativity—the exercise of the logic and prerogative of racial subordination—distress, accordingly, the most intimate paradigms of social coordination. One scene especially witnesses the profound disarray, the scene in which Harriet Jacobs depicts the response of Mrs. Flint to Dr. Flint's prurient interest and wayward sexual pursuit of the pseudonymous slave girl, Linda Brent. The increasingly dangerous, vexed circumstances of Linda Brent are as follows, Jacobs writes:

> She now took me to sleep in a room adjoining her own. There I was an object of her especial care, though not of her especial comfort, for she spent many a sleepless night to watch over me. Sometimes I woke up, and found her bending over me. At other times she whispered in my ear, as though it was her husband who was speaking to me, and listened to hear what I would answer. If she startled me, on such occasions, she would tell me I had been talking in my sleep, and ask who I was talking to. At last I began to be fearful for my life. It had been often threatened; and you can imagine, better than I can describe, what an unpleasant sensation it must produce to wake up in the dead of night and find a jealous woman bending over you. Terrible as this experience was, I had fears it would give place to one more terrible.[25]

Strangely enough, the sexual persecution of Linda Brent is redoubled.

The scene depicts an anaclitic repetition, to use the language of Freudian psychoanalysis. The determining anaclitic attachment of the scene is the settlement of the sexual drive positioning Linda Brent as the object of desire. This formation of desire, buttressed by the force of statutory license, accounts for the most menacing interactions in the narrative between Brent and her slave master. The disruptiveness to heteronormative designs of this formation of desire is undeniable in its repetition undertaken by Mrs. Flint in her most diabolical moments of jealousy. She imitates Dr. Flint's offending structure of desire, the expression of desire through which racial contradistinction is overwhelmingly equivocal, thus challenging the heteronormative designs of subjectivity, civil society, and the state. The arbitrariness of these designs is clear, because the modern figure of the existence of subjectivity, civil society, and the state—the enfranchised white male figure—articulates his desire (his will to continuity) in the systemically impossible point of cathexis, racial blackness.

In her mimicry of her husband, Mrs. Flint draws desire even more remarkably: the prevailing structure of desire in the crisis is intersubjective, therefore an ideological and, moreover, statutory force. Mrs. Flint assumes the postures of body and mind expressing her husband's desire and his power; she appears to exceed the specification of her own gendered disenfranchisement through the power afforded her by the dichotomous legal assignments of racial blackness and racial whiteness.

The sinister performance abrogates the heteronormative designs of subjectivity, civil society, and the state, in several ways, foremost, however, because the homoeroticism of the performance is plain, one woman immediate to another entreating sexual contact. As plainly, the triangularity of the libidinal exercise confounds the protocols of heteronormative domesticity. But, furthermore, the intrigue fully undermines and confounds the historical and paradigmatic principle of the civil, political, and subjectivizing exclusions that describe the modern appearance of racial blackness.

The crisis in the Flint household abrogates the fundamental designs of modernization and its renditions of power. For the mechanisms of power in the modern era adamantly would exclude the thought and the figures of racial blackness from the heuristic sanctum through which "the semiotics of things and practices associated with the state form . . . reproduces itself through highly elaborated practices of familial reproduction,"[26] from the moral sanctum by means of which "political communities and kinship structures overlap."[27] The aleatory and anaclitic possibilities of social proximity interrupt these political and intimate determinations of modern racialization, as Mrs. Flint's imitation of Dr. Flint depicts.*

The protocols circumscribing the libidinal conscript the libidinal for ends always at some point frustrated, distressed, by the illogically circular demands ad infinitum of the libidinal. The logics of family and race propose that the excessiveness of sexual engagement, its rewards and risks of *jouissance*, draws subjectivity into indulgences that never can be fully or strictly civic. The routinely acknowledged complexities of the Freudian family romance, its inevitable generation of traumas and neuroses, reflect the depth of the quandary. The fraught management of the sexual energies within the modern family, indicated by the arduous path of "normal" development, yields by Freud's account a spectacular array of problems rather than any definitive solution or denouement to the crisis of management:

---

* At this point, Barrett makes an opening reference to Geneva Cobb Moore's highlighting of Jacobs's acclaimed physical beauty: "In this regard, literary critic Geneva Cobb Moore highlights the contemporary antebellum accounts of Harriet Jacobs's 'physical beauty,' 'acclaimed good looks and bodily voluptuousness' (9). Moore, that is, notes the countervailing power of the libidinal in the ideal mechanisms of political and [. . .] well as their potentially violent cross-purposes in here in the corporeal fact that no *necessary* relation exists between orgasm, procreation, or any powerful civic imperative proposing and enforcing the keen alignments of the libidinal, the national, and the racial." As the discontinuity that occurs between "political and . . ." and " . . . well as their" above suggests, there is clearly a gap in the original manuscript. While it may be only a few lines, the pagination in Barrett's original typed manuscript suggests that as many as thirteen pages may have been lost. In any case, exactly what has been lost is impossible to tell. Therefore, the reference to Moore, and Barrett's ensuing discussion of her treatment of the possible libidinous investments surrounding Jacobs, have been omitted from the final manuscript. For the above quotes of Moore, see Geneva Cobb Moore, "A Freudian Reading of Harriet Jacobs' *Incidents in the Lives of a Slave Girl*," *The Southern Literary Journal* 38, no. 1 (2005): 3–20.

"Every step on this long path of development can become a point of fixation, every juncture in this involved combination can be an occasion for a dissociation of the sexual instinct, as we have already shown from numerous instances."[28] The paradigm of race frets these already fretful set of negotiations undertaken by the competing paradigm of the family, granted that the transmissions of the phenotypical traits on which the viability of race depends can only be effected through the mechanism of heterosexual procreative sexuality (or currently its technological correlates), which the formulation of the nuclear family acclaims.

The logics of family and race struggle to codify continually what they represent as natural, even as their strenuous enforcements appear to contradict the historical inevitability or soundness of the protocols. The elaborations counter-pose themselves to the insinuations that, rather than forego the libidinal, can respect too fully the circular, or nonrational, dynamics of the sexual engagements they would overmaster as social protocols. Both attempt separate, but occasionally isomorphic, prohibitions on the discharge of sexual energy, the nuclear family as the traditionally accepted site for the proprietary management of all libidinal quandaries, the acknowledgements, functionalities, and materialities of racialization the concomitant calculus for the transmission and stability, from generation to generation, of the darkness or lightness of skins, the textures of hair, the shapes of eyes, noses, cheekbones, buttocks, and so on, the arrangement of the unstable phenotypical traits imperative to the modern epistemological programs. Insofar as the familial attempts to represent fully ordered and disciplined libidinal energies, it attempts a representational gesture, just as does race (and ideally in concert with race), that never wholly or successfully coordinates phenomenal and noumenal renditions of personhood. The discrepancy strictly comprehends the phenotypical differentiations of race as well as, more broadly, the distressing recklessness of the libidinal, the aleatory play of desire finally warranting the gravity of civic, legislative, national, or even violent pronouncement.

The ultimate instability of these regimes of identity is plain, given the effects of the legal and extralegal licenses held by those persons inhabiting the most fully sovereign white male relations to the familial, civility, nation, and race in the modern experiment of the United States. The logical, legal, and libidinal confusions utilized by the resurgent abolitionist movement of the 1830s betray the profound predicament of modern policy in which "through successive generations, a visible, albeit culturally inauthentic, 'whiteness' was reproduced from 'black' female bodies."[29] The cultural and political predicament is the transfiguration of the nonrational into the irrational, because the unarbitrated relations of sexual engagement, orgasm and procreation, organized by political fiat, confuse dramatically the affective and the material distinctions of the familial and the racial.

To restate the matter more generally, in the economic reorganizations of the seventeenth-century mercantile era, the complementary but troubled agendas of the familial and the racial recast the "host of discursive inductions through which the African American body historically became signifiable within the bounds of a decidedly bourgeois humanism governed by the bodily integrity of sexual difference."[30] Both, even as they cannot adequately manage the affective or speculative exigencies pressed upon them, remain the social vectors of the very highest priority, given the orderliness, even propriety, they aspire to represent and formalize in the imagination of the nation. The only certainty of the vexation, ultimately, is that the familial and the racial refract their social power through each other, competing to determine the limits of identification, particularly in its civic and political extrapolations.

In the influential study *The Body in Pain* Scarry employs the concept of "analogical verification (or substantiation)" to codify the inevitability that the acuteness of corporeal sensation remains always an ideological concern. Analogical verification (or substantiation) is most evident, in Scarry's view, at "particular moments when there is within a society a crisis of belief . . . [so that] the sheer material factualness of the human body will be borrowed to lend that cultural construct the aura of 'realness' and 'certainty'";[31] in the case of torture, for example, "[t]he physical pain [of the victim] is so incontestably real that it seems to confer its quality of 'incontestable reality' on the power that has brought it into being."[32] Pain, as anatomized by Scarry, is a form of compelling, involuntary withdrawal from the social landscape, "a state that has at its center the single, overwhelming discrepancy between an increasingly palpable body and an increasingly substanceless world."[33] Sexual arousal and orgasm, although in different ways, pursue the withdrawal of the state, however, in socially questionable ways that are not applicable to the condition of pain. Regardless of how similar or different the engagements, if subjectivity yields itself in the physical impress of pain, subjectivity also yields itself in the physical impress of "the non-utilitarian dimensions of sexuality[,] which are often summarized under the sign of pleasure."[34]

Therefore, because they also trouble the "overwhelming [and exploitable] discrepancy" between the palpability of the body and the competing symbolic configurations of subjectivity, the libidinal and the sexual remain virtually matchless cultural resources to be overmastered and formalized. The civic and the political terms of the antebellum development of the U.S. modernity confirm the relation, specifying "race, sex, and gender [as] . . . inextricably linked first through a system of slavery that placed white men in control of the productive labor of black men and the productive and reproductive labor of both black and white women, and then nationally through an economic and political system and a cultural ideology that established a fundamental racist and sexist hierarchy of privilege and oppression."[35]

Pressed to these designs, the logics of family and race—their putative "normalizing" of desire—produce private and public epistemologies never as secure as they seem, their normative determinations often failing conspicuously. Restated, the never necessarily consequent domestic/racial relations that sexual congress would underpin only redescribe the libidinal imperative, which never manages to expend itself fully in the sparing system of the psychic and cultural restrictions that the familial and the racial aim to sustain. These cultural restrictions, nonetheless, are indispensable to the economic modernity of the seaboard colonies and their federal articulation.

Jennifer Rae Greeson highlights one version of the problem in the literary context of *Incidents in the Life of a Slave Girl*. She investigates the development that, although "substantially absent from U.S. discourse on slavery before the 1830s, the sexual violation of enslaved women became a centerpiece of Northern representation of the South by the 1850s."[36] She proposes that the answer lies not simply in the "social order of Southern slavery [which] remained relatively static in the antebellum decades" but, rather, in the social "life in the Northern states [which] at that time was evolving at a dramatic pace under the related forces of industrialization and urbanization,"[37] the vanguard of the modern advance. Greeson contends that "it was the politicization of illicit female sexuality in urban gothic discourse that provided the conceptual framework through which the sexual order of Southern slavery could be made intelligible—and intolerable—for Northern readers."[38] In other words, with the emergent "formulas of the urban gothic," the abolitionist literary project becomes "the critique of an unjust economic system . . . engineered at least in part through the familiar figure of a sexually transgressing woman—here not an urban prostitute but the light-complexioned, enslaved concubine of the depraved slaveholder."[39] The troubling dynamic of the uneasy, modern national formation reflects the aleatory libidinal and social compass of the economic design. Greeson's conclusion is that the "urban gothic conventions for figuring the fallen woman's tale were useful to abolitionist writers because they allowed them to channel the immediate, visceral anxieties of Northern readers about the social changes they encountered each day on the street into political action against an economic system that had been abolished in their own section two generations before."[40] Through "their perceptions of Northern anxieties, abolitionist writers thus identified sexual exploitation of women as the prominent issue of the day that could make Southern slavery intolerable to Northern readers."[41] The African American body, in the national interrogation, appears as the spectacular limit of open sociality, the confounding point of possible civic disintegration.

The historian Peter Bardaglio, in *Reconstructing the Household: Families, Sex, and the Law in the Nineteenth-Century South*, confirms the significance of the libidinal in the national discrepancy over the political determinations of racial blackness and racial whiteness. Reforms in the Southern states as well involve the urgent social appearance of sexuality, Bardaglio writes:

> Especially during the 1850s a sense of uncertainty about the future gathered momentum in the black belt areas of the South as wealth in land and slaves became increasingly concentrated, construction integrated ever greater areas of the cotton South into a market economy over which individuals exercised little control. All of these economic forces combined to foster a profound sense of anxiety among planters and yeomen about their ability to preserve a system of domestic governance becoming more and more whipsawed by the contradictions of maintaining a slaveholding society within an international capitalist market.[42]

Part of the uneasiness of the federal contradictions is the civic administration of the social united within the singularity of the federation. The economic paradigms of the free and slaveholding states overwhelm the purely economic, given that "slavery, as both a system of social and legal relations, violated the sacred principles of the domestic order emerging in the North, an order that emphasized the individualism and autonomy of family members."[43] If the literary drawing of the African American body as the spectacular limit of civility reports the antebellum interrogation of the North, the slaveholding coordination of the legalities of the familial and the racial reports the Southern complementary fixation of the African American body as the limit of civility: "The major exception to the antistatist posture of elites [concerning domestic matters] in the slave South was in the realm of interracial marriage and sex, where authorities showed little hesitancy in erecting the legal prohibitions necessary both to buttress the racial division upon which slavery rested and to control the sexual behavior of white women."[44] The African American body constitutes the equivocal issue of insistent priority.

Thus, the patterns of the representation of African American bodies in the slave narratives are not simply indexical, but they respond to the confusion of market exchange, sexual desire, and social violence pervading the social landscape and the national form. These thematics persist in the African American literary canon, an imperative point of the drama in, for instance, William Wells Brown's 1852 *Clotel*, Solomon Northup's 1853 *Twelve Years a Slave*, Harriet Wilson's 1859 *Our Nig*, Martin Delaney's 1861–1862 *Blake*, Charles Chesnutt's 1900 *The House Behind the Cedars*, Pauline Hopkins's 1902–1903 *Of One Blood*, James Weldon Johnson's 1912 *Autobiography of an Ex-Colored Man*, Nella Larsen's 1928 *Quicksand* and 1929 *Passing*, Richard Wright's 1940 *Uncle Tom's Children*, Chester Himes's 1945 *If He Hollers Let Him Go*, Ann Petry's 1946 *The Street*, as well as James Baldwin's stark and uncompromising 1965 "Going to Meet the Man"—to enumerate a rough chronology of the first one hundred years of the African American literary narrative in the United States. The narrative tradition documents the imbrication of market exchange, social violence, and sexual desire in the cultural legibility of the "Africanist presence," to borrow the term of Toni Morrison, in the impulse to and the machinations of Western modernity, the hegemonic paradigm for the exchange of human values, politically ensconced by the nineteenth century.

However, the definition and conscription of the radical "Other" once engaged preeminently in the United States through racial blackness for economic as well as a variety of purposes is accomplished much more broadly by the close of the nineteenth century. Historian Matthew Jacobson in *Barbarian Virtues: The United States Encounters Foreign Peoples at Home and Abroad* writes that the moment of the turn of the nineteenth century into the twentieth century—that is, the moment when Western capitalism comes increasingly under the aegis of the United States—is one in which "the modern state was built, and modern nationalism generated, in close relation to the imperialist project," or restated still, "the very moment when global [economic] power was so lustily seized."[45] Jacobson writes further: "The emergence of the United States on the world stage, then, was marked by both a bitter competition among the European and Euro-identified nations, and an articulated kinship among these same powers in their self-proclaimed civilizing mission among the savages, semi-savages, and barbarians of Africa, Asia, and Latin America."[46] A series of political, military, and international occurrences bear out these observations. Historian Frank Ninkovich in *The United States and Imperialism* gauges the 1880s as the decisive point in the fluorescence of U.S. imperialism:

> Imperialism, like crime (or any human endeavor, for that matter), requires means, motive, and opportunity. In the 1880s, the United States acquired some significant new military capabilities when Congress, which was looking for ways to use up some large budget surpluses, splurged on a modern steel navy. The Civil War navy, which at its zenith had been one of the world's most imposing fleets, went to rot following Lee's surrender at Appomattox. Had it been preserved, it would have been quickly outmoded in any case by a revolution in naval architecture that replaced wooden-hulled sailing vessels with a new breed of steel warships—heavily armored, powered by coal-burning boilers, and equipped with powerful new rifled cannons set in deck turrets.[47]

The subsequent international escapades ranging across vast terrains of the globe are numerous: Hawaii and Puerto Rico are annexed by the United States in 1898; Panama becomes a U.S. protectorate from 1903 to 1936 in efforts to secure the Panama Canal (the canal zone being controlled by the United States from 1903 to 2000); the Dominican Republic becomes a U.S. protectorate in 1903 and is occupied by the United States from 1916 to 1924; Cuba becomes a U.S. protectorate under the Platt Amendment from 1903 to 1934; Nicaragua becomes a U.S. protectorate from 1911 to 1924, to which U.S. troops are sent from 1912 to 1925 and again from 1926 to 1931; Haiti is occupied by the United States from 1915 to 1934; and the U.S. Virgin Islands are purchased in 1917. In the brief Spanish-American War, lasting from April 25 to August 12, 1898, around which many of the Caribbean acquisitions and interventions turn, the Philippines take on an important role in the Pacific arena, insofar as the possession of the Philippines seems a crucial point of leverage concerning the potentially enormous markets long represented by China. For the nineteenth-century Treaty of Nanjing that concludes the Opium Wars (1839–1842) leaves the potentially enormous economic values of China open to the leading Western industrial powers by overthrowing the "Canton system" of trade between China and the West, the system of trading lasting from 1760 to 1840 that scripts Chinese superiority in the trade relations by limiting Western access to the cultural and market systems of China.

The re-articulated interests of codifying racial "Otherness" at the opening of the twentieth century proceed in large part from the dramatic reconfiguration of the U.S. naval power and its imperialist successes, reconfigurations yielding economic as well as nationally ideological upshots. Jacobson, on this point, underscores that "[t]he United States' spectacular economic growth at the turn of the century was attended by an equally spectacular pattern of downturns and failures: nearly half of the years between the 1870s and World War I were depression years—1878–79, 1882–85, 1893–97, 1907–8, and 1913–15."[48] The increasing definition of international consumer and labor markets from the vantage of the United States remain attempts to address these economic vacillations, with the international upheaval of World War I marking the decisive point of U.S. world economic dominance since, as François Crouzet observes, in 1913 prior to the devastation of the European landscape and economy resulting from the conflict:

> Western Europe alone had twice as many inhabitants as the United States and a bigger economy. It remained "the workshop of the world," as it supplied 60 percent of world exports of manufactured goods. Europe (including Russia) mined 50 percent of the world's coal output, made 57 percent of its steel, had two-thirds of its cotton-spinning capacity, and was responsible for 40 percent of its industrial production. It also was the world's banker—the United States being then a net debtor—and had a quasi-monopoly in services (shipping, insurance, etc.). Europe was the hub and engine of the world economy; it exercised an influence and even domination over economic developments in other continents.[49]

The ascendancy of the United States to the economic leadership and stewardship of the Western industrial powers after World War I is signaled conclusively in 1924 by the Dawes Plan implemented by the U.S. federal authorities in conjunction with U.S. banking interests in efforts to resuscitate the European economy after the financial collapse of Germany. In *Financial Missionaries to the World: The Politics and Culture of Dollar Diplomacy, 1900–1930,* historian Emily Rosenberg characterizes the schemes of international finance attendant to imperialist policies, "dollar diplomacy," as "a controversial U.S. policy that attempted to use private bank loans to leverage the acceptance of financial advisers by foreign governments that U.S. officials and investors considered unstable."[50] Rosenberg's analysis is not economic simply, but also cultural. Acknowledging the role of the anti-banking discourses of farmer and labor groups, the Populist Movement, sections of the Democratic Party and Southerners in opposition to the professional-managerial discourses of government officials, bankers and brokers, as well as midlevel managers and aspiring professionals nationwide supporting dollar diplomacy, Rosenberg notes the differing applications of the loan-control policies internationally. She writes that by the early 1920s "[t]he active governmental promotion of bank loans in the Western hemisphere contrasted so sharply with hands-off policies toward Europe that some obvious dilemmas came up when the government tried to craft an overall policy on foreign lending."[51] From the standpoint of the national imagination of the United States, the vivid conjunction of racial paradigms and the increasingly abstracted market of Western capitalism is radically revised: "The growing economic interconnections that Americans were establishing with unfamiliar and racially different lands, which were represented through the rapidly growing mass media, fed a fascination with the 'primitive,'"[52] that at the level of international military and financial force sponsors the "dividing line between those who managed the global system of promises to pay and those who seemed naturally to need supervision could earmark a cognitive division of the world into civilized and uncivilized segments."[53]

These developments re-articulate the relations between the economic and the cultural that encompass the post-emancipation African American citizenry, re-articulations as profound for the post-emancipation African American citizenry, although not nearly as abrupt or stark, as the U.S. Civil War, and Jacobson, to this end, observes: "The Reconstruction era's profound philosophical revisions of the concept of citizenship . . . formed the crucial background for later public discussions of the many other peoples of color who were drawn into the political and social orbit of the United States."[54] For example, legal scholar Ian F. Haney López in *White by Law: The Legal Construction of Race,* a study examining the "racial prerequisite to citizenship"[55] upheld by the United States Supreme Court particularly at the turn of the nineteenth and twentieth centuries, rehearses the legal maneuvers by which naturalization "[a]pplicants from Hawaii, China, Japan, Burma, and the Philippines, as well as mixed-race applicants, failed in their arguments"[56] for acquiring U.S. citizenship on racial grounds.

These are the circumstances in which the majority of the post-emancipation African American citizenry are placed and reconstrued at the opening of the twentieth century, even as nonetheless—largely in exile from the contrivances of national citizenship—this portion of the U.S. population pursue and cherish self-defining cultural protocols admitted through brazenly raucous but also sometimes "soft, stirring melod[ies] in an ill-harmonized and unmelodious land"[57]—to borrow a phrase from W. E. B. DuBois's *The Souls of Black Folk*. Historian Hannah Rosen, for example, in the essay "'Not That Sort of Women': Race, Gender, and Sexual Violence," rehearsing the events of the Memphis race riot of 1866, reports that newly emancipated African Americans, who augmented the black population of Memphis by 275 percent from antebellum levels, "fashioned social lives and urban communities that revolved around the grocery-saloons and street corners of South Memphis. In these spaces, freedwomen gathered, danced, and drank with black soldiers, often into the morning hours . . . [as well as] helped build independent black churches in Memphis, such as the Methodist Episcopal Church and various Baptist churches."[58] More to the immediate historical point, the turn of the nineteenth century into the twentieth century, cultural critic Angela Davis observes in *Blues Legacies and Black Feminism: Gertrude "Ma" Rainey, Bessie Smith, and Billie Holiday*:

> The historical context within which the blues developed a tradition of openly addressing both female and male sexuality reveals an ideological framework that was specifically African American. Emerging during the decades following the abolition of slavery, the blues gave musical expression to the new social and sexual realities encountered by African Americans as free women and men. The former slaves' economic status had not undergone a radical transformation—they were no less impoverished than they had been during slavery. It was the status of their personal relationships that was revolutionized. For the first time in the history of the African presence in North America, masses of black women and men were in a position to make autonomous decisions regarding the sexual partnerships into which they entered. Sexuality was thus one of the most tangible domains in which emancipation was acted upon and through which its meanings were expressed. Sovereignty in sexual matters marked an important divide between life during slavery and life after emancipation.[59]

The appearance of the civic unruliness of the African American body is redoubled in the eligibilities of the culture. In short, African American persons, the corporeal markers of the social limit of the U.S. modernity, are dispersed socially, insinuating the discontinuities of modernity more than ever.

CHAPTER 5

Modernism and the Affects of Racial Blackness

In the introduction to the prose collection *A Renaissance in Harlem*, Lionel Bascom briefly describes the cultural significance of the Harlem Renaissance and its program, stating that "the spiritual, social, and literary fervor that raced through Harlem during these years could be called the greatest period of self-discovery in African-American history after the Civil War and before the start of the Civil Rights era of the 1960s."[1] He writes further that the participating artists "used Harlem's growing popularity as a unique opportunity to do what reconstruction after the Civil War had not done—create a positive public image of blacks as thinking, creative human beings in American society. It was a noble effort. In

---

We are not certain that this work was intended as chapter 5 of this book. It was included in hard copies of Barrett's manuscript in progress, but the various plans for the book did not include it specifically as a chapter. The rest of the manuscript depends on Barrett's carrying his argument up to the period of the Harlem Renaissance, arguably the moment at which African Americans contended most directly with the modernization process. It is also possible that Barrett intended to carry his argument beyond the Harlem Renaissance, as his published essays on hip-hop and other contemporary cultural aspects of African American culture would suggest. Without any concrete evidence of a chapter on the Harlem Renaissance or African American modernism in the twentieth century, this chapter has been included in this final manuscript. We believe that it was written originally for a volume of essays Barrett was editing under the title *Modernism and Bodies That Don't Matter*, which would have included contributions from other scholars of African American culture, along with Barrett's own contribution. The decision to include this essay is an unconventional one by editorial standards, but we hope that with this explanation the addition will make Barrett's argument in this book more historically relevant to African American modernity.

their widely read essays, novels, plays, and newspaper articles, this well-meaning group set out to kill pernicious stereotypes of black folks."[2] George Schuyler and Langston Hughes famously address this issue of the cultural profile of African Americans in early-twentieth-century modernity in their essays "The Negro-Art Hokum" and "The Negro Artist and the Racial Mountain," published in *The Nation* in 1926, at the height of the Harlem Renaissance. The essays dispute the specificity of African American culture and identity by considering the forms and meanings of contemporary social interactions, rather than primarily historical points of reference. Rather than assessing African American aesthetics foremost by the legacies and aftermath of U.S. enslavement, the essays articulate divergent attitudes toward the routinely measured advancement or progressiveness of the early twentieth century, sharing then the matter of modernity, but not necessarily the inclinations of modernism. The essays debate the nature or effect of African American participation in the quotidian world of the early twentieth century, so that, unlike the primary African American speculations of the eighteenth and nineteenth centuries and earlier, the propositional knowledge is the introjection of African Americans into the U.S. civic order, an introjection understood as more or less quotidian, confirming Bascom's observations on the cultural success of the Harlem Renaissance, the broad proposition "of blacks as thinking, creative human beings in American society." They contest the cultural upshot of the modern quotidian made clearly and increasingly literal and literary within the boundaries of "One Hundred and Tenth Street on the south; on the east, Lenox Avenue to One Hundred and Twenty-sixth Street, then Lexington Avenue to the Harlem River, and the Harlem River on the east and north to a point where it passes the Polo Grounds, just above One Hundred and Fifty-fifth Street; on the west, Eighth Avenue to One Hundred and Sixteenth Street, then St. Nichols Avenue up to a juncture with the Harlem River at the Polo Grounds," as put by Schuyler in his critique of Harlem Renaissance writers.[3]

As does his title *Black Manhattan*, James Weldon Johnson's detailed descriptions coordinate the civic and the quotidian as the racial. Conceptually, African American presence embodies the civic—as registered by the prolix, casual tone of the description. Despite the violence of U.S. social, legal, and political histories, the cartography of the most famous urban space in the United States, New York, is black, Johnson outlines, and the cultural upshot George Schuyler contends in "The Negro-Art Hokum" is: "Negro art 'made in America' is as non-existent as the widely advertised profundity of Cal Coolidge, the 'seven years of progress' of Mayor Hylan, or the reported sophistication of New Yorkers. Negro art there has been, is, and will be among the numerous black nations of Africa; but to suggest the possibility of any such development among the ten million colored people in this republic is self-evident foolishness."[4] Casting the public image of African American identity and expressivities as virtually indistinguishable from those of the dominant national community, Schuyler's argument follows four principal points—the acknowledgment of the geographic and, therefore, cultural diversity of Africans and African Americans; the cultural miscegenation of the United States as reflected by the educational ties of leading African American intellectuals and artists to Euro-American institutions or figures; the conflation of stereotypes with racial identity; and the economic and social forces of early-twentieth-century capitalism, that is, the appeals of mass and consumer cultures, their interpellative influence and influence on community formation. "Aside from his color, which ranges from very dark brown to pink, your American Negro is just plain American. Negroes and whites from the same localities in this country talk, think, and act about the same."[5] Writing in opposition to "The Negro-Art Hokum" and producing his most famous essay, Langston Hughes argues that Schuyler's convictions represent a metaphorical "mountain standing in the way of any true Negro art in America—this urge within the race toward whiteness, the desire to pour racial individuality into the mold of American standardization, and to be as little Negro and as much American as possible."[6] "The Negro Artist and the Racial Mountain" opposes Schuyler's essay not only in argument, but also in its imagistic movement (from broad geographies to the domestic household); it opens with the domestic scene, which is superseded by the scene of jazz, as well as Hughes's closing, irreverent boast, a trajectory that casts the public image of African American identity and expressivity in terms of a set of willful attentions incommensurate with the attentions of the dominant national community. "Without going outside his race, and even among the better classes with their 'white' culture and conscious American manners, but still Negro enough to be different, there is sufficient matter to furnish a black artist with a lifetime of creative work."[7]

The point is to note that as much as the issue of race, the issue of the cultural conditions of the early twentieth century is integral to the disagreement. Schuyler and Hughes in this dispute propose aesthetic visions that, as much as contest the figuration of racial blackness, reflect divergent cultural postures toward the modern. Despite the most patent terms of the disagreement, the cultural disposition of African Americans, what remains integral to the essays is the cultural assignation of meaning to the "*process* of social and economic development, involving the rise of industry, technology, urbanization, and bureaucratic institutions, that can be traced back as far as the seventeenth century."[8] The opposed aesthetic assessments restate, that is, the defining tension or schism between modernity and modernism. Modernity, a material historical development, is the point of reference for modernism, as put by literary critic David Singal in

"Towards a Definition of American Modernism," "a constellation of related ideas, beliefs, values, and modes of perception—that came into existence during the mid- to late nineteenth century, and that has had a powerful influence on art and thought on both sides of the Atlantic since roughly 1900."[9] The constellation includes three broad formations in Singal's outline, a "stance toward modernization [that] has typically been marked by ambivalence, with Modernists simultaneously admiring the vitality and inventiveness of technological progress while decrying the dehumanization it appears to bring in its wake," the connotation of "radical experimentation in artistic style, a deliberate cultivation of the perverse and the decadent, and the flaunting of outrageous behavior designed to shock the bourgeoisie," and a fomenting "'adversary culture' originating in bohemia but later adopted by twentieth-century intellectuals in their growing estrangement from mass society, and ultimately reappearing as a virtual parody of its earlier self in the form of the 1960s counterculture."[10] Modernism, to a greater or lesser degree, rejects the increasingly corporatized, rationalized, mechanized, militarized, and (re)racialized circumstances of the early twentieth century in a turn to the production of aesthetic forms, literary images, language, and narrativities that both rebuke and transform quotidian modern prescriptions of the human. Modernism, as an aesthetic movement, recognizes the rapidly altered social, historical, and economic certainties yielding the cultural conditions of the early twentieth century in order to provide a limit to or critique of those conditions. In addition, then, to their alternative visions of African American identity and expressivity, "The Negro-Art Hokum" holds no seeming interests in or implications of "a counter-response to the triumph of modernization,"[11] while "The Negro Artist and the Racial Mountain" keenly holds these interests and implications.

For these reasons, the disagreement between Schuyler and Hughes should be understood in terms of a broader dispute concerning modernization, which depends on a new "periodizing concept, characterized by a nexus of related historical, intellectual, technological, and aesthetic developments, rather than by a set of formal traits or styles," as cultural critic Susan Hegeman poses the issue in her *Patterns for America: Modernism and the Concept of Culture.*[12]

It bears repeating, then, that the differing postures of Schuyler and Hughes toward African American aesthetic production articulate yet at the same time divergent assessments of "the relationship between progress in the modern world (and also the lack of it, or the threats that appear as the unwanted consequences or side effects of 'progress') and the developments of modernist aesthetics."[13] It bears repeating also that the figure of the domestic household is more than incidental to the imbrication of these issues in the dispute: more than incidental to the economic terms of modernity, particularly its progressive inflections through mass and consumer culture, to the monopolization of social relations as capitalist social relations, in response to which the disillusionment characteristic of modernist aesthetic reinvention in large part arises, and clearly more than incidental to the precarious introjections of African Americans into the post-emancipation U.S. civil order. Figured through the domestic household, the nexus marks the principal point of strategy in the dialogue between "The Negro-Art Hokum" and "The Negro Artist and the Racial Mountain." As already stated, the trajectory of "The Negro-Art Hokum" presents the scene of the domestic household as the climax of its argument, the point of evidence determining that U.S. national identity supersedes racial identity: "Again, the Aframerican is subject to the same economic and social forces that mold the actions and thoughts of the white Americans. He is not living in a different world as some whites and a few Negroes would have me believe."[14] In illustration of the claim, Schuyler's domestic scene details the effective constitution of U.S. national culture and its citizens foremost through the abstract similarity conferred through market relations (in lieu of, the contention is, phenotypes or other indices of racialization—eclipsed figures of national importance). In its evidentiary role, the domestic scene bears the interpellative impresses of consumer and mass cultures:

> When the jangling of his Connecticut alarm clock gets him out of his Grand Rapids bed to a breakfast similar to that eaten by his white brother across the street; when he toils at the same or similar work in mills, mines, factories, and commerce alongside the descendants of Spartacus, Robin Hood, and Eric the Red; when he wears similar clothing and speaks the same language with the same degree of perfection; when he reads the same Bible and belongs to the Baptist, Methodist, Episcopal, or Catholic church; when his fraternal affiliations also include the Elks, Masons, Knights of Pythias; when he gets the same or similar schooling, lives in the same kind of houses, owns the same makes of cars (or rides in them), and nightly sees the same Hollywood version of life on the screen; when he smokes the same brands of tobacco, and avidly peruses the same puerile periodicals; in short, when he responds to the same political, social, moral, and economic stimuli in precisely the same manner as his white neighbor, it is sheer nonsense to talk about 'racial differences' as between the American black man and the American white man.[15]

The essay makes its ultimate appeal to identity in terms of the most dramatic of the social transformations fully underway by the 1920s, the advent of mass and consumer cultures. Beyond the consolidation of corporate fiscal and legal hegemony, the emergence of consumer culture and of mass culture exacerbates in the early decades of the twentieth century the national monopolization of social and cultural life in support of the bureaucracies and interests of corporate entities, newly the unassailable purveyors of capital accumulation by the turn of the nineteenth century. In *Structures of the Jazz Age*, cultural critic Chip Rhodes examines the new social currency held by the automobile and the radio at the advent of the 1920s as indices of the transforming social imaginary and landscape of culture and mass cultures, observing: "By 1925, the auto industry was responsible for 15 percent of the total steel output for the country; factory sales of cars rose from 4,000 in 1900 to nearly one million in 1918, doubled in the next two years, and climbed steadily through the twenties to reach a peak of four and a half million in 1929."[16]

Drawing on Michel Aglietta's study *A Theory of Capitalist Regulation*, Chip Rhodes argues that, while in the nineteenth century U.S. capitalist production and growth are driven foremost by capital goods—production of goods that increase the fixed capital stock of corporations, such as railroads and factories—twentieth-century capitalist production and growth are driven foremost by the production of commodities for the recreational and social use of capitalist workforces. The vogue of the automobile by the 1920s underscores the transformation. The marked increases in the sale of consumer goods, such as the automobile, signal a transformation not only of markets and channels for capital accumulation, but also of the imaginative position of the modern and modernizing U.S. populations. Precedent forms and mechanisms of social interaction are transformed by participation in the recreational possibilities of the market. Even more so, this holds true for the rapid currency of the radio:

> The car was not the only high-profile consumer durable that found a new consumer market ready to embrace it. Sales of radios and electrical equipment rose from $28 million to over $388 million between 1922 and 1929. All consumer durables sold well, in fact, thanks in large measure to advanced advertising and consumer credit (without which none of this would have been possible). Telephones increased from 13 million to 20 million between 1920 and 1929, while sales of vacuum cleaners, electric cookers, refrigerators, and entertainment all rose by leaps and bounds in the decade.[17]

The rapid popularity of the radio illustrates the more or less permeable distinction between mass culture and consumer culture, which has to do with the imaginative effects that proceed from the act of consumption, consumer culture yielding scripts more particularly for self-formation and mass culture scripts for community-formation. "In achieving mass culture's goal of uniting the population and erasing boundaries, radio was arguably even more powerful than the movies. A forerunner of television in its ability to collapse distinctions between public and private realms, radio violated the sanctity of the home, irreparably compromising the family's autonomy as an ideological apparatus. Radio paradoxically erased and exacerbated temporal and spatial discrepancies, challenging its listeners' lived experiences of 'common sense' reality."[18] The domestic scene, as it appears in George Schuyler's argument, holds precisely this aspect: the point of coincidence of individual and national situations premised on the calculus of equivalence that is reckonable foremost through market exchange, thus the calculus of equivalence providing the arc of civic subjectivity.

Even as the formulation is precise, the feint is remarkable. To begin, the feint that "naturalizes" the household as the repository of market exchanges is a declension of commodity fetishism, the misrecognition of the ties between the social conditions of the labor yielding the commodity and the failure of the commodity to resemble those conditions in the exchange. The proceeding, extenuating feint that evacuates race as a meaningful index of identity (and, thus, aesthetics) redoubles the declension, particularly the fetishistic negation of material conditions:

> Harlem's promise and sense of liberation made it possible to overlook a widening range of social evils the community was already suffering even in the early 1920s. Although Harlemites earned less ($1,300 a year compared to $1,570) than other New Yorkers, they paid far more for housing ($9.50 a month per room, compared to $6.67). In Harlem, five-, six-, and seven-room apartments—originally built for large families, with large incomes, rather than for Harlem's growing population of young, unmarried migrants with relatively few children—taking lodgers became a familiar practice, accelerating deterioration. In spite of a youthful adult population, the death rate was 42 percent higher for Harlemites than for the rest of the city. In specific categories (such as infant mortality, death from tuberculosis, and violent death), the rates doubled, tripled, and venereal disease and malnutrition were commonplace. In spite of the fewer number of teenagers, the incidence of juvenile crime was higher. Working mothers had little time to care for children. Schools were overcrowded, with as much as 100 percent turnover each year in some instances, as students followed their rootless families from one residence to another. Quacks, healers, confidence men, loan sharks, and religious charlatans, exploiting the crisis of the community, only made the situation worse. In addition, Harlem was a "wide-open city," where the sale of alcohol flourished with few restrictions during Prohibition, along with vice, gambling, and narcotics.[19]

In deference to the feint of the marketplace, Schuyler overlooks the material conditions of the racially designated community in Manhattan. The fetishistic turn is pronounced: Schuyler's proposition of the meaning of race renewed through the marketplace makes more exorbitant the premise of equivalence in which the marketplace traffics even as it generates the unequal material conditions often reporting the social difference and the inequity of civic subjects.

The other points of emphasis of Schuyler's argument further clarify the fetishistic play effacing African American aesthetic sensibilities—the appeal to the geographic, to the cultural miscegenation of the United States reflected in African American intellectuals and artists, and to the confusion between stereotypes and racial identity. Initially in the essay, geography confers identity. Forecasting its final claims, the essay opens with geographic and jurisdictional references that serve as the paramount register of identity, so that, with the satiric irony characteristic of Schuyler throughout his career, "The Negro-Art Hokum" opens with nonblack points of reference: the president of the United States, the mayor of New York, and the municipal notion of identity granted by residence in the city. The final reference implies, particularly, the cross-racial identity that the essay idealizes. The inconsistency is that subsequent geographic references oppose, fracture, rather than consolidate, identity. The geographical distinction between Africans and African Americans marks these groups as non-identical; the origins of the popular dance in Charleston, South Carolina, marks the dance as a regional anomaly rather than a specifying figure of African American culture in the same way that the anomalies of the Appalachians cannot be mistaken for specifying figures of dominant white culture. Briefly put, the Charleston is the invention of only a small "caste" of the larger African American collective, and the claim is that this geographically specific group can be no more representative than any geographically specific group can be representative of all whites. However, beyond the inconsistent uses of the geographic appeals, the quandary is that, as the essay argues for pan-racial identity, it assiduously subdivides into more particular identities the identities it finally proposes to configure as the inexorable singularity marking the modern moment.

To discount the specificity of African American identity and expressivities, "The Negro-Art Hokum" also lists W. E. B. Du Bois, Meta Warwick Fuller, and Henry Ossawa Tanner in order to disqualify them as "expressive of the Negro soul" by noting their ties to leading U.S. and European universities and figures, their works then expressive of these ties, more so the argument posits, than any specific knowledge, sensibilities, or insights that might reckon the cultural forms of racial blackness. The point is underscored by a subsequent international list of black artists, including Coleridge-Taylor, Claude McKay, and Pushkin, whose work "shows the impress of nationality rather than race"—a muted return to the geographic appeals so important to the opening of the essay. Any appearance to the contrary, Schuyler states, is due to the fact that "[t]he mere mention of the word 'Negro' conjures up in the average white American's mind a composite stereotype of Bert Williams, Aunt Jemima, Uncle Tom, Jack Johnson, Florian Slappery, and the various monstrosities scrawled by cartoonists."[20] In short, any appearance of

African American cultural specificity is the misguided product of the imagination of the dominant culture. At this point in the essay, Schuyler provides his gainsaying description of the significance of the domestic household fetish.

In Hughes's rejoinder to Schuyler there is not simply a reversal of claims but also a reversal of appeals, trajectory, and tone. The difference in tone immediately is evident in the anecdotal opening of the essay that signals the more conversational than satiric tenor. The opening of "The Negro Artist and the Racial Mountain" repeats the cultural equivalence of racial blackness and racial whiteness posited by its companion essay; however, Hughes redoubles the proposal by figuring it as an issue of subjectivity rather than as geographic or jurisdictional identity. The central appeal of Hughes's essay is to matters of desire and willful identification, for Hughes does not dispute the facility of the form of pan-racial amalgam the earlier essay claims, but the meaning of the misrecognition he already understands it to imply—the misrecognition metaphorized in the title of the essay. The abstracted natural image of the racial mountain already contests the domestic ward delineated by the evidentiary turn of "The Negro-Art Hokum." The metaphor of the racial mountain figures, as differences of subjectivity, the differences—or distance—between the quotidian ideal of the modern and the African American aesthetic. An important crux of the differences of subjectivity is the perception of the modern.

Rather than general references, the essay opens with the allusion to an earlier conversation—which it implies it extends—an allusion, in particular, to the aesthetic sensibilities of Countee Cullen, sensibilities serving as the initial cognate for the position of Schuyler, establishing the focus of the essay, in this way, as the question of subjectivity, the psychic complex not so much of nomination as interpellation, the annunciative negotiation of accessibility to the social hegemony. "The Negro Artist and the Racial Mountain" yields, then, a much less tangible—or positivist—definition of race than "The Negro-Art Hokum." The essay highlights, rather than domestic or social inventories, psychic negotiations, because Langston Hughes views the human "standardization" fomented by mass culture, rather than as inexorable, as historical and social progresses that might be interrupted or relatively resisted, particularly since their culturally transmitted currencies recast the imagination in finally racially valenced ways. The opening anecdote illustrates these valences: "One of the most promising of the young Negro poets said to me once, 'I want to be a poet—not a Negro poet,' meaning, I believe, 'I want to write like a white poet'; meaning subconsciously, 'I would like to be a white poet'; meaning behind that, 'I would like to be white.'"[21] This series of interpretations posits the question of racial imitation at the heart of the young poet's comments and, furthermore, by suggestion, at the heart of Schuyler's remarks. While "The

Negro-Art Hokum," despite its aims, fractures racial identity largely by granting virtual ontological import to geographic specificities, "The Negro Artist and the Racial Mountain" fractures black racial identity also, though the dispersion is not taken for granted like the lines, dashes, and squiggles scoring the surface of a map. If there seems a dearth of culturally specific African American art—a fact his essay disputes—Hughes contends that the appearance is the outgrowth of "American standardizations" as they are communicated through the class lines that complicate black racial identity (as they do the terms of all racial identities). Hughes draws, then, the domestic scene as the confluent point of mass cultural script, as the site of instruction not so much premised on racial commonality, as Schuyler proposes, as racial hierarchy:

> But let us look at the immediate background of this young poet. His family is of what I suppose one would call the Negro middle class: black people who are by no means rich yet never uncomfortable nor hungry—smug, contented, respectable folk, members of the Baptist church. The father goes to work every morning. He is a chief steward at a large white club. The mother sometimes does fancy sewing or supervises parties for the rich families of the town. The children go to a mixed school. In the home they read white papers and magazines. And the mother often says "Don't be like niggers" when the children are bad. A frequent phrase from the father is, "Look how well a white man does things." And so the word white comes to be unconsciously a symbol of all virtues. It holds for the children beauty, morality, and money. The whisper of "I want to be white" runs silently through their minds. This young poet's home is, I believe, a fairly typical home of the colored middle class. One sees immediately how difficult it would be for an artist born in such a home to interest himself in interpreting the beauty of his own people. He is never taught to see that beauty. He is taught rather not to see it, or if he does, to be ashamed of it when it is not according to Caucasian patterns.[22]

Whereas in Schuyler's essay the domestic scene provides the final ground for the certainty of cross-racial unification and conformity, it provides for Hughes the questionable, equivocal ground of intraracial disunion and depreciation, and this is crucial to note. The redoubled domestic scene disseminates forms of approval and disapproval corresponding respectively to the racial positions of whiteness and blackness, a reading of race in terms of class that retains the focus on subjectivity at the center of the essay, since class amounts foremost to a profile that, as a key determinant, articulates race. However, while the rendition of the domestic scene primarily betrays the cues of cultural hierarchy, the rendition in the essay of what Hughes terms "the low-down folks, the common element, and they are the majority"[23] embodies the African American aesthetic, understood as practices and formations of community incommensurate to domestic wards. From the domestic scene, the essay turns to the social world informed by jazz, reflecting Hughes's choice not only for the argument of the essay but his work generally, as he acknowledges: "Most of my own poems are racial in theme and treatment, derived from the life I know. In many of them I try to grasp and hold some of the meanings and rhythms of jazz."[24] The aesthetic dynamic, as Hughes understands it, is not preeminently or necessarily the same as the domestic one. The domestic world, and the economic and affective routines it would be made to support within the structures of consumer and mass cultures, do not approximate in Hughes's understanding the racial character of jazz: "But jazz to me is one of the inherent expressions of Negro life in America: the eternal tom-tom beating in the Negro soul—the tom-tom of revolt against weariness in a white world, a world of subway trains and work, work, work; the tom-tom of joy and laughter, and pain swallowed in a smile."[25] The point remains psychic, the standardization or massification of social relations in question not serving as the evidence of an inexorable outcome, but of the adamant brokering or leveraging of a particular outcome. The exemplarity of the domestic for the argument is not that there is no African American cultural specificity, but that African American aesthetics arise in ways that circumvent the scripting of human and social similarity through the marketplace. To this end, the central figure of the essay is wayward:

> The people who have their nip of gin on Saturday nights and are not too important to themselves or the community, or too well fed, or too learned to watch the lazy world go round. They live on Seventh Street in Washington or State Street in Chicago and they do not particularly care whether they are like white folks or anybody else. Their joy runs, bang! into ecstasy. Their religion soars to a shout. Work maybe a little today, rest a little tomorrow. Play awhile. Sing awhile. O, let's dance! These common people are not afraid of spirituals, as for a long time their more intellectual brethren were, and jazz is their child. They furnish a wealth of colorful, distinctive material for any artist because they still hold their own individuality in the face of American standardizations. And perhaps these common people will give to the world its truly great Negro artist, the one who is not afraid to be himself. Whereas the better-class Negro would tell the artist what to do, the people at least let him alone when he does appear. And they are not ashamed of him—if they know he exists at all. And they accept what beauty is their own without question.[26]

The disagreement over aesthetics concerns not accuracies of perception but, as the notion of ideology suggests instead, the incongruities between the various organizations of thought that veil material relations so as ultimately to order them. Ideology implies, write Karl Marx and Frederick Engels in *The German*

Ideology, "'consciousness,' but even so, not inherent, not 'pure' consciousness,"[27] but consciousness more or less in contradiction with the material and class rule provisioning civic and civil organization. In summarizing the first segment of their argument in *The German Ideology*, Marx and Engels write: "The conditions under which definitive productive forces can be applied are the conditions of the rule of a definitive class of society, whose social power, deriving from its property, has its *practical*-idealistic expression in each case in the form of the State"[28] and that which the State cherishes for its perpetuation. Marx, in *Capital*, presents, as the prime example of the ideological, the fetishism of commodities, in which it "is a definite social relation between men, that assumes, in their eyes, the fantastic form of a relation between things."[29] Economists Jack Amariglio and Antonio Callari observe, accordingly, in the article "Marxian Value Theory and the Problem of the Subject," that "Marx has had a theory of the subject, the theory of commodity fetishism. To the extent that it attempts to conjoin the analysis of commodity production and circulation with a discussion of 'ideology,' commodity fetishism does discuss the peculiar subjectivity typical of capitalist social formations."[30] The economists continue, "[T]he act of exchange is not simply the site of an economic process but also one of the key locations within capitalism where a symbolic order is particularly constituted and learned."[31] Since the concept of commodity fetishism describes the phantasmatic torque of rational exchanges, it abrogates—precisely as an elaboration of subjectivity—the "unnecessary gulf [that] has come to exist between two important areas of theoretical work in contemporary Marxism, with the theory of value (the economics, if you will) on one side and the nature and role of subjectivity (an antieconomism) on the other."[32] The ideally infinite arena of ideally infinite exchange—the modern abstracted market—forms, at once, the most regulated nexus of material and conceptual dissemination.

"The Negro Artist and the Racial Mountain," more so than draw this sparing circuit at the node of the domestic scene, privileges the defiant self-declaration that marks the most famous quotation from the essay: "We younger Negro artists who create now intend to express our individual dark-skinned selves without fear or shame. If white people are pleased we are glad. If they are not, it doesn't matter. We know we are beautiful. And ugly too. The tom-tom cries and the tom-tom laughs. If colored people are pleased we are glad. If they are not, their displeasure doesn't matter either. We build our temples for tomorrow, strong as we know how, and we stand on top of the mountain, free within ourselves."[33] The declaration highlights the modernist aspect prevailing in the African American cultural revolution of the early twentieth century, that is to say, the complex, productive, creative distance from the idealizations of similitude informing "the blare of Negro jazz bands and the bellowing voice of Bessie Smith singing blues penetrat[ing] the closed ears of the colored near-intellectuals until they listen and perhaps understand . . . Paul Robeson singing 'Water Boy.' Rudolph Fisher writing about the streets of Harlem, and Jean Toomer holding the heart of Georgia in his hands, and Aaron Douglass drawing strange black fantasies cause the smug Negro middle class to turn from their white, respectable, ordinary books and papers to catch a glimmer of their own beauty."[34] To repeat the point, the essay fixes the question of the aesthetic in terms of subjectivity, the complex, productive, creative distance from the idealizations of similitude realizing the civic, which is to say, the realm of the psychic. In other words, the debate relies, in its articulations of race, on perspectives taken toward the material apportionments and the new forms of social superintendence sponsored by the early twentieth-century modernity: thus, the modernist character of the exchange, as well as a signal component of the renewed cultural exposition of Harlem Renaissance.

The modernity of the cultural moment as measured by the estranged stance of modernism is integral to the exchange, and the same issue bears directly on the subsequent fiction of Schuyler and Hughes, because their fiction elaborates clearly the divergent positions of the exchange. The two writers, by the end of the next decade, acquire very different literary profiles. Although known primarily as a journalist, Schuyler writes serial fiction for the *Pittsburgh Courier* under the names Samuel I. Brooks and Rachel Call, as well as the novels *Black No More* (1931) and *Slaves Today* (1931). Although known primarily as a poet, particularly by the volumes *The Weary Blues* (1926) and *Fine Clothes to the Jew* (1927), Hughes writes as a journalist and dramatist, as well as the novel *Not without Laughter* (1930), the collection of short stories, *The Ways of White Folk* (1934), and by 1940 the first installment of his autobiography, *The Big Sea*.

Insofar as modernism can be characterized formally as experimentations in systems of representation that increasingly trouble or compromise "realism" or strict mimesis, the modernist sensibilities of Hughes are evident in the curious narrative simplicity of *The Ways of White Folk*. Literary critic Joseph Boone in the study *Libidinal Currents: Sexuality and the Shaping of Modernism* writes that the "novelistic endeavor to shift attention from externally rendered reality to the realm of the interior that exists beyond direct representation is a hallmark of that body of formally experimental fiction most often subsumed under the rubrics of *modernism* and *stream-of-consciousness* narration."[35] Although *The Ways of White Folk* does not engage this aesthetic ideal, its reconsiderations of the dynamics of the libidinal and of the social insistently disturb the conventional upshots of narrative representation. *The Ways of White Folk* upholds simply the indeterminacies of social contact and private desire, rather than the apparent stabilities of the domestic, the familial, the parental, the racial, or (as their abstracted point of conflation) the notion of heterosexual affection around which these other notions are arrayed by the normative canvas that realism and strict mimesis conventionally convey. The narrative simplicity of Hughes's *The Ways of White Folk* concerns itself directly with issues of sexuality, issues exposing the racial, gendered, and libidinal valences of social conflict and identity in the early twentieth century.

Rather than suggest the alignments with the early twentieth-century modern that Schuyler's writings pursue, *The Ways of White Folk* queries the easy prospect of those alignments, because the situations and interactions recounted by the collection, as though routine, belie the straightforwardness with which they and the unfolding civic landscape are rehearsed. The psychic and social disturbances forming the events of the collection, only partially veiled by the uncomplicated language and plotting, call into question—rather than extrapolate ideally—the cultural configurations convening the characters. The narratives outline the culturally rooted disturbances bringing the characters together and, as important, separating them, so that the collection highlights the complication of human relations entrenched by the protocols of the early-twentieth-century modernity. These complications are eccentric to Schuyler's 1936 serialized novella "The Ethiopian Murder Mystery." As the primary force of the plot, "The Ethiopian Murder Mystery" unfolds the process of detection uncovering the relations between the odd series of objects, the clues, reiterating the prime narrative significance of the first enigmatic object described: the dead body of the character Prince Destu, the Ethiopian whose secret purpose in Harlem is to undermine the Italian annexation of Ethiopia. In opposition to the interests of modernism, "The Ethiopian Murder Mystery" presents the cultural nexus convening its characters through a mimetic register foremost. Key to the juxtaposition of the fiction of Hughes and Schuyler, then, is the issue of the different valences of their acts of the imagination that describe the modern: the widely ordered "way of living and of experiencing life which has arisen with the changes wrought by industrialization, urbanization, and secularization."[36]

As in the disagreement between "The Negro-Art Hokum" and "The Negro Artist and the Racial Mountain," the disposition of the domestic space reiterates these valences. In the framing stories of *The Ways of White Folk*, "Cora Unashamed," which opens the collection, and "Father and Son," which closes the collection, sexuality is never equivalent simply to what seems plain or conventional desire. Rather, the issues of sexuality draw the characters of the narrative into palimpsest-like structures betraying the gendered symmetry, the domestic or the familial bonds, as well as the procreative finality assigned as the most "realistic," or naturalized, aspects of the libidinal and the sexual. In "Cora Unashamed," for example, the specter of miscegenation is pervasive, defining as well as thwarting the sexual tensions bristling throughout the narrative, a figure for the unprecedented possibilities of the racial, migratory, and economic fluxes of the early twentieth century. The protagonist and her family are the only African American residents of Melton and, as Cora's siblings mature, the "boys, lonesome, went away as far as they could from Melton. One by one, the girls left too, mostly in disgrace."[37] Miscegenation is implied in the reasons for the sequential disappearance of Cora's brothers and explicit in the certainty that there "was something about the cream-and-tan Jenkins girls that attracted the white farm hands."[38] Cora, for all of these reasons, is "one of the least citizens of Melton," which is neither "large enough to be a town [n]or small enough to be a village,"[39] and she is employed as a maid by the Studevants. With her earnings she supports her parents and siblings, her abiding predicament being that "[t]here was something about the teeth in the trap of economic circumstance that kept her in their power practically all her life—in the Studevant kitchen, cooking; in the Studevant parlor, sweeping; in the Studevant backyard, hanging clothes."[40] The narrative details, nonetheless, the events leading to Cora's disregard of this basic power in her life, disregard confirming the integrity of her affection for the Studevant's daughter, whom Cora helps to raise and whom she watches die from the abortion demanded by her parents.

At one point during her career with the Studevants, Cora also takes a lover and has a daughter, Josephine, who sometimes plays with Jessie Studevant when she is a child. When Cora can no longer take her child to work, and Josephine dies of whooping cough, Cora's abundant grief makes clear that she "was not humble before the fact of death."[41] Similarly, years later, when Jessie dies, after languishing for a month after her abortion in Kansas City, Cora demonstrates again that she "was not humble before the fact of death." The point of sympathy between Cora and the dead Jessie that elicits Cora's outbursts at the second funeral mark the strongest bonds of affection described in the narrative. Cora's outburst at Jessie's funeral is not the result simply of her long attendance on Jessie, but also a result of Cora's recognition, identification with, and approval of Jessie's sexual transgressions. At the funeral Cora denounces the Studevants and the community for killing both Jessie and her unborn child, until, sobbing, "with great tears coming for the love of Jessie,"[42] she is dragged away by the Studevant men in what amounts virtually to a brawl.

The second funeral and Cora's second outburst recast the first funeral and her first outburst, entangling the lines of identification between the characters. Jessie at the second funeral corresponds to Cora's dead child Josephine in the first. As an unwed mother Jessie corresponds also to Cora. Moreover, the father of Cora's daughter Joe is a "white boy . . . some kind of foreigner . . . [with] an accent,"[43] and, years later, so is the father of Jessie's aborted child, "the Greek boy"[44] who disappears after her death. The implication is that Cora mourns again for her own daughter when she mourns for Jessie, and remembers the enticements of lust, affection, and risk. These correspondences hold the center of the narrative and confirm the integrity of the bond between the two women as secured by their long acquaintance, their separate sexual transgressions, and the fateful outcomes of those transgressions. Still, there are plain economic consequences to the fact that Cora "was not humble before the fact of death." She is discharged by the Studevants, living "from the little garden [she and her mother] raise, and from the junk Pa collects."[45] At the same time that Cora's outburst is an emotional rupture, it is concomitantly an economic rupture.

As already suggested, the intrigue insinuating the market, race, and sexuality is not new to African American literary production, as the feminist sensibility of *Incidents in the Life of a Slave Girl* or the literary figure of the "tragic mulatta" developing alongside African American slave narratives indicate. "Cora Unashamed," however, in ways never fully imaginable or reckonable in nineteenth-century literature, establishes the point of emotional fidelity between the racially distinct Cora and Jessie through transgressive sexual intrigues. The otherwise settled narration of the story is disturbed by the moment of affective, libidinal, and psychological intensity, at once, recalling the recklessness of lust, affection, and open desire as well as describing emotional fidelity across racial lines, all in determined contradistinction to the mired complexities that would fix, as though incontrovertible, the domestic, the familial, the heterosexual, and the racial orders that social desire and sexuality are presumed to superintend.

In the conventionality of the narrative, rife with signal silences, the ordering phallic Law/economic Law presides across the variable and palimpsest-like scheme inscribing the dilemmas that injuriously surpass the individual precisely as the mechanisms and insinuations of the prolix capitalist order never suffer as great a crisis as those impressed by the phallic Law/economic Law. Thus, "Cora Unashamed" closes with images of the dilapidated Jenkins family, which also suggestively provide images of the more ostensibly respectable Studevants. Langston Hughes writes: "Anyhow, on the edge of Melton, the Jenkins niggers, Pa and Ma and Cora, somehow manage to get along."[46] The simplicity of the narrative presentation itself is not disrupted but, instead, the conventional canvas of racialization, sexuality, psychic interiority, and desire that narrative simplicity conventionally would be understood to superintend.

Whereas "Cora Unashamed" rehearses the integrity of bonds of affection that defy strictly maintained lines of social difference by crossing and re-crossing the dynamics of the familial, "Father and Son," the concluding story of the collection, rehearses the destruction of affective ties seemingly secured by the familial, the domestic, and the racial. "Father and Son" also recounts the more dire racial violence insinuated in the unsettled social possibilities of the racial, migratory, and economic fluxes marking the twentieth century as increasingly distinct from the nineteenth—the public physical and psychic excess animating the civic practices that, by definition, would strictly, perpetually, guilefully formalize the matters of sexuality. The narrative recounts the return of Bert, the long absent, biracial son of Colonel Thomas Norwood, to the family plantation. Bert is enrolled in college out of state, and his long absence and his education away from the plantation ill-prepare him for meeting his white father and fully respecting the codes of racial disinheritance. The colonel's death of a heart attack during an argument with Bert makes Bert a fugitive briefly and eventually the victim of the lynching that concludes the narrative. Drawing the terms of emotional unrest leading to the violent events, the conflicted positions of Bert, his mother Cora, and Colonel Norwood are drawn in turn. The opening of the narrative describes the deep anticipation yet feigned indifference of Colonel Norwood to the arrival of Bert and, as immediately, the seeming mimetic simplicity of the narrative is disrupted:

> The Colonel entered the small room where he kept his books and papers of both a literary and a business nature. He closed the door. He did this deliberately, intending to let all the Negroes in the house know that he had no interest whatsoever in the homecoming about to take place. He intended to remain in the library several hours after Bert's arrival. Yet, as he bent over his desk peering at accounts his store-keeper had brought him, his head kept turning toward the window that gave on the yard and the road, kept looking to see if a car were coming in a cloud of dust.[47]

Colonel Norwood, torn between the codes of public identity and the countervailing impulses of private desire, opens the narrative, not simply as a figure of authority but as a figure for the disjunction of signification and meaning. Each of his gestures, as well as the line of his thought—all the points of agency in the scene—disturb the reading of the scene and, in particular, the concomitant racial and domestic knowledge that confirms his standing as a figure of authority. The trouble is that what for Colonel Norwood is a dilemma of severe self-division is, nonetheless, the point of plain cultural settlement, which is to say, the paramount, dis-affective charge of racialization. Colonel Norwood's self-contradictions demonstrate that, as much as he is the presiding point of authority, social as well as narrative authority, he is—to return the vexed issue to questions of representation—"already structured by difference and distance as much as is writing" or, restated, demonstrates that "the illusion of self-presence of meaning or of consciousness is thus produced by the repression of the differential structures from which they spring."[48] On this point, Ian F. Haney López in *White by Law* posits the self-differential of racial whiteness as follows:

> Finally, uncritically accepting a White identity requires the burial of one's own identity. Whiteness requires constructing oneself not in terms of the failings and virtues that all people share, but in the mythical terms decreed by Whiteness. The unquestioned embrace of Whiteness alienates one from others, non-Whites and Whites alike, and from oneself. Claiming a White identity creates an uncrossable divide within the self and an unbridgeable gulf between the self and others.[49]

That is, the psychological fulcrum of the scene, like the psychological intensity and parallelism of "Cora Unashamed," reflects an abiding modernist conundrum, the increasing quandary or intricacy of the articulation of difference. The unreliability of Colonel Norwood's narrative perspective reflects the dilemma that the most creditable terms of social difference and order do not align abidingly or readily with the most deeply felt terms of self-proposition. Specifically, the racial component of this representational drama resides in the perplexity that literary critic Joseph Boone characterizes as "the instability and variability of psychosexual impulses and . . . [the] wayward trajectories that the libido etches in the subconscious [so as to render] . . . a poetics and politics of the perverse."[50]

These libidinal instabilities also pertain to Schuyler's "The Ethiopian Murder Mystery," insofar as the solving of the titular mystery assures the possibility of the domestic union of two of the central characters, Roger Bates, the determined newspaper reporter aiding the detective assigned to the case, and Crissina Van Dyke, the Harlem socialite who is the prime criminal suspect for most of the text. The novella opens at "the Finchley Arms, a swank Sugar Hill apartment house,"[51] where the Ethiopian Prince Destu is found murdered in his rooms, with one of his fingers severed (because of the ring it bears), and, as tantalizingly, a green handkerchief scented with expensive perfume is recovered from the murder scene. Madame Custiss, briefly a suspect herself, identifies Crissina Van Dyke leaving the scene the night of the murder, and the investigating detective Jim Willitson and the newspaperman Bates, having competing theories of Crissina Van Dyke's guilt or innocence, collaborate to unravel the confusion. In contrast to the short stories of *The Ways of White Folk*, which never routinely assure or fundamentally propose the resolution of indeterminate meaning, "The Ethiopian Murder Mystery" has as its premise and imperative the process of detection that resolves the relations between the material objects highlighted throughout the text as the clues to apprehending the circumstances of the murder of the Ethiopian Prince

Destu. The process of detection has as its resolution not only the revelation of the murderer of Prince Destu but also the domestic union of Roger Bates and Crissina Van Dyke, which is suspended by the accusations against her. In other words, "The Ethiopian Murder Mystery" and *The Ways of White Folk* recapitulate the terms of the earlier disagreement between "The Negro-Art Hokum" and "The Negro Artist and the Racial Mountain" in assessing U.S. cultural modernity through the index of race. The novella resolves itself by as deliberate a turn to the domestic scene as does "The Negro-Art Hokum." In other words still, because the resolution of indeterminate meaning coincides finally with the proposition of the domestic scene, the important cultural calculus of the domestic scene is insinuated in the coherence—racial and otherwise—granted to the modern in Schuyler's work.

Serialized October 5, 1935, to February 1, 1936, the plot of "The Ethiopian Murder Mystery" rescripts the "imperialistic adventure of Fascist Italy [that] came at a critical juncture in the history of black America," a time when, in the words of historian Robert G. Weisbord: "The Great Depression was ravaging people long frustrated and anguished by economic privation and racial discrimination. No wonder Mussolini's wanton aggression triggered an outpouring of cold fury."[52] Unlike his subsequent "Revolt in Ethiopia: A Tale of Black Insurrection against Italian Imperialism," in which the unfolding espionage and romance range through Europe and Ethiopia, Schuyler restricts "The Ethiopian Murder Mystery" to Manhattan, Ethiopia holding symbolic, not material, importance for the narrative action, to which there are three principal outcomes: first, the unraveling of the significance of Prince Destu's missing ring, which functions for "Ethiopians in the espionage and diplomatic service as a means of unfailing identification";[53] second, the successful securing through pan-Africanist efforts of technological superiority for the Ethiopian military in the conflict with Italy, in the science fictional form of Professor Tankkard's death ray; third, the impending marriage of Roger Bates and Crissina Van Dyke. It is important to recognize the positivist imperative of the genre of the detective novel, as well as the more immediate resemblances of "The Ethiopian Murder Mystery" to Dashiell Hammett's *The Maltese Falcon* and the first African American detective novel, Rudolph Fisher's *The Conjure Man Dies*. But, more to the point, it is important to acknowledge that, as the point of narrative resolution, the unraveling of the murder mystery consolidates the most glossed interpellative equipoise of capitalist social relations. Stated more elaborately, it is important to acknowledge the "fusion of racial nationalism with modernity" that historian Robert Hill observes "was a requirement of Schuyler's credo,"[54] a credo articulated in the novella by means of the prime mass cultural formula coupling the futurist possibilities of modernity with the libidinal scripting implied properly in the domestic scene that reposes the macropolitical routines of production and consumption.

The emphatic point of appeal is definitive for mass and consumer cultures and the reforged civic terrain of early-twentieth-century modernity they yield, as historian T. Jackson Lears argues in *Fables of Abundance: A Cultural History of Advertising in America*, when noting the subtle insinuations of the corporate hegemony of modern economic and social relations. Lears writes, "mass-produced abundance was an agent of the civilizing process. To gratify their zest for amusement, young men became habituated to the demands of industrial routine and eventually sought the pleasure of 'enlarging relationships'; they married and their wives reinforced the family's commitment to ever-increasing consumption. Proliferating things . . . were markers of economic and cultural ascent."[55] In other words, the ideal regulatory reach of the abstract marketplace would impress not only the exchange of cash for goods, and public forms of imagination and narrative, but libidinal protocols as well—the reach also implied by the full scope of the thesis of Amariglio and Callari. *In Structures of the Jazz Age,* Chip Rhodes also notes the widespread and coordinated impress when considering the role of Hollywood in the 1920s and its reformulation of the quotidian. Remarking the rapid imperatives toward standardization and regulation in Hollywood, Rhodes notes generally that "[t]he product itself . . . became more streamlined and formulaic, as studios sought to make costs and profits more predictable,"[56] and he notes, in an analysis of Cecil B. DeMille's domestic dramas from 1917 to 1922, that "[e]ven though the explicit lesson is always that sexual excitement and consumption can be contained within the institution of marriage, these films reinforced the broad-based acceptance of consumer desire that made the boom of the twenties possible."[57]

Unlike the stories in *The Ways of White Folk,* the matters of sexuality privileged in Schuyler's novella do not disturb finally the most fixed forms of identity, the apparent simple inevitability of civic protocols, or the realistically advertised forms of self-knowing that become at the opening of the twentieth century, to follow the analysis of historian Sharon Ullman in *Sex Seen,* "increasingly ensnared in a rhetoric combining commerce and sexuality."[58] However, if the trajectory of the novella realizes the impending domestic scene of Roger Bates and Crissina Van Dyke, the earlier portions of the trajectory are more wayward. For the first point of the investigation, the scented green handkerchief discovered with the body of Prince Destu directly introduces to the narrative "the instability and variability of psychosexual impulses"[59] foreclosed largely by the conclusion of the novella given to its libidinal formula. In the exclusive Manhattan boutique that sells the expensive perfume found on the green handkerchief, detective Jim Williston confronts the signs of sexual transgression in the young French sales attendant.

As he identifies the perfume, the salesman's "penciled eyebrows arched and a smile of recognition swept over his face" so that he "fluttered across the room" to retrieve the perfume for the detective, and eventually the list of purchasers of the perfume.[60] The detective confronts again the signs of sexual transgression in the list of customers: Of the twenty-eight, "[f]our he recognized immediately. They were Madame Helen Custiss, the hairdresser; Crissina Van Dyke, the socialite of Harlem; Mom Johnson, who ran the strange, shuttered house on 134th Street where well-to-do Nordics came furtively after nightfall; and Percival Prentiss, the well known Harlem hairdresser, sometimes known as the Faggot Queen."[61] The initial turn of the investigation, irrespective of the appellate domestic scene, recasts the libidinal.

Yet the scene rests also on a countervailing point of racial recognition. When asked to retrieve the list of customers, the attendant muses, "Suppose some wealthy patrons should come in and find a big Negro sitting down there!"[62] The disturbance, beyond the phenotypical difference, is the possible interruption of market relations. The profile of racial blackness at this point stands the furthest from the calculation of modernity with which the narrative ends, the calculation recurring as the hallmark of George Schuyler's fiction. In the scene, racial blackness stands without the libidinal circuit grasped by the renewed cultural forces of the early-twentieth-century modernity and without the circuit of exchange that is the focus of the renewed cultural forces of the early twentieth-century modernity. In the perfume shop, the perspective of Jim Williston discloses racial blackness irrespective of the normative libidinal circuit, and the perspective of the salesman discloses racial blackness as errant to the dominant circuit of exchange in capitalist social relations. The impending domestic union of the socialite and the newspaperman marks a trajectory—through the narrative premise of the unraveling process of detection—that forecloses or overshadows the disclosures of both the detective's and the salesman's perspectives. The detective's interview with Crissina Van Dyke in the next chapter begins to contextualize Prince Destu's activities in Harlem, activities that begin to widen the mystery and diminish the suspicion aimed at her, even though still posing challenges to the domestic paradigm the novel privileges at its conclusion. The specter of miscegenation is diffuse in the narrative, as in most of Schuyler's fiction as well as in the circumstances of the urban landscape of the modern, and provides the motive for the murder of Prince Destu. Through the collaboration of Jim Williston and Roger Bates, the discovery is that Saidi Mattch, an Ethiopian operative who is the associate of Oscar Holcombe, chairman of the "Help Ethiopia League," murders Prince Destu. The outrage is that "Destu was a sensualist . . . [who] permitted himself to get involved with that white woman."[63]

The international, urban, racial, libidinal nexus of the intrigue reports precisely the odd convening terms of early- twentieth-century modernity, and the point is that Schuyler's narrative, like his 1926 essay, does not foremost query the instabilities, restricting forces, or inequities of the convention, as does Hughes's collection of stories and his 1926 essays. The two authors imagine opposing the stakes of the cultural moment, which Josef Jařab codifies in a series of rhetorical questions:

> But was such a program of novel integration, which may have sprung from modern minds in America at the turn of the century, a generally desired and a feasible goal, especially in its larger cultural and, above all, social implications? Was the common awareness comprehensive and deep enough to even register what, for instance, integration in the pluralistic society would really amount to; how such a process would be implemented and realized; and who the actors in its unavoidable drama would be? Obviously, even if the modernist claims of an integrative intent were true and sincere, the social scene was hardly ready at the beginning of the twentieth century, and, in fact, neither were the cultural sensitivity and civic mentality of American society mature enough for such dramatic changes.[64]

In short, the imaginative network of "The Ethiopian Murder Mystery" does not polarize modernity and the psychic—as in the case of modernist aesthetics or modernist cultural critique—but aims to establish the contiguity of the two. "The Ethiopian Murder Mystery" emphasizes the process of the construction of readily coherent meaning, a process yielding, in particular, the substantiation of the domestic scene, on which turns—as in "The Negro-Art Hokum"—the economic mechanisms of the early-twentieth-century modernity as well as the incompletely aligned mechanisms of racial affiliation and disjunction.

Black No More, Schuyler's 1931 novel, acknowledged as the first satiric novel in the African American literary tradition, also fully constitutes and preserves the domestic scene and its implicit elaboration of the libidinal, as the most resolute outcome of the diegesis. Still, insofar as it is driven by the proposition of the primarily illusory division of black and white racial communities, *Black No More* also recapitulates the tenets of "The Negro-Art Hokum." As in the essay, the fundamental proposition of the narrative is the certainty that the racial and cultural distinctions that divide African Americans and the dominant community are finally negligible. The novel imagines the eradication of these seeming differences as a process so formulaic that it is neatly mastered by the principles of science, a figuration or representation of the annihilation of racial difference that, in effect, retraces in elaborate fictional form the vision of the historical-technological progress at the center of the domestic scene exemplary of the cross-racial identity developed in "The Negro-Art Hokum." Both "The Negro-Art Hokum" and *Black*

No More position the question of race as the question of a linear progressive history that does not so much reference the past and its cultural legacies, but imagines those cultural legacies—particularly of the African American past—as made irrelevant by the terms of modern urban life and the exorbitant position of the marketplace in capitalist social relations.

To this end, literary critic Jane Kuenz argues in the article "American Racial Discourse, 1900–1930: Schuyler's *Black No More*": "By recoding racial markers as class signs and showing throughout the novel their structural instability as signs, Schuyler situates both 'blackness' and 'whiteness' in relation to an industrial and market economy increasingly willing and able to manipulate and finally obliterate any semblance of culture, tradition, and individual identity, racial or otherwise, among the people it needs to keep itself going."[65] *Black No More* posits the homogenization of black and white races through a mass-marketed scientific process that transforms Negroid phenotypes into Caucasian phenotypes, the satiric narrative charting the economic and political consequences of the mass transformation through the adventures of the virtually picaresque Max Disher, aka Matthew Fisher. There are burgeoning economic and political consequences, particularly, as the novel indicates, in the South:

> The economic loss to the South by the ethnic migration was considerable. Hundreds of wooden railroad coaches, long since condemned as death traps in all parts of the country, had to be scrapped by the railroads when there were no longer any Negroes to 'Jim Crow.' Thousands of railroad waiting rooms remained unused because, having been set aside for the use of Negroes, they were generally too dingy and unattractive for white folk or were no longer necessary. Thousands of miles of streets located in the former black Belts, and thus without sewers or pavement, were having to be improved at the insistent behest of the rapidly increased white population, real and imitation. Real estate owners who had never dreamed of making repairs on their tumble-down property when it was occupied by the docile Negroes, were having to tear down, rebuild and alter to suit white tenants. Shacks and drygoods boxes that had once sufficed as schools for Negro children, had now to be condemned and abandoned as unsuitable for occupation by white youth. Whereas thousands of school teachers had received thirty and forty dollars a month because of their Negro ancestry, the various cities and countries of the Southland were now forced to pay the standard salaries prevailing elsewhere.[66]

The premise of the plot is that race functions as an easily cipherable quantity and that, given its scientific formulation, the material and interpellative circumstances of the nation are reordered, the transformation "made complete and authoritative with the help of churches, courts, schools, labor unions, newspapers and magazines, social and biological sciences, political and cultural organs, and all the other ideological state apparatuses integral in the erection and maintenance of a really effective oppressive system."[67] The observation is important, because it underscores that Max Disher, aka Matthew Fisher, does not so much enter a racially neutral landscape after his transformation from black to white but, instead, actively participates in forms of white sociality from which he is disbarred formerly, even as he glances with fleeting nostalgia at the forms of African American sociality from which he is removed. After his transfiguration, "[d]espite his happiness, Max found it pretty dull. There was something lacking in these ofay places of amusement or else there was something present that one didn't find in the black-and-tan resorts in Harlem. The joy and abandon here was obviously forced. . . . He felt a momentary pang of mingled disgust, disillusionment and nostalgia."[68] That is, despite the premise of the novel—the ultimately formulaic commensurability of racial blackness and whiteness—Max Disher finds himself situated in radically incommensurate racial communities and atmospheres while, moreover, he finds himself in the situation to exacerbate further the "really effective oppressive system" that defines in part the radically different valences to the racialized positions. As the white Matthew Fisher, Max travels to Georgia, joins the white supremacist organization the Knights of Nordica, fomenting further the negrophobic hatred among "the lower stratum of white working people: Hard-faced, lantern-jawed, dull-eyed adult children, seeking like all humanity for something permanent in the eternal flux of life,"[69] which immediately brings him financial gain, as it does Rev. Henry Givens, the leader of the Knights of Nordica. Race marks a pecuniary cipher "in a society like the United States, where countless generations have made a considerable social, economic, and psychic investment in producing and maintaining racial hierarchies,"[70] which is the central point of ridicule articulated through the science fictional premise of Dr. Crookman's patented process. The first Crookman Sanitarium constructed in Manhattan appears as a symbol of the early twentieth-century modernity and its understood historical progress, the exorbitance of the marketplace, and the formulaic constitution of civic identity available at their conjunction:

> Although it was five o'clock on a Sunday morning, the building was brightly lighted from cellar to roof and the hum of electric motors could be heard, low and powerful. A large electric sign hung from the roof to the second floor. It represented a huge arrow outlined in green with the words BLACK-NO-MORE running its full length vertically. A black face was depicted at the lower end of the arrow while at the top shone a white face to which the arrow was pointed. First would appear the outline of the arrow; then, BLACK-NO-MORE would flash on and off. Following that the black face would appear at the bottom and beginning at the lower end the long arrow with its lettering would appear

> progressively until its tip was reached, when the white face at the top would blazon forth. After that the sign would flash off and on and the process would be repeated.[71]

The image arrays the preeminent themes of the satire—the equivocation of racial specificity, the regularizations of the modernity, the cash nexus—that recur in the descriptions of the materially and politically transformed conditions of the South. As the correspondences suggest, the premise of the novel understands race primarily as a positivist element of the environment, an element of the environment understood in terms of distinct facts and observable phenomena and the objective relations between these phenomena and their physically determining laws. Still, the question of race is never so simple in the narrative, for what is fully constituted and preserved by the conclusion of the narrative is the libidinal domestic order that is the most resolute outcome of Max Disher's sexual imaginary and picaresque agenda. If the ultimate satiric turn of the novel is that the racial valences of black and white are inverted, for at its conclusion the new vogue is the Zulu tan, in reaction to the fact that "the new Caucasians were from two to three shades lighter than the old Caucasians,"[72] then the preceding intrigue is undercut hugely in the revelation of the more than seeming absurdity, in short, the irrational imperative of racial designation failing codification as any scientific or historically progressive formula. However, if the conclusion of the narrative undermines the opening of the narrative and its premise, it does not do so entirely. For the consequential, early appearance in a Manhattan nightclub of Helen Givens, the daughter of Rev. Henry Givens, "as though she had stepped from heaven or the front cover of a magazine,"[73] provides the principal point of cathexis for the two racial incarnations of Max Disher. The narrative, through free indirect discourse, presents the cathexis as Max contemplates undergoing Dr. Crookman's process: "As a white man he could go anywhere, be anything he wanted to be, do most anything he wanted to do, be a free man at last . . . and probably be able to meet the girl from Atlanta. What a vision!"[74] The novel, that is, resolves the heterosexual quandary with which it begins—through the progress of Disher's infatuation, marriage, and domestic procreative union—even as it befuddles the central appeal to the technological formulation of race on which it more elaborately rests. To this end, the first and enduring racial crisis of the novel is Helen Given's preemptory dismissal of Max Disher in the nightclub because he is black, for—insofar as race would appear a positivist matter, fully reconcilable to the modern technological imagination and imperative—it appears so in the service of resolving this dilemma.

In other words, even as the center of the satirical critique is the description of the far-flung economic and psychic chaos produced by the mass transformation of African Americans that makes specification and marginalization of African

Americans increasingly impossible, the constitution of the domestic scene is the most substantial outcome of the events. The proposition of the singularity of racial/national identity through the torsion of the marketplace imagines concomitantly, and as fundamentally, the singularity of libidinal identity, understood as heteronormativity. The complex proposal belies, or supplants, the abundantly evident permutations of civic identity expressed, for example, in the urban routines and rituals of Manhattan. The further irony bears the disavowal of fetishism:

> Although Greenwich Village's gay enclave was the most famous in the city, even most white gay men thought gay life was livelier and more open in Harlem than in the Village. . . . It was easier for white interlopers to be openly gay during their brief visits to Harlem than for the black men who lived there round the clock. But black gay men nonetheless turned Harlem into a homosexual mecca. Denied access to most of the segregated restaurants and speakeasies white gay men patronized elsewhere in New York, they built an extensive gay world in their own community, which in many respects surpassed the Village's in scope, visibility, and boldness. The Village's most flamboyant homosexuals wore long hair; Harlem's wore long dresses. The village had cafes where poets read their verse and drag queens performed; Harlem had speakeasies where men danced together and drag queens were regular costumers. The Village's Liberal Club ball was attended by scores of drag queens and hundreds of spectators; Harlem's Hamilton Lodge ball drew *hundreds* of drag queens and *thousands* of spectators. Among outsiders, Greenwich Village's reputation as a gay mecca eclipsed Harlem's only because it was a white, middle-class world—and because Harlem's singular reputation as a black metropolis took precedence over everything else.[75]

Similarly, Steven Watson in *The Harlem Renaissance: Hub of African American Culture, 1920–1930* explains, "Advertised largely by word of mouth to those 'in the life,' homosexual and lesbian nightlife thrived in Harlem. Greenwich Village and Harlem were the city's main areas for homosexual gatherings."[76] He notes more particularly that the "best known of the homosexual and lesbian hangouts was the Clam House, a long, narrow room on 133rd Street's Jungle Alley, described in *Vanity Fair* as 'a popular house for revelers but not for the innocent young.' Downtown celebrities went on bisexual sprees—among them were Beatrice Lillie, Tallulah Bankhead, Jeanne Eagels, Marilyn Miller, Princess Murat from Paris, and—dressed in matching bowler hats—came chanteuse Libby Holman and her heiress lover Louisa Carpenter du Pont Jenney. The only performer to publicly exploit her lesbian identity was Gladys Bentley, the Clam House's headliner."[77] If the domestic scene, and its tracing of regularized libidinal order, most resolutely records Schuyler's satire and its co-implication of market, sexual, and racial relations, then the provocative disavowal in reporting the exemplary modernity of Manhattan is the burgeoning legibility of what exceeds the domestic scene, the civic and subjective worlds the domestic scene cannot figure resolutely, in which the network of market, sexual, and racial relations do not reflect the ideal singularity of mass cultural approximations.

The figurative importance of the domestic scene recuperates the broad conceptual, legal, and expressive potentials of the early-twentieth-century modernity not simply in the co-implication of market, libidinal, and racial orders but, moreover, their sparing, fetishistic alignment. The critical modernist distance between the racial and aesthetic charters of Schuyler and Hughes remain at this point. For, insofar as the alignment would figure the historical progress and settlement of modernity, the challenge of "The Negro Artist and the Racial Mountain" to the racial and aesthetic schema of "The Negro-Art Hokum" holds as its foremost proposition the racial, cultural, and aesthetic importance of blues and jazz, expressions that brazenly "challenged the gender politics implicit in traditional cultural representations of marriage and heterosexual love relationships. Refusing, in the blues tradition of raw realism, to romanticize relationships, they instead exposed the stereotypes and explored the contradictions of those relationships."[78] The music and civic conventions defining Band Box Club, the Clam House, Edmond's Cellar, Garden of Joy, Hollywood Cabaret, Hot-Cha Bar and Grill, Kaiser's, Leroy's, Manhattan Casino/Rockland Club, One Hundred and One Ranch Club, Pod and Jerry's Catagonia Club, Renaissance Casino and Ballroom, and Savoy Ballroom belie, as their shared premise, the implacability of the social imagination sponsored through the formalized nexus of consumer and mass cultures.

Ultimately, the point of controversy is a historical hermeneutic, as is modernism. The representational value, for instance, of Harlem's "jungle alley"—133rd Street between Lenox and 7th Avenues—and its social insinuations queries, or re-invents, the understood progress of modernity. The starkest cultural meaning of modernity—as the work of anthropologists like Franz Boas, James Frasier, and Bronisław Malinowski directly attest—is as the notion of "civilization" at its most fully developed, an apex meticulously marked out in contrast to its most rudimentary precedents. Modernity, as the vanguard of human and social development, implies "the rise of capitalism, of social study and state regulation, of a belief in progress and productivity leading to mass systems of industry, institutionalization, administration and surveillance,"[79] the circumstances recast obliquely and famously in "jungle alley" and, more generally, Harlem, because of its renowned racial character. Modernity as a progressive paradigm indexing human social development holds adamant racial valences, which makes the issue of urban proximities and systems of circulatory exchange a renewed matter of awareness in the early twentieth century, as put succinctly by Theodore Roosevelt in the essay "On Race": "The problem is so to adjust the relations between two races of different ethnic type that the rights of neither be abridged nor jeopardied [*sic*]; that the backward race be trained so that it may enter into the possession of true freedom, while the forward race is enabled to preserve unharmed the high civilization wrought out by its forefathers."[80] Modernism, a historical hermeneutic, variously queries the terms at which the assured progress has arrived.

Published in 1930, *Not without Laughter* is Hughes's first extended literary offering outside the genre of poetry and maintains the concern with African American vernacular language and life, the ritual importance of dance, and particularly the jazz and blues expressions outlined in "The Negro Artist and the Racial Mountain." Rather than a linear, progressive diegesis of cause and effect—like the premise of detection in "The Ethiopian Murder Mystery" or the escalating picaresque successes of Max Disher in *Black No More*—*Not without Laughter* does not so much strictly align its accumulating narrative events and its central narrative presence Sandy as juxtapose them. The loose, meandering procession of the narrative scores the brooding racial tensions of U.S. life attending the both oppressive and potentially liberating circumstances of the accelerating twentieth-century modernity above all. Thirty chapters trace a movement from the rural to the Northern urban center, from the close quarters of the community dance hall to the spectatorial arrangements of the urban nightclub, from the unrehearsed songs of casual social arrangements to their commodified, commercial renditions. The development of Sandy, the central figure, parallels these progressions, yielding at the same time the primary elaboration of race in the novel as a psychic space, rather than as a positivist quantity, as in the propositions and fiction of Schuyler.

Rather than documenting a series of outcomes following from Sandy's actions, the unfolding events provide foremost the context—material and symbolic—for Sandy's highlighted presence in the text. The initial dramatic action remains as symbolic as it does mimetic. Moreover, the opening action, a violent storm, stands beyond the control or capacities of any of the central characters, particularly Sandy, who remains huddled in the house with his grandmother. The storm generates chaos that is destructive and deadly. Along with the death of white neighbors, whose piano is strewn across the lawn, the home of Aunt Hagar, Sandy's grandmother, the equally symbolic setting for much of the novel, is damaged: "Not a semblance of a porch was left and the front door opened bare into the yard."[81] The central figures and community are overwhelmed by a force initially threatening the primary setting of the action, and ultimately fragmenting it. Literary critic Elizabeth Schultz in "Natural and Unnatural Circumstances in Langston Hughes's *Not without Laughter*" posits that "Hughes perceives nature in his novel as the source of neither transcendental reverie nor Darwinian determinism as European American writers were doing in the 1920s and 1930s. . . . Instead Hughes, recognizing the conventionality and neutrality of nature as imagery and subject matter for middle- and upper-class readers, exploited its rhetorical possibilities for representing complex social concerns."[82] The social concern at issue in the novel is the impress of modernization and its renewed racial order on African American community and identity formations although, significantly, the initial figuration of this violent force is indiscriminate in its destructiveness, for the storm kills "[g]ood white folks, the Gavitts . . . their large frame dwelling lay[ing] on its side like a doll's mansion, with broken furniture strewn careless on the wet lawn . . . a piano flat on its back in the grass."[83]

Foreshadowing the overarching social crisis of the narrative, the symbolic force of the storm registers the destructive capacities of modernization and its attendant, renewed forms of racial subordination, while the accumulating report of the several succeeding chapters—"Conversation," "Jimboy's Letter," "Thursday Afternoon," "Guitar," "Work," and "White Folks"—outlines countervailing narrative imperatives that are detailed through the interactions of Sandy's family as well as Sandy's perspective as participant-observer. The countervailing forces of African American sociality—the casual exchange over the meal with a neighbor, the return of Jimboy's itinerant father, the recurrent singing and dancing around the house and the yard, the cathartic recollection and retelling of white racist violence and customs—culminate in the eighth chapter, "Dance," in the infective enthusiasms of "[f]our homeless, plug-ugly niggers . . . playing mean old loveless blues in a hot, crowded little dance-hall in a Kansas town on Friday night. Playing the heart out of loneliness with a wide-mouth leader, who sang everybody's troubles until they became his own."[84] That is, whereas the expository prose and fiction of Schuyler posits the virtually seamless coincidence of African American culture and the formalities of the ascendant consumerist interpellation of the early twentieth century, *Not without Laughter* highlights African American vernacular practice without the ideal confirmations of the dominant culture, for the force that the marketplace bears in these early chapters (and ultimately throughout the novel) is as the principal point of the rupture of community, as borne out clearly in the chapter "White Folks" in Sister Johnson's narration of the mass exodus of African Americans from "a Mississippi town near Vicksburg,"[85] the mass exodus that brings her to the Kansas neighborhood. The racist violence that causes the mass migration begins: "wid de whites talkin' an' de coloreds doin' better'n better year by year, sellin' mo' cotton ever' dayan' gittin' nice furniture an' buyin' pianers, till by an' by a pros'rous nigger name John Lowdins up an' bought one o' dese here new automobiles—an' dat settled it!"[86] The novel begins with the symbolism of the destructive force of the natural world that shortly is matched by the material violence of racial subordination that brokers access to participation in the national community as understood as participation in the ascendant consumerist marketplace. Moreover, if the opening chapter primarily draws the psychic space of the overwhelmed Sandy in reaction to the storm, then so too does the white racist violence sketched in succession in "White folks" by Sister Johnson's recollection, Jimboy's commentary, and Harriet's passionate invectives: "'White folks run the world, and the only thing colored folks are expected to do is work and grin and take off their hats as though it don't matter. . . . O, I hate them!' Harriet cried, so fiercely that Sandy was afraid."[87]

The initial symbolic force of the storm, recapitulated in the racial animus of the white community, is recapitulated still as a psychic force through the perspective of Sandy. The chapters begin to form, then, an associational pattern that draws out the narrative as opposed to a positivist causal network of events. In this way, there is an immediate significance to the gainsaying abandon of Sandy's clandestine visit to the dance hall, where "the piano was the water flowing, and the high, thin chords of the banjo were the mountains floating in the clouds. But in sultry tones, alone and always, the brass comet spoke harshly about the earth."[88] The psychic space drawn in the chapter that is also drawn as a communal space and that is also presented as a naturalized space remains in stark contrast to the destructive forces opening the narrative.

Throughout, twentieth-century modernity—leveraged otherwise in the writings of Schuyler—imperils the conventions of this cultural space that is finally most fully associated with Sandy's Aunt Harriet. Stated differently, just as it is symbolized concomitantly in the destructive force of the storm that opens the narrative, the temporality fundamental to the concept of modernity is gauged through the cultural disposition of this space, the prolix spontaneity of community shared in abandon. The novel ends in Chicago with Sandy and his mother witnessing, no longer in Hagar's yard but "at the Monograph Theatre on State Street,"[89] Harriett's transformation into "Princess of the Blues": "She swayed towards the footlights, while Billy teased the keys of the piano into a hesitating delicate jazz. Then she began to croon a new song—a popular version of an old Negro melody, refashioned with words from Broadway."[90] The urbanization, the commercialization, and the mass cultural re-codings that outline the temporal movement of modernity provide the terms that convey Harriett's transformation so that, from Sandy's highlighted perspective, the cognate of the temporal movement of modernization is the reformation of African American social forms in uneasy, insinuating alignment with the "shift in geography [that] spelled a shift in occupation."[91] Cultural critic Ann Douglass in *Terrible*

Honesty: Mongrel Manhattan in the 1920s observes: "In 1890, 63 percent of black men were employed in agriculture, forestry, and fishing; only 7 percent were in manufacturing and mechanical pursuits. By 1930, however, the number of black men in agriculture was down to 42 percent, while the number employed in industry went up to 25 percent, and the trend continued apace, after the interruption of the Depression, in the 1940s and 1950s."[92] Insofar as it sets African Americans within modern industrial society and its rhythms of citizenship, the historical movement amounts to a geographic resettling that does not render stark geographic synonymity but, rather, complex orchestrated curtailments of the hegemonic strategies of social order as the hallmark of African American social expressions.

Whereas in Schuyler's prose and fiction the incessantly progressive temporality of the modern is consolidating, the same historical impress in *Not without Laughter* is more fraught, and again the figure of the domestic household bears the difference. The primary domestic site in the novel, the house of Sandy's grandmother Aunt Hagar, is damaged by the opening action, the porch wrenched from the rest of the structure. Similarly, each of Hagar's three daughters pursues separate libidinal designs, which uphold or betray more or less the protocols animating "the assumption . . . that the social and psychological can be brought into productive alignment"[93] through the monopolistic, interpellative appeal of the domestic scene. The last daughter introduced in the narrative, Tempy, once a maid, is left a small house in the will of her employer and "had managed to buy another house, too. When Mr. Siles asked her to be his wife, everybody said it was a fine match, for both owned property, both were old enough to know what they wanted, and both were eminently respectable. . . . Now they prospered together."[94] Annjee, Sandy's mother, is married to Jimboy, "a traveling man—and she, Annjee, was too meek and quiet, that's what she was—too stay-at-homish. Never going nowhere, never saying nothing back to those who scolded her or talked about her, not even sassing white folks when they got beside themselves."[95] Harriett is associated with precincts that cannot be recharted readily within the limitations and normative appeals of the domestic scene:

> At night in the Bottoms victrolas moaned and banjos cried ecstatically in the darkness. Summer evenings little yellow and brown and black girls in pink or blue bungalow aprons laughed invitingly in doorways, and dice rattled with the staccato gaiety of jazz music on a long table in the rear rooms. Pimps played pool; bootleggers lounged in big red cars; children ran in the streets until midnight, with no voice of parental authority forcing them to an early sleep; young blacks fought like cocks and enjoyed it; white boys walked through the streets winking at colored girls; men came in autos; old women ate pigs' feet and watermelon and drank beer; whisky flowed; gin was like

> water; soft indolent laughter didn't care about anything; and deep nigger-throated voices that had long ago stopped rebelling against the ways of this world rose in song.[96]

The disagreement between "The Negro Artist and the Racial Mountain" and "The Negro-Art Hokum" registered through the figure of the domestic household is recast in the cultural mosaic of Aunt Hagar's daughters. Hughes emphasizes again the temporal movement of modernity in the issue. Each of Hagar's daughters represents a different inclination toward the increased material and imaginative proximities of the early-twentieth-century modernity brokered through the marketplace, the temporal movement in which "as significant as the black migration was, its major impact, particularly in terms of how it affected the racial or ethnic mix of a community, was on northern cities and not on the South."[97] Sandy remains the primary witness in the novel to the ultimately historical phenomenon. The aspect of history is the crux of the disagreement between "The Negro Artist and the Racial Mountain" and "The Negro-Art Hokum," in the same way the aspect of history bears centrally on the relation between modernity and modernism. The work of Schuyler aligns exposition and narration with temporality understood as the ontological order—the order of being—progressing further and implacably in the service of apparent rational absolutes: the marketplace, the libidinal ideal of bourgeois domesticity, technological development, the calculation of identity that mirrors the certainty of cartographical precincts, and their mutually reinforcing resolutions. The work of Hughes draws exposition and narration through temporality understood as a much less seamless or implacable linearity, not so much a resolute progress as a forceful and contingent determination never absolute in its power, trajectory, or ideal order of being.

The differing aspect of history in these two formulations is critical, precisely in the sense of the relation that modernism holds to modernity, which is to say, in enunciating—as phrased by Malcolm Cowley in *Exile's Return*—that "[l]ife in this country is joyless and colorless, universally standardized, tawdry, uncreative, given over to the worship of wealth and machinery."[98] Schuyler's essay and fiction champion the hegemonic tenor of the civic order that modernism critiques, and Hughes's essay and fiction provides the modernist critique in terms of African American vernacular conventions, the conventions spawning the precincts of "jungle alley" in Manhattan—interstitial cartographies in the implacable progressive "search for a rational, scientifically ordered universe . . . [inimical to] the notion of a distinctively African-American art aesthetic."[99] That is, modernism represents an aesthetics of historical challenge and, as Hughes would have it, African American vernacular culture performs an aesthetics of historical challenge. The representational and historical critique of modernism and African American vernacular culture, according to Hughes, amounts to pursuing human relations and knowledge beyond the exorbitance of the advertised rational absolutes of modernity.

The racial, as the patent sign of civic or psychic disturbance, appears only rarely in the narrative, unlike in *The Ways of White Folk*. In "The Ethiopian Murder Mystery" Schuyler bears witness to the possibilities of consumer and mass culture and their technological supports that the reader ultimately witnesses. The modernist agenda of the early twentieth century is more aligned with the finally socially deleterious disturbances that Hughes pursues. For, if a significant element of the startling disorientation of the modern moment of the early twentieth century remains the new terms of proximity defining the meeting or re-convergence of diverse populations, then matters of both sexuality and history are of prime importance, matters that Hughes highlights.

Poet Helene Johnson captures in a series of swift images some of the speculative disturbances at stake in the debate in the poem "Sonnet to A Negro in Harlem":

> You are disdainful and magnificent—
> Your perfect body and your pompous gait,
> Your dark eyes flashing solemnly hate,
> Small wonder that you are incompetent
> To imitate those whom you so despise—
> Your shoulders towering high above the throng
> Your head thrown back in rich, barbaric song
> Palm trees and mangoes stretched before your eyes.
> Let others toil and sweat for labor's sake
> And wring from grasping hand their mead of gold.
> Why urge ahead your supercilious feet?
> Scorn will efface each footprint that you make.*

* The manuscript of this chapter ends with this quotation of Helene Johnson's sonnet (which can be found in, inter alia, Nina Miller, *Making Love Modern: The Intimate Public Worlds of New York's Literary Women* (New York: Oxford University Press, 1998), 237. We have no way of knowing if Barrett intended to continue his argument in this chapter or perhaps had planned other chapters to discuss other responses by the writers of the Harlem Renaissance to the broader social, economic, and racial issues raised in this chapter on George Schulyer and Langston Hughes. It would make sense, according to the rhetorical organization of the previous chapters, that Barrett would turn to African American women writers from the Harlem Renaissance, such as Gwendolyn Bennett (1902–1981), just as he turned in previous chapters to Harriet Jacobs and other nineteenth-century African American women writers for their contributions to the fugitive slave narrative. As indicated in the prefatory note to this chapter, it is not even entirely certain that this chapter was in fact intended to be part of this book manuscript, even though its themes and focal subjects—Schuyler and Hughes—seem entirely in keeping with Barrett's intention to carry his argument into the Harlem Renaissance, perhaps even beyond it to our contemporary moment.

Epilogue

I first met Lindon Barrett some years ago when he was a young assistant professor at UC Irvine and I (Dwight McBride) was an even younger graduate student at UCLA. He was teaching a graduate seminar at UCLA, and we had been introduced to one another by mutual friends and colleagues. Lindon was, in a word, brilliant. He had a quality of mind one scarcely finds inside or outside of the academy. His was an expansive intellect interested in everything from basketball and music to the finer points of the western philosophical tradition and poststructuralist theory. The sharpness and laser focus of his analyses of texts, popular culture, and everyday life experiences were without peer. Conversations with Lindon had a narcotic quality; they always drew you in, made you think before you realized you were doing so. Those who knew him well appreciate what a gift he so generously dispensed in the form of his naturally unbridled curiosity. Encounters with Lindon made you want to think harder and be better. But such a statement alone doesn't come close to capturing the full measure of the man.

Lindon was also kind, gentle, generous in the extreme, and immensely approachable. He was the kind of person who somehow made it easier to exhale when you were in his presence. What I remember most about first meeting Lindon was asking him what I should call him—Professor Barrett? Dr. Barrett? To which he replied, "Oh baby just call me 'Thing.' 'Miss Thing' if you're feeling formal." And with that beautifully playful turn of phrase our many years of friendship were launched. I could scarcely have imagined then the circumstances that would occasion my involvement in the posthumous publication of this book. Indeed, it still remains painful for me to recall just how we got here.

As John Carlos Rowe notes in the introduction to this volume, Lindon Barrett's untimely death left many a void in the lives of his friends, colleagues, and family. One particular lacuna, the extant versions of his latest book in progress, we have been honored, and humbled, to see into print. The completion of any book manuscript is a daunting task, but this one was made more daunting still by a variety of logistical hurdles. After Winston James's phenomenal work of collecting materials, and John Carlos Rowe's herculean task of arranging these into a manuscript, it was our duty to make them into a book.

First, the materials—which arrived as printed copy—had to be retyped into an electronic format. Secondly, after much deliberation about releasing this work as a collection of essays, we decided that the best way to honor Lindon would be to make the materials at hand cohere as a monograph: that is, to shape Lindon's impressive research trajectory and nuanced writing style into a clear, cogent argument. The work you have before you represents that effort: checking citations and inspecting references, creating an index, explaining connections, and, in some instances, filling gaps. In every place where changes were made to the manuscript beyond simple copyediting, we have noted our work so as to distinguish it from Lindon's own writing. Any remaining errors or omissions fall upon us as editors; the groundbreaking research and inspiring arguments, however, rest solely with Lindon.

The publication of a posthumous manuscript is always about more than the book at hand. In the case of an author long since passed, there is the excitement of the discovery of new material, the invigorating promise of new insights, and the joy that comes with the renewal of a cherished conversation since grown stale. In the case of an author whose untimely death has left a void in the hearts and minds of his contemporaries, the contents of the book are uniquely framed by emotional forces: fond remembrance of a life now lost; mourning for the loss of a colleague, mentor, friend, and family member; and forfeiture of the possibility of more groundbreaking thought from a probing intellect, challenging writer, gifted scholar, and inspiring teacher. In the case of *Racial Blackness and the Discontinuity of Western Modernity*, the publication of this important volume comes also with an unsettling lack of closure coupled with an ominous foreboding about the intrinsic loneliness that may be constitutive of the lives of black gay intellectuals.

The lack of closure is perhaps easier to explain, if not to understand completely. In July 2008 Lindon Barrett was found dead in his Long Beach apartment; subsequent autopsy results indicate that he was strangled. Following the lead of Barrett's stolen car, police apprehended Marlon Martinez as a suspect in the murder. While awaiting trial in the Los Angeles County Men's Central Jail, just weeks before his trial was to begin, Martinez was found dead in his cell on Christmas Day 2009. Any inmate's death is suspicious, but Martinez's even more so; though autopsy reports indicate he died of an accidental heroin overdose, Martinez allegedly feared retaliation from Los Angeles Sheriff's Department deputies because he had witnessed the beating of another prisoner. Both men dead, we will never know why Lindon was killed nor, though it seems clear they knew each other, the exact nature of the relationship between Lindon and Martinez.

What we do know, however, is that Lindon's death was extraordinarily similar to several other murders of prominent gay black intellectuals in recent years. In 2004, Curt Blackman, a graduate coordinator for recruitment and minority programs at Duke University (who himself had just been admitted to a PhD program at Northwestern University), was brutally murdered by Thomas Anthony Pitt. Don Belton, an openly gay, black assistant professor of English at Indiana University Bloomington, was stabbed to death in December 2009 by Michael J. Griffen. Bennett Bradley, an award-winning director who staged challenging and sometimes controversial productions at Hollywood's Fountain Theatre, was killed in January 2010 by Jose Fructuoso. Blackman, Belton, and Bradley were, like Barrett, killed by men several years their junior, men with whom they had a previous relationship. Speculation about the nature of these relationships has run rampant, but what is clear is that each of these men was slain by much younger men, men whose crimes were motivated by sexual fear.

This shocking rash of strikingly similar murders raises more questions than simply the motivation of the assailants. In particular, one is called to wonder at the loneliness that may have led established intellectual black men to pursue relationships with men so much younger. Far from a prescriptive commentary on whom one should or shouldn't love, we raise this question to ponder not only the profound homophobia of American society, which frames the lives and choices of the young male perpetrators, but also the isolation of the gay black intellectuals targeted as victims. Alienated from gay communities by their race, ostracized from communities of color by both their sexual orientation and scholarly aspirations, men and women who juggle the admixture of race, sex, and class distinctions in their most poignant and complex intersections are often estranged from the very communities others frequently draw upon as sources of solace, courage, and creativity.

Lindon ignited the fires of a generation of African American scholars as he carried the mantle of a tradition of black intellectual engagement. As this book goes forth to honor his contributions, we can only hope that his writings and teaching may foster greater, more inclusive communities of love and inspiration.

Justin A. Joyce & Dwight A. McBride
Evanston, Illinois

Notes

Chapter 1. The Conceptual Impossibility of Racial Blackness: History, the Commodity, and Diasporic Modernity

1. Foucault, *Archaeology of Knowledge*, 8.
2. Rodney, *History of the Upper Guinea Coast*, 121.
3. Butchart, *Anatomy of Power*, ix.
4. Ibid.
5. Ibid., 42, 55.
6. Barker, *Tremulous Private Body*, 10.
7. Stoler, *Race and the Education of Desire*, 9.
8. Butchart, *Anatomy of Power*, 17.
9. Ibid.
10. Romero, *Homefronts*, 39.
11. Mbembe, "Necropolitics," 23.
12. Ibid., 17 (emphasis in original).
13. Crouzet, *History of the European Economy*, 53.
14. Eltis, "Europeans," 1400.
15. Ibid., 1405.
16. Ibid., 1401.
17. Ibid., 1404.
18. Ibid., 1411.
19. Ibid., 1422.
20. Ibid., 1423. The torque and quandary are reckonable, to follow the arguments of historian William Piersen, as a type of aesthetic transaction in which "certain black and white

designs can be made to contain two vastly different pictures, the observed pattern depending upon which color our mind perceives at a particular moment to be dominant. . . . What would happen if we shifted our normal perspective so as to make our nation's black legacy a primary point of reference? Just as in the visual image, the patterns of American history would instantly seem to reverse themselves. Such a process would not change the history, but it would offer a flash of Afrocentric insight—how changed the world could be if only we thought differently about things, at least for a moment" (*Black Legacy*, ix).

21. Morgan, *American Slavery, American Freedom*, 381.
22. Eltis, "Europeans," 1423.
23. Gemery and Hogendorn, "Economic Costs, 143–61.
24. Blackburn, *Making of New World Slavery*, 384.
25. Rodney, *History of the Upper Guinea Coast*, 259.
26. Lovejoy, *Transformations in Slavery*, 57.
27. Ibid., 46.
28. Ibid., 68.
29. Ibid., 66.
30. Ibid.
31. Gemery and Hogendorn, "Economic Costs," 161.
32. Amariglio and Callari, "Marxian Value Theory," 188.
33. Ibid., 215.
34. Ibid., 186.
35. Appleby, *Capitalism and a New Social Order*, 47.
36. Robinson, *Black Marxism*, 4.
37. Ibid., 3.
38. Ibid., 164.
39. Ralph Davis, *Rise of the Atlantic Economies*, 6.
40. Thomas, *Slave Trade*, 60.
41. Ibid., 70.
42. Ibid., 68.
43. Ibid., 71.
44. Mintz, *Sweetness and Power*, 24.
45. Ibid., 36.
46. Dunn, *Sugar and Slaves*, 19.
47. Ibid., 46.
48. Mintz, *Sweetness and Power*, 32.
49. Thomas, *Slave Trade*, 76.
50. Ibid., 77.
51. Knight, *Caribbean*, 37.
52. Thomas, *Slave Trade*, 91.
53. Blackburn, *Making of New World Slavery*, 132 (emphasis in original).
54. Thomas, *Slave Trade*, 98.
55. Ralph Davis, *Rise of the Atlantic Economies*, 63.
56. Knight, *Caribbean*, 63.

57. Thomas, *Slave Trade,* 99.
58. Mintz, *Sweetness and Power,* 155.
59. Thomas, *Slave Trade,* 114.
60. Ibid., 135.
61. Davis, *Rise,* 90.
62. Thomas, *Slave Trade,* 159.
63. Israel, *Dutch Republic,* 313.
64. Ibid., 727.
65. Emmer, "Second Atlantic System," 95: "The international importance of the Dutch in the creation and operation of the Atlantic economy sharply contrasted with the modest Dutch share in the production of Atlantic cash crops, as well as with the negative returns on Dutch plantation investments."
66. Knight, *Caribbean,* 53.
67. Mintz, *Sweetness and Power,* 114.
68. Eltis, *Rise of African Slavery,* 118.
69. Dunn, *Sugar and Slaves,* 35.
70. Thomas, *Slave Trade,* 205.
71. Ibid., 206.
72. Blackburn, *Making of New World Slavery,* 438.
73. Dunn, *Sugar and Slaves,* 205
74. Robin Blackburn notes further: "The pre-eminence of French plantation produce in European markets reflected not only the productivity of the French Colonies but also the comparatively small size of the French internal market. Thus France, with two or three times the population of Britain, consumed only half as much sugar. It also signaled the success of French merchants in dominating the European market for luxury products of all types" (*Making of New World Slavery,* 445).
75. Ibid., 433.
76. Thomas, *Slave Trade,* 254–55.
77. Stinchcombe, *Sugar Island Slavery,* 182.
78. Greene, *Pursuits of Happiness,* 44.
79. Davis, *Rise of the Atlantic Economies,* 286.
80. Mintz, *Sweetness and Power,* 143. Mintz continues: "The important feature of those triangles is that human cargoes figured vitally in their operation. It was not just that sugar, rum, and molasses were not being traded directly for European finished goods; in both transatlantic triangles the only 'false commodity'—yet absolutely essential to the system—was human beings. Slaves were a 'false commodity' because a human being is not an object, even when treated as one. In this instance, millions of human beings were treated as commodities. To obtain them, products were shipped to Africa; by their labor power, wealth was created in the Americas. The wealth they created mostly returned to Britain; the products they made were consumed in Britain; and the products made by Britons—cloth, tools, torture instruments—were consumed by slaves who were themselves consumed in the creation of wealth" (43).
81. Connor, "Nation Is a Nation," 379–88.

82. Renan, "*Qu'est qu'une nation?*" 26.
83. Ibid., 29.
84. Strange, *Retreat of the State*, 17.
85. Eltis, "Europeans," 1399.
86. Amariglio and Callari, "Marxian Value Theory," 215.
87. López-Alves, *State Formation and Democracy*.
88. Brewer, *Sinews of Power*, 169.
89. Blackburn, *Making of New World Slavery*, 483.
90. Cayton, "Radicals in the 'Western World,'" 78.
91. Gailey, *History of Africa*, 119.
92. Appleby, "Republicanism in Old and New Contexts," 32.
93. Wood, *Black Majority*, xiii.
94. Shalhope, "Republicanism and Early American Historiography," 334.
95. Ibid., 345.
96. Ibid., 354.
97. Appleby, "Republicanism in Old and New Contexts," 31.
98. Breen, "'Baubles of Britain,'" 75.
99. Ibid., 74.
100. Beard, *Economic Interpretation*, 100.
101. Ben-Atar, "Introduction," 59–60.
102. Banning, *Citizens of the World*, 2.
103. Jennings, *Creation of America*, 8.
104. Sloan, "Hamilton's Second Thoughts," 67.
105. Ferguson, "Nationalists," 242.
106. Ferguson, "Political Economy," 389.
107. Ibid., 390.
108. Ibid., 391.
109. Ferguson, "Nationalists," 244.
110. Ferguson, "Political Economy," 411.
111. Appleby, "Repubicanism in Old and New Contexts," 31.
112. Jay, *The Federalist*, 38.
113. Smith, *Civic Ideals*, 23.
114. Jay, *The Federalist*, 38.
115. Ibid.
116. Bailyn, *Peopling of British North America*, 9 (emphasis in original).
117. Berkin, "Ethnicity."
118. Dull, *Diplomatic History*, 157.
119. Rakove, "From One Agenda to Another," 102.
120. Hobson, "Negative on State Laws," 215.
121. Ibid., 216.
122. Beard, *Economic Interpretation*, 87.
123. Madison, *Notes*, 91.
124. Hobson, "Negative on State Laws," 233.

125. Casey, "Limits of Equality," 43.
126. Alexander Hamilton, "Number XXXV," *The Federalist*, 169.
127. Hobson, "The Negative on State Laws," 222.
128. Banning, "Citizens of the World," 171.
129. Banning, "Republican Ideology," 187.
130. Ibid., 180.
131. Hobson, "Negative on State Laws," 234–35.
132. Howard A. Ohline, "Slavery," 335–36.
133. Ibid., 336.
134. Ibid., 357.
135. Ferguson, "Nationalists," 245.
136. Ibid., 246.
137. Ohline, "Slavery," 359.
138. Morrison, *Beloved*, 275.

Chapter 2. Making the Flesh Word: Binomial Being and Representational Presence

1. Davis, *Rise of the Atlantic Economies*, 134–35.
2. Davis, *Problem of Slavery*, 13.
3. Bolster, *Black Tacks*, vii–viii.
4. Ibid., 114.
5. Ibid., 103.
6. Ibid., 39.
7. Ibid., 100.
8. Wood, *Blind Memory*, 22.
9. Gusdorf, "Conditions and Limits," 28–29.
10. Folkenflik, *Culture of Autobiography*, 1 (emphasis in original).
11. Ibid., 5.
12. Weintraub, *Value of the Individual*, xvii.
13. Gusdorf, "Conditions and Limits," 29.
14. Chakrabarty, "Provincializing Europe," 345 (emphasis in original).
15. Ibid., 351.
16. Carretta, "Olaudah Equiano or Gustavus Vassa?" 104.
17. Ibid., 98.
18. Douglas and Ney, *Missing Persons*, 5.
19. Chakrabarty, "Provincializing Europe," 351.
20. Macpherson, *Political Theory*, 126.
21. Smith, *Self-Discovery*, 15.
22. Equiano, *Interesting Narrative*, 46.
23. Ibid., 47.
24. Ibid.
25. Ibid., 49.

26. Ibid., 50.
27. Ibid., 51.
28. Chakrabarty, "Provincializing Europe," 351.
29. Carretta, "Olaudah Equiano or Gustauvus Vassa?" 104.
30. Gusdorf, "Conditions and Limits," 43 (emphasis in original).
31. Foster, *Written by Herself*, 59.
32. Costanzo, *Surprising Narrative*, 52.
33. Equiano, *Interesting Narrative*, 79 (emphasis in original).
34. Ibid., 48.
35. Ibid., 67–68.
36. Ibid., 73.
37. Ibid., 155.
38. Spillers, *Black, White, and in Color*, 441.
39. Equiano, *Interesting Narrative*, 157.
40. Ibid., 69–70.
41. McBride, *Impossible Witnesses*, 120.
42. Park, *Travels*, 6.
43. Gates, *Signifying Monkey*, 130.
44. Ibid., 131.
45. Equiano, *Interesting Narrative*, 83.
46. Park, *Travels*, 6.
47. Ibid., 67.
48. Ibid., 68.
49. Ibid., 2 (emphasis in original).
50. Ibid., 68.
51. Ibid.
52. Ibid., 304.
53. Equiano, *Interesting Narrative*, 76.
54. Park, *Travels*, 306.
55. Gusdorf, "Conditions and Limits," 31.
56. Ibid., 42 (emphasis in original).
57. Weintraub, *Value of the Individual*, xi.
58. Chandler, "Moving Accidents," 141.
59. Smith, *Wealth of Nations*, 307.
60. Ibid., 390.
61. Ibid., emphasis added.
62. Smith, *Subjectivity, Identity, and the Body*, 8–9.
63. Lejeune, *On Autobiography*, 161–62.
64. Macpherson, *Political Theory*, 3.
65. Verger, *Men of Learning*, 66–67.
66. Hudson, *Writing and European Thought*, 5.
67. Chartier, *Order of Books*, 36.
68. Martin, *History and Power of Writing*, 343.

69. Johns, *Nature of the Book*, 35.
70. Ibid., 46.
71. Steele, "Money Economy," 486.
72. Gusdorf, "Conditions and Limits," 29.
73. Wallerstein, *Historical Capitalism*, 18.
74. Blackburn, *Making of New World Slavery*, 270.
75. Perelman, *Invention of Capitalism*, 9.
76. Ibid., 81.
77. Habermas, *Structural Transformation*, 77.
78. Eakin, *How Our Lives Become Stories*, 100.
79. Olney, *Autobiography*, 6.
80. Buck, "Reading Autobiography," 478.

Chapter 3. Captivity, Desire, Trade: The Forging of National Form

1. Hartman, *Scenes of Subjection*, 115.
2. Mills, *Blackness Visible*, 7.
3. Renault, *Era of the Individual*, xxvii–xxviii.
4. Hegel, *Philosophy of History*, 93.
5. Ibid., 87.
6. Ibid., 14.
7. Ibid., 19.
8. Ibid., 53.
9. Ibid., 99.
10. Ibid., 56.
11. Ibid., 79 (emphasis in original).
12. Ibid., 80.
13. Ibid., 91.
14. Ibid., 104.
15. Ibid., 96.
16. Ibid., 93.
17. Ibid., 104.
18. Ibid.
19. Ibid., 101.
20. Ibid., 63–64 (emphasis in original).
21. Ibid., 292–93.
22. Ibid., 112.
23. Ibid., 120 (emphasis in original).
24. Ibid., 140.
25. Ibid., 144.
26. Ibid., 147.
27. Ibid., 167.

28. Ibid., 174.
29. Ibid., 192.
30. Ibid., 215 (emphasis in original).
31. Ibid., 250.
32. Ibid., 265, 267.
33. Ibid., 279 (emphasis in original).
34. Ibid., 281.
35. Ibid., 289.
36. Ibid., 315.
37. Ibid., 320 (emphasis in original).
38. Ibid., 325, 331.
39. Ibid., 399.
40. Ibid., 416.
41. Ibid., 422.
42. Ibid., 446.
43. Ibid., 207.
44. Ibid., 428.
45. Hegel, *Philosophy*, 14.
46. Mills, *Racial Contract*, 19 (emphasis in original).
47. Robin Blackburn, *Making of New World Slavery*, 3.
48. Hegel, *Philosophy*, 346.
49. Ibid., 84.
50. Ibid., 9.
51. Zerubavel, *Terra Cognita*, 118.
52. Eltis, *Rise of African Slavery*, 136.
53. Hegel, *Philosophy*, 15–16.
54. Northrup, *Africa's Discovery of Europe*, 6.
55. Buck-Morss, "Hegel and Haiti," 842.
56. Ibid., 843.
57. Ibid., 846.
58. Ibid., 821.
59. Ibid., 835.
60. Ibid., 844.
61. Hegel, *Philosophy*, 59.
62. Ibid., 61 (emphasis in original).
63. Ibid., 75–76.
64. Ibid., 47, 39.
65. Ibid., 192.
66. Hartman, *Scenes of Subjection*, 5.
67. Equiano, *Interesting Narrative*, 97.
68. Scarry, *Body in Pain*, 22.
69. Hartman, *Scenes of Subjection*, 20.
70. Starling, *Slave Narrative*, 106.

71. Foster, *Witnessing Slavery*, 52.
72. Andrews, "Representation of Slavery," 82.
73. Kawash, *Dislocating the Color Line*, 47.
74. Ibid., 50.
75. Ibid., 80.
76. See the final third of chapter 1.
77. Ohline, "Slaver," 335–60.
78. Kawash, *Dislocating the Color Line*, 48.
79. Ibid., 56.
80. William H. Freehling, *Road to Disunion*, 138.
81. Onuf, *Statehood and Union*, 64.
82. Hartman, *Scenes of Subjection*, 123.
83. Foner, *Nothing but Freedom*, 61.
84. Lowance, *House Divided*, 27.
85. Ibid.
86. Ibid., 28.
87. Ibid., 26.
88. Fehrenbacher, *Slaveholding Republic*, 208.
89. Ibid., 217.
90. Ibid., 232.
91. Hartman, *Scenes of Subjection*, 123.
92. Hancock, *Citizens of the World*, 15.
93. Harms, *Diligent*, 5.
94. Hancock, *Citizens of the World*, 16.
95. Miller, *Arguing about Slavery*, 9.
96. DeVoto, *Year of Decision*, 12.
97. Freehling, *Road to Disunion*, 458.
98. Ibid., 489.
99. Hancock, *Citizens of the World*, 15.
100. Cover, *Justice Accused*, 187.
101. Fehrenbacher, *Slaveholding Republic*, 273.
102. Freehling, *Road to Disunion*, 559–60.
103. Finkelman, *Dred v. Sandford*, 10.
104. Fehrenbacher, *Dred Scott Case*, 352.
105. Ibid., 540.
106. Grimes, "Life of William Grimes," 120.
107. Graff, *Legacies of Literacy*, 4.
108. Starling, *Slave Narrative*, 106.
109. Banning, *Citizens of the World*, 37.
110. Ibid., 81.
111. Holt, "Marking," 14.
112. Starling, *Slave Narrative*, 106; Holt, "Marking," 10.
113. Bruce, *Origins of African American Literature*, 218.

114. Blassingame, *Slave Testimony*, 687.
115. Ibid., 589.
116. Ibid., 687.
117. Ibid.
118. Samuel Sewall, "The Selling of Joseph: A Memorial" (Boston, 1700), 1. Available online through Early American Imprints.
119. Ibid., 2.
120. Saffin, reprinted in Lowance, *House Divided*, 14–15.
121. Zilversmit, *First Emancipation*, 66.
122. Ibid., 70.
123. Ibid., 78–79.
124. Ibid., 86.
125. Ibid., 200.
126. Walker, *Appeal*, 1.
127. Tise, *Proslavery*, 52.
128. Rachleff, "David Walker's Southern Agent," 100.
129. Crockett, "Incendiary Pamphlet," 309.
130. Ibid.
131. Ibid., 311.
132. Ibid., 313.
133. Ellis and Wildavsky, "Cultural Analysis," 102.
134. Van Deburg, "William Lloyd Garrison," 224.
135. Ibid., 230.
136. Ibid.
137. Cain, *William Lloyd Garrison*, 106.
138. Stewart, "Modernizing 'Difference,'" 708.
139. Ibid., 702.
140. Ibid., 693.
141. Ibid., 698.
142. Ibid., 700.
143. Stewart, "Emergence of Racial Modernity," 181–217.
144. Brooks, "Massachusetts Anti-slavery Society," 312.
145. Wyatt-Brown, "Abolitionists' Postal Campaign," 227–28.
146. Ibid., 220.
147. Ibid., 227.
148. Ibid., 231.
149. Van Deburg, "William Lloyd Garrison," 224.
150. Ibid., 230.
151. Ibid., 231.
152. Ibid.
153. Pickard, "John Greenleaf Whittier," 250.
154. Ibid., 251.
155. Ibid.
156. Ibid.

157. Maynard, "World's Anti-Slavery Convention," 452.
158. Ibid.
159. Ibid., 457.
160. Cover, *Justice Accused*, 84.
161. Nogee, "Prigg Case," 185.
162. Ibid., 189.
163. Brophy, "Let Us Go Back," 203.
164. Ibid., 197.
165. Miller, *Arguing about Slavery*, 103.
166. Ibid., 27.
167. Ibid., 98.
168. Omi and Winant, *Racial Formation*, 72.
169. Hardt, "Withering of Civil Society," 27.
170. Gougeon, "Emerson and Abolition," 562.
171. Ibid., 567.
172. Ibid., 561.
173. Ibid., 564.
174. Ibid., 574.
175. Emerson, *Selected Writings*, 132.
176. Ibid., 145.
177. Ibid., 152.
178. Rowe, *At Emerson's Tomb*, 21.
179. Gougeon, "Abolition, the Emersons," 346.
180. Belasco, "'Animating Influences of Discord,'" 91.
181. Neocleous, "From Civil Society to the Social," 396.
182. Kumar, "Civil Society," 378.
183. Neocleous, "From Civil Society to the Social," 396.
184. Ibid., 397.
185. Smith, *Civic Ideals*, 15.
186. Ibid.
187. Hardt, "Withering of Civil Society," 29.
188. Ibid., 28.
189. Ibid.
190. Ibid., 32.
191. Giles, "Narrative Reversals," 803.
192. Douglass, *Narrative*, 67.
193. Stepto, "Narration," 185.
194. Olney, "I Was Born," 150.
195. Andrews, "Introduction," 7.
196. Douglass, *Narrative*, 23.
197. Ibid.
198. Ibid.
199. Franchot, "Punishment of Esther," 141.
200. Douglass, *Narrative*, 27.

201. Ibid., 30.
202. Ibid., 28.
203. Ibid., 30.
204. Kumar, "Civil Society," 377.
205. Ibid., 378.
206. Douglass, *Narrative*, 30.
207. Kumar, "Civil Society," 379.
208. Neocleous, "From Civil Society to the Social," 396.
209. Spillers, *Black, White, and in Color*, 206.
210. Ibid.
211. Ibid.
212. Ibid., 207.
213. McDowell, "In the First Place," 50.
214. Ibid., 49.
215. Neocleous, "From Civil Society to the Social," 404.
216. Franchot, "Punishment of Esther," 149.
217. Ibid., 141.
218. DeLombard, "'Eye-Witness to the Cruelty,'" 246.
219. Ibid., 252.
220. Ibid., 248.
221. Spillers, *Black, White, and in Color*, 206.
222. Castiglia, "Abolition's Racial Interiors," 33.
223. Ibid., 35.
224. Ibid., 34.
225. Ibid., 33.
226. See Nichols, "Who Read the Slave Narratives?" 149–62.
227. Ibid., 150.
228. Rathburn, "Debate," 486.
229. Ibid., 488 (emphasis in original).
230. Stephanson, *Manifest Destiny*, 29.
231. Rathburn, "Debate," 463.
232. Ibid., 462.
233. Ibid., 464.
234. Ibid., 468.
235. Ibid., 471.
236. Ibid., 481.
237. Ibid., 485.
238. Stephanson, "Manifest Destiny," 48.
239. Ibid., 33.
240. Freehling, "Road to Disunion," 455.
241. Ibid., 458.
242. Hodder, "Authorship," 525.
243. Ibid.
244. Ibid., 539.

245. Sebok, "Judging the Fugitive Slave Acts," 1852–53.

246. Ibid., 1853.

247. Ibid.

248. Cover, *Justice Accused*, 198.

249. Ibid., 176.

250. Ibid., 177.

251. Maginnes, "Case of the Court House Rioters," 31.

252. Higginson, *Army Life in a Black Regiment*, 27.

253. Maginnes, "Case of the Court House Rioters," 33.

254. Neocleous, "From Civil Society to the Social," 403. In this formulation, Neocleous is reading Karl Marx's "Concerning Feuerbach" and "Economic and Philosophic Manuscripts" together with Clarke, *Marx, Marginalism and Modern Sociology*.

255. Kumar, "Civil Society," 379.

256. Maginnes, "Case of the Court House Rioters," 33.

257. Ibid., 34.

258. Ibid., 37.

259. Ibid., 41.

260. Freehling, "Road to Disunion," 537.

261. Stauffer, *Black Hearts of Men*, 94.

262. Ibid., 169.

263. Hodder, "Authorship," 530.

264. Freehling, "Road to Disunion," 552.

265. Stauffer, *Black Hearts of Men*, 197.

266. Nichols, "Kansas-Nebraska Act," 206.

267. Ibid., 209.

268. Ibid.

269. Ibid., 210.

270. Fehrenbacher, *Dred Scott*, 343.

271. Wiecek, "Slavery and Abolition," 43.

272. Vishneski, "What the Court Decided," 375.

273. Brophy, "Let Us Go Back," 207–8.

274. Vishneski, "What the Court Decided," 376.

275. Fehrenbacher, *Dred Scott*, 325.

276. Allen, "Political Economy," 234.

277. Spillers, *Black, White, and in Color*, 206.

278. Ibid.

Chapter 4. The Intimate Civic: The Disturbance of the Quotidian

1. Scarry, *Body in Pain*, 4.

2. Ibid.

3. Ibid., 12 (emphasis in original).

4. Ibid., 27.

5. Smith, *Subjectivity, Identity, and the Body*, 6.
6. Litwack, *North of Slavery*, vii.
7. Rael, *Black Identity*, 48.
8. Pennington, "Fugitive Blacksmith," 211.
9. Ibid. (emphasis in original).
10. Ibid.
11. Pennington, "Fugitive Blacksmith," 198.
12. Foster, "Adding Color," 32.
13. Blassingame, *Slave Testimony*, 687.
14. Walters, "Erotic South," 182.
15. Locke, *Two Treatises of Government*, 319 (emphasis in original).
16. Wynter, "Sambos and Minstrels," 150.
17. Ibid., 152.
18. Walters, "Erotic South," 181.
19. Ibid., 183.
20. Wynter, "Sambos and Minstrels," 149.
21. Taylor, *Race*, 143.
22. Crockett, "Incendiary Pamphlet," 305.
23. Greeson, "'Mysteries and Miseries,'" 277.
24. Ibid., 294.
25. Jacobs, *Incidents*, 38.
26. Stevens, *Reproducing the State*, 44.
27. Ibid., 51.
28. Freud, *Three Essays*, 101.
29. Ginsberg, "Politics of Passing," 5.
30. Carr, "At the Thresholds," 136.
31. Scarry, *Body in Pain*, 14.
32. Ibid., 27.
33. Ibid., 30.
34. Singer, *Erotic Welfare*, 36.
35. Ginsberg, "Politics of Passing," 5.
36. Greeson, "'Mysteries and Miseries,'" 277.
37. Ibid., 278.
38. Ibid., 279.
39. Ibid.,283.
40. Ibid., 302–3.
41. Ibid., 283.
42. Bardaglio, *Reconstructing the Household*, 118.
43. Ibid., 119.
44. Ibid., 117.
45. Jacobson, *Barbarian Virtues*, 263.
46. Ibid., 18.
47. Ninkovich, *United States and Imperialism*, 11.

48. Jacobson, *Barbarian Virtues*, 18.
49. Crouzet, *History of the European Economy*, 167.
50. Rosenberg, *Financial Missionaries*, 1.
51. Ibid., 105.
52. Ibid., 199.
53. Ibid., 198.
54. Jacobson, *Barbarian Virtues*, 8.
55. López, *White by Law*, 1.
56. Ibid., 2.
57. DuBois, *Souls of Black Folk*, 275.
58. Rosen, "'Not That Sort of Women,'" 270.
59. Davis, *Blues Legacies*, 4.

Chapter 5. Modernism and the Affects of Racial Blackness

1. Bascom, *Renaissance in Harlem*, 4.
2. Ibid., 5.
3. Schuyler, "Negro-Art Hokum," 662.
4. Ibid., 662.
5. Ibid.
6. Hughes, "Negro Artist," 692.
7. Ibid., 693.
8. Singal, "American Modernism," 7 (emphasis in original).
9. Ibid.
10. Ibid., 8.
11. Ibid., 7.
12. Hegeman, *Patterns for America*, 19.
13. Jařab, "Modernity," 4.
14. Schuyler, "Negro-Art Hokum," 662.
15. Ibid.
16. Rhodes, *Structures*, 87.
17. Ibid.
18. Ibid., 18.
19. de Jongh, *Vicious Modernism*, 9.
20. Schuyler, "Negro-Art Hokum," 662.
21. Hughes, "Negro Artist," 692.
22. Ibid., 692–93.
23. Ibid., 693.
24. Ibid., 694.
25. Ibid.
26. Ibid., 693.
27. Marx and Engels, *German Ideology*, 50. Citation refers to 1970 edition.

28. Ibid., 94.
29. Marx, *Capital*, 77.
30. Amariglio and Callari, "Marxian Value Theory," 188.
31. Ibid., 215.
32. Ibid., 186.
33. Hughes, "Negro Artist," 694.
34. Ibid.
35. Boone, *Libidinal Currents*, 4 (emphasis in original).
36. Childs, *Modernism*, 14–15.
37. Hughes, *Ways of White Folk*, 6.
38. Ibid.
39. Ibid., 3.
40. Ibid., 4.
41. Ibid., 8.
42. Ibid., 17.
43. Ibid., 6.
44. Ibid., 15.
45. Ibid., 18.
46. Ibid., 18.
47. Ibid., 209.
48. Johnson, "Translator's Introduction," ix (emphasis in original).
49. López, *White by Law*, 185.
50. Boone, *Libidinal Currents*, 7.
51. Schuyler, *Ethiopian Stories*, 53.
52. Weisbord, "Black America," 236.
53. Schuyler, *Ethiopian Stories*, 121.
54. Hill, "Introduction," 25.
55. Lears, *Fables in Abundance*, 115.
56. Rhodes, *Structures*, 114.
57. Ibid., 116.
58. Ullman, *Sex Seen*, 9.
59. Boone, *Libidinal Currents*, 7.
60. Schuyler, *Ethiopian Stories*, 63.
61. Ibid., 64.
62. Ibid., 63.
63. Ibid., 121.
64. Jařab, "Modernity," 5 (emphasis in original).
65. Keunz, "American Racial Discourse," 171.
66. Schuyler, *Black No More*, 133–34. Citations refer to Northeastern University Press edition.
67. Keunz, "American Racial Discourse," 171.
68. Schuyler, *Black No More*, 40.
69. Ibid., 76.

70. Miller, "Foreword," in Schuyler, *Black No More,* 10.
71. Schuyler, *Black No More,* 43–44.
72. Ibid., 218.
73. Ibid., 20.
74. Ibid., 26.
75. Chauncey, *Gay New York,* 244–45.
76. Watson, *Harlem Renaissance,* 134.
77. Ibid., 134–35.
78. Davis, *Blues Legacies,* 41.
79. Childs, *Modernism,* 16.
80. Roosevelt, *Address.*
81. Hughes, *Not without Laughter,* 22. Citations refer to Scribner's Paperback Fiction edition.
82. Schultz, "Natural," 1177–87.
83. Hughes, *Laughter,* 23–24.
84. Ibid., 105.
85. Ibid., 83.
86. Ibid., 84.
87. Ibid., 90.
88. Ibid., 96.
89. Ibid., 291.
90. Ibid., 293.
91. Ibid., 73.
92. Douglas, *Terrible Honesty,* 73–74.
93. Boone, *Libidinal Currents,* 116.
94. Hughes, *Not without Laughter,* 238.
95. Ibid., 46–47.
96. Ibid., 218.
97. Wintz, *Black Culture,* 16.
98. Cowley, *Exile's Return,* 77. Citation refers to the Penguin edition.
99. Hill and Rasmussen, "Afterword," 301.

Bibliography

Albanese, Denise. "Mathematics as a Social Formation: Mapping the Early Modern Universal." In *The Culture of Capital: Property, Cities, and Knowledge in Early Modern England*, edited by Henry S. Turner, 255–73. New York: Routledge, 2002.

Allen, Austin. "The Political Economy of Blackness: Citizenship, Corporations, and Race in Dred Scott." *Civil War History* 50, no. 3 (2004): 229–60.

Alpers, Svetlana. *The Art of Describing: Dutch Painting in the Seventeenth Century*. Chicago: University of Chicago Press, 1983.

Alpert, Jonathon. "The Origin of Slavery in the United States—The Maryland Precedent." In *The Law of American Slavery: Major Historical Interpretations*, edited by Kermit L. Hall, 1–33. New York: Garland, 1987.

Amariglio, Jack, and Antonio Callari. "Marxian Value Theory and the Problem of the Subject: The Role of Commodity Fetishism." In *Fetishism as Cultural Discourse*, edited by Emily Apter and William Pietz, 186–216. Ithaca, N.Y.: Cornell University Press, 1993.

Anderson, Benedict. *Imagined Communities: Reflections on the Origin and Spread of Nationalism*. New York: Verso, 1991. Originally published 1983.

Andrews, William L. Introduction to *African American Autobiography: A Collection of Critical Essays*, edited by William L. Andrews, 1–7. Englewood Cliffs, N.J.: Prentice Hall, 1993.

———. "The Representation of Slavery and the Rise of Afro-American Literary Realism, 1865–1920." In *African American Autobiography: A Collection of Critical Essays*, edited by William L. Andrews, 77–99. Englewood Cliffs, N.J.: Prentice Hall, 1993.

Appiah, Anthony. *In My Father's House: Africa in the Philosophy of Culture*. New York: Oxford, 1992.

Appleby, Joyce. *Capitalism and a New Social Order*. New York: New York University Press, 1984.

———. "Republicanism in Old and New Contexts." *William and Mary Quarterly* 43, no. 1 (1986): 20–34.

Bailyn, Bernard. *The Peopling of British North America: An Introduction*. New York: Vintage, 1988.

Balibar, Etienne. "Subjection and Subjectivation." In *Supposing the Subject*, edited by Joan Copjec, 1–15. London: Verso, 1994.

Banning, Lance. *Citizens of the World: London Merchants and the Integration of the British Atlantic Community, 1735–1785*. New York: Cambridge University Press, 1995.

———. "Republican Ideology and the Triumph of the Constitution, 1789–1793." *William and Mary Quarterly Third Series* 31, no. 2 (1974): 167–88.

Bardaglio, Peter. *Reconstructing the Household: Families, Sex, and the Law in the Nineteenth-Century South*. Chapel Hill: University of North Carolina Press, 1995.

Barker, Francis. *The Tremulous Private Body: Essays on Subjection*. Ann Arbor: University of Michigan Press, 1995.

Bascom, Lionel. *A Renaissance in Harlem: Lost Voices of an American Community*. New York: Avon, 1999.

Baucom, Ian. *Spectres of the Atlantic: Finance Capital, Slavery, and the Philosophy of History*. Durham, N.C.: Duke University Press, 2005.

Bay, Mia. *The White Image in the Black Mind: African-American Ideas about White People, 1830–1925*. New York: Oxford University Press, 2000.

Beard, Charles. *An Economic Interpretation of the Constitution of the United States*. New York: Free Press, 1986. Originally published 1913 by Free Press.

Belasco, Susan. "'The Animating Influences of Discord': Margaret Fuller in 1844." *Legacy* 20, nos. 1–2 (2003): 76–93.

Ben-Atar, Doran. "Introduction: The Paradoxical Legacy of the Federalists." In *Federalists Reconsidered*, edited by Doran Ben-Atar and Barbara B. Oberg, 1–16. Charlottesville: University of Virginia Press, 1988.

Benjamin, Timothy, Timothy Hall, and David Rutherford. Introduction to *The Atlantic World in the Age of Empire*, edited by Thomas Benjamin, Timothy Hall, and David Rutherford, 1–10. Boston: Houghton Mifflin, 2001.

Bennett, Herman L. *Africans in Colonial Mexico: Absolutism, Christianity, and Afro-Creole Consciousness, 1570–1640*. Bloomington: Indiana University Press, 2003.

———. "'The Sons of Adam': Text, Context, and the Early Modern African Subject." *Representations* 92, no. 1 (2005): 16–41.

Bergquist, Charles. "The Paradox of American Development." In *The Atlantic World in the Age of Empire*, edited by Thomas Benjamin, Timothy Hall, and David Rutherford, 153–65. Boston: Houghton Mifflin, 2001.

Berkin, Carol. "Ethnicity in Seventeenth-Century English America, 1600–1700." In *Race and Ethnicity in America: A Concise History*, edited by Ronald H. Bayor, 1–20. New York: Columbia University Press, 2003.

Berlin, Ira. *Many Thousands Gone: The First Two Centuries of Slavery in North America*. Cambridge, Mass.: Belknap, 1998.

Bersani, Leo. *The Freudian Body*. New York: Columbia University Press, 1986.

Bibb, Henry. *Narrative of the Life and Adventures of Henry Bibb, an American Slave, Written by Himself.* Salem, N.H.: Ayer, 1991.

Blackburn, Robin. *The Making of New World Slavery: From the Baroque to the Modern 1492–1800.* London: Verso, 1997.

Blassingame, John W. *Slave Testimony: Two Centuries of Letters, Speeches, Interviews, and Autobiographies.* Baton Rouge: Louisiana State University Press, 1977.

Blaut, J. M. *The Colonizer's Model of the World: Geographical Diffusionism and Eurocentric History.* New York: Guilford, 1993.

Boehner, Philotheus. "Ockham's Political Ideas." *Review of Politics* 5, no. 4 (1943): 462–87.

Boghossian, Paul, and Christopher Peacocke. Introduction to *New Essays on the A Priori,* edited by Paul Boghossian and Christopher Peacocke, 1–11. New York: Oxford University Press, 2000.

Bolster, Jeffrey. *Black Tacks: African American Seamen in the Age of Sail.* Cambridge, Mass.: Harvard University Press, 1997.

Boone, Joseph Allen. *Libidinal Currents: Sexuality and the Shaping of Modernism.* Chicago: University of Chicago Press, 1998.

Breen, T. H. "'Baubles of Britain': The American Consumer Revolutions of the Eighteenth Century." *Past & Present* 119, no. 1 (May 1988): 73–104.

———. "Creative Adaptations: Peoples and Cultures." In *The Atlantic World in the Age of Empire,* edited by Thomas Benjamin, Timothy Hall, and David Rutherford, 57–80. Boston: Houghton Mifflin, 2001.

Brewer, John. *The Sinews of Power: War, Money, and the English State, 1688–1783.* Cambridge, Mass.: Harvard University Press, 1988.

Brooks, Elaine. "Massachusetts Anti-slavery Society." *Journal of Negro History* 30, no. 2 (1945): 311–30.

Brophy, Alfred L. "Let Us Go Back and Stand upon the Constitution: Federal-State Relations in *Scott v. Sandford.*" *Columbia Law Review* 90, no. 1 (1990): 192–225.

Brown, Christopher Lee. *Moral Capital: Foundations of British Abolitionism.* Chapel Hill: University of North Carolina Press, 2006.

Brown, Kathleen. *Good Wives, Nasty Wenches, and Anxious Patriarchs: Gender, Race, and Power in Colonial Virginia.* Chapel Hill: University of North Carolina Press, 1996.

Bruce, Dickson. *The Origins of African American Literature 1680–1865.* Charlottesville: University of Virginia Press, 2001.

Buck, Willis R., Jr. "Reading Autobiography." *Genre* 13, no. 4 (1980): 477–98.

Buck-Morss, Susan. "Hegel and Haiti." *Critical Inquiry* 26, no. 4 (2000): 821–65.

Burr, David. "Ockham, Scotus, and the Censure at Avignon." *Church History* 37, no. 2 (1968): 144–59.

Butchart, Alexander. *The Anatomy of Power: European Constructions of the African Body.* London: Zed, 1998.

Cain, William E. *William Lloyd Garrison and the Fight against Slavery: Selections from* The Liberator. Boston: Bedford/St. Martin's, 1995.

Carr, Brian. "At the Thresholds of the 'Human': Race, Psychoanalysis, and the Replication of Imperial Memory." *Cultural Critique* No. 39 (1998): 119–50.

Carretta, Vincent. "Olaudah Equiano or Gustavus Vassa? New Light on an Eighteenth-Century Question of Identity." *Slavery and Abolition* 20, no. 3 (1999): 96–105.

Casey, Marion R. "The Limits of Equality, 1789–1836." In *Race and Ethnicity in America: A Concise History*, edited by Ronald H. Bayor, 41–62. New York: Columbia University Press, 2003.

Castiglia, Christopher. "Abolition's Racial Interiors and the Making of White Civic Depth." *American Literary History* 14, no. 1 (2002): 33–59.

Cayton, Andrew R. L. "Radicals in the 'Western World': The Federalist Conquest of the Trans-Appalachian North America." In *Federalists Reconsidered*, edited by Doran Ben-Atar and Barbara B. Oberg, 77–95. Charlottesville: University of Virginia Press, 1988.

Césaire, Aimé. *Discourse on Colonialism*. Introduction by Robin Kelley. New York: Monthly Review Press, 2000. First published in France, 1955.

Chakrabarty, Dipesh. "Provincializing Europe: Postcoloniality and the Critique of History." *Cultural Studies* 6, no. 3 (October 1992): 337–57.

Chandler, James. "Moving Accidents: The Emergence of Sentimental Probability." In *The Age of Cultural Revolutions*, edited by Colin Jones and Dror Wahrman, 137–70. Berkeley: University of California Press, 2002.

Chartier, Roger. *The Order of Books*. Stanford, Calif.: Stanford University Press, 1994.

Chauncey, George. *Gay New York: Gender, Urban Culture, and the Making of the Gay Male World, 1890–1940*. New York: Basic, 1994.

Childs, Peter. *Modernism*. London: Routledge, 2000.

Clarke, Simon. *Marx, Marginalism and Modern Sociology: From Adam Smith to Max Weber*. New York: Macmillan, 1982.

Cobb Moore, Geneva. "A Freudian Reading of Harriet Jacob's Incidents in the Life of a Slave Girl." *Southern Literary Journal* 38, no.1 (2005): 3–20.

Connor, Walker. "A Nation Is a Nation, Is a State, Is an Ethnic Group, Is a . . ." *Ethnic and Racial Studies* 1, no. 4 (1978): 379–88.

Copjec, Joan. Introduction to *Supposing the Subject*, edited by Joan Copjec, vii–xiii. London: Verso, 1994.

Costanzo, Angelo. *Surprising Narrative: Olaudah Equiano and the Beginnings of Black Autobiography*. Westport, Conn.: Greenwood, 1987.

Countryman, Edward. Introduction to *How Did American Slavery Begin?* Readings (Historians at Work), edited by Edward Countryman, 1–13. Boston: Bedford/St. Martin's, 1999.

Cover, Robert M. *Justice Accused: Antislavery and the Judicial Process*. New Haven, Conn.: Yale University Press, 1975.

Cowley, Malcolm. *Exile's Return: A Literary Odyssey of the 1920's*. With an introduction and notes by David W. Faulkner. New York: Penguin, 1994. First published by Norton, 1934. Citations refer to Penguin edition.

Crockett, Hasan. "The Incendiary Pamphlet: David Walker's Appeal in Georgia." *Journal of Negro History* 86, no. 3 (2001): 305–18.

Crosby, Alfred W. "Infectious Diseases and the Demography of the Atlantic Peoples." In *The Atlantic World in the Age of Empire*, edited by Thomas Benjamin, Timothy Hall, and David Rutherford, 169–79. Boston: Houghton Mifflin, 2001.

Crouzet, François. *A History of the European Economy, 1000–2000*. Charlottesville: University of Virginia Press, 2001.

Crowe, Michael J. *Theories of the World from Antiquity to the Copernican Revolution*. Mineola, N.Y.: Dover, 1990, 2001.

Cullen, Louis M. "Irish Businessman and French Courtier: The Career of Thomas Sutton, Comte de Clonard, c. 1722–1782." In *The Early Modern Atlantic Economy*, edited by John McCusker and Kenneth Morgan, 86–104. New York: Cambridge University Press, 2000.

Curtin, Philip D. *The Rise and Fall of the Plantation Complex: Essays in Atlantic History*. New York: Cambridge University Press, 1990.

Davis, Angela Y. *Blues Legacies and Black Feminism: Gertrude "Ma" Rainey, Bessie Smith, and Billie Holiday*. New York: Pantheon, 1998.

Davis, David Brion. *The Problem of Slavery in Western Culture*. New York: Oxford University Press, 1966.

Davis, Ralph. *The Rise of the Atlantic Economies*. Ithaca, N.Y.: Cornell University Press, 1973.

de Jongh, James. *Vicious Modernism: Black Harlem and the Literary Imagination*. Cambridge, U.K.: Cambridge University Press, 1990.

DeLombard, Jeannine. "'Eye-Witness to the Cruelty': Southern Violence and Northern Testimony in Frederick Douglass's 1845 Narrative." *American Literature* 73, no. 2 (2001): 245–75.

Descartes, René. *Meditations on the First Philosophy*. Translated by John Cottingham. New York: Cambridge University Press, 1986.

DeVoto, Bernard. *The Year of Decision, 1846*. New York: St. Martin's, 2000. First published in 1942 by Little, Brown.

Diop, Cheikh Anta. *Precolonial Black Africa*. Translated by Harold Salemson. Brooklyn, N.Y.: Lawrence Hill, 1987.

Donnan, Elizabeth. "The Early Days of the South Sea Company, 1711–1718." *Journal of Economic and Business History* 11, no. 3 (1930): 419–50.

Douglas, Ann. *Terrible Honesty: Mongrel Manhattan in the 1920s*. New York: Farrar, Strauss & Giroux, 1995.

Douglas, Mary, and Steven Ney. *Missing Persons: A Critique of Personhood in the Social Sciences*. Berkeley: University of California Press, 1998.

Douglass, Frederick. *Narrative of the Life of Frederick Douglass*. Edited by Benjamin Quarles. Cambridge, Mass.: Belknap, 1960.

DuBois, W. E. B. *The Souls of Black Folk*. New York: New American Library, 1969. First published in 1903 by A. C. McClurg, Chicago.

Dull, Jonathan R. *A Diplomatic History of the American Revolution*. New Haven, Conn.: Yale University Press, 1985.

Dunn, Richard. *Sugar and Slaves: The Rise of the Planter Class in the English West Indies, 1624–1713*. Chapel Hill: University of North Carolina Press, 1972.

Eakin, Paul John. *How Our Lives Become Stories: Making Selves*. Ithaca, N.Y.: Cornell University Press, 1999.

Ellis, Richard, and Aaron Wildavsky. "A Cultural Analysis of the Role of Abolitionists in the Coming of the Civil War." *Comparative Studies in Society and History* 32, no. 1 (1990): 89–116.

Ellison, Ralph. *Shadow and Act.* New York: Vintage, 1963.

Eltis, David. "Europeans and the Rise and Fall of African Slavery in the Americas: An Interpretation." *American Historical Review* 98, no. 5 (1993): 1339–423.

———. *The Rise of African Slavery in the Americas. New York*: Cambridge University Press, 2000.

Emerson, Ralph Waldo. *Selected Writings of Emerson.* Edited by Donald McQuade. New York: Random House, 1981.

Emmer, P. C. "The Dutch and the Making of the Second Atlantic System." In *Slavery and the Rise of the Atlantic System*, edited by Barbara I. Solow, 75–96. Cambridge, Mass.: W. E. B. DuBois Institute for Afro-American Research, Harvard University, 1991.

Engerman, Stanley. "France, Britain, and the Economic Growth of Colonial North America." In *The Early Modern Atlantic Economy*, edited by John McCusker and Kenneth Morgan, 227–49. New York: Cambridge University Press, 2000.

Equiano, Olaudah. *Equiano's Travels.* Edited by Paul Edwards. Oxford, U.K.: Heinemann, 1967.

———. *The Interesting Narrative of the Life of Olaudah Equiano, or Gustavus Vassa, the African, Written by Himself.* Edited by Angelo Costanzo. Peterborough, Ont.: Broadview, 2001.

Fage, J. D. With William Tordoff. *A History of Africa.* New York: Routledge, 2002. Originally published in London by Hutchinson, 1978.

Farnie, D. A. "The Commercial Empire of the Atlantic, 1607–1783." *Economic History Review*, n.s., 15, no. 2 (1962): 205–18.

Fehrenbacher, Don E. *The Dred Scott Case: Its Significance in American Law and Politics.* New York: Oxford, 1978.

———. With Ward M. McAfee. *The Slaveholding Republic: An Account of the United States Government's Relations to Slavery.* New York: Oxford University Press, 2001.

Ferguson, E. James. "The Nationalists of 1781–1783 and the Economic Interpretation of the Constitution." *Journal of American History* 56, no. 2 (1969): 241–61.

———. "Political Economy, Public Liberty, and the Formation of the Constitution." *William and Mary Quarterly* 40, no. 3 (1983): 389–412.

Fichtelberg, Joseph. "Word between Worlds: The Economy of Equiano's Narrative." *American Literary History* 5, no. 3, Eighteenth-Century American Cultural Studies (1993): 459–80.

Finkelman, Paul. "Crimes of Love, Misdemeanors of Passion: The Regulation of Race and Sex in the Colonial South." In *The Devil's Lane: Sex and Race in the Early South*, edited by Catherine Clinton and Michele Gillespie, 124–38. New York: Oxford University Press, 1997.

———. *Dred v. Sandford: A Brief History with Documents.* Boston: Bedford/St. Martin's, 1997.

Fischer, Kirsten. "'False, Feigned, and Scandalous Words': Sexual Slander and Racial Ideology Among Whites in Colonial North Carolina." In *The Devil's Lane: Sex and Race in the Early South.* Edited by Catherine Clinton and Michele Gillespie, 139–53. New York: Oxford University Press, 1997.

Fisher, Rudolf. *The Conjure Man Dies: A Mystery Tale of Dark Harlem.* Ann Arbor: University of Michigan Press, Ann Arbor, (paperback) 1992. First published in 1932 in New York.

Folkenflik, Robert, ed. *The Culture of Autobiography.* Stanford: Stanford University Press, 1993.

Foner, Eric. *Nothing but Freedom: Emancipation and Its Legacy*. Baton Rouge: Louisiana State University Press, 1983.

Foster, Frances Smith. "Adding Color and Contour to Early American Self-Portraitures: Autobiographical Writings of African American Women." In *Conjuring: Black Women, Fiction, and Literary Tradition*, edited by Marjorie Pryse and Hortense J. Spillers, 25–38. Bloomington: Indiana University Press, 1988.

———. *Witnessing Slavery: The Development of Antebellum Slave Narratives*. Westport, Conn.: Greenwood, 1979.

———. *Written by Herself: Literary Production by African American Women: 1746–1892*. Bloomington,: Indiana University Press, 1993.

Foster, Hal. "The Art of Fetishism: Notes on Dutch Still Life." In *Fetishism as Cultural Discourse*, edited by Emily Apter and William Pietz, 251–65. Ithaca, N.Y.: Cornell University Press, 1993.

Foucault, Michel. *The Archeology of Knowledge and the Discourse on Language*. Translated by A. M. Sheridan Smith. New York: Pantheon, 1982.

———. *The Order of Things: An Archaeology of the Human Sciences*. New York: Vintage, 1970.

———. *Power/Knowledge: Selected Interviews and Other Writings, 1972–1977*, edited by Colin Gordon. New York: Pantheon, 1980.

Fracchia, Joseph. "Marx's Aufhenbung of Philosophy and the Foundations of a Materialist Science of History." *History and Theory* 30, no. 2 (1991): 153–79.

Franchot, Jenny. "The Punishment of Esther: Frederick Douglass and the Construction of the Feminine." In *Frederick Douglass: New Literary and Historical Essays*, edited by Eric J. Sundquist, 141–65. New York: Cambridge University Press, 1990.

Frank, Andre Gunder. *World Accumulation, 1492–1789*. New York: Algora, 1978.

Fraser, Alexander Campbell. Prolegomena to *An Essay Concerning Human Understanding: Collated, Annotated, with Prolegomena, Biographical, Critical, and Historical by Alexander Campbell Fraser*, by John Locke. New York: Dover; 1959.

Freehling, William H. *The Road to Disunion: Secessionists at Bay 1776–1854*. New York: Oxford University Press, 1990.

Freud, Sigmund. *Three Essays on the Theory of Sexuality*. New York: Basic, 1975.

Frey, Sylvia R., and Betty Wood. "The Survival of African Religions in the Americas." In *The Atlantic World in the Age of Empire*, edited by Thomas Benjamin, Timothy Hall, and David Rutherford, 122–32. Boston: Houghton Mifflin, 2001.

Friedman, Michael. "Transcendental Philosophy and A Priori Knowledge: A Neo-Kantian Perspective." In *New Essays on the A Priori*, edited by Paul Boghossian and Christopher Peacocke, 367–83. New York: Oxford University Press, 2000.

Gailey, Harry A. *History of Africa, Vol. I: From Earliest Times to 1800*. Malabar, Fl.: Krieger, 1999. First published in 1970.

Gaspar, David Henry, and David Patrick Geggus. Introduction to *A Turbulent Time: The French Revolution and the Greater Caribbean*, edited by David Henry Gaspar and David Patrick Geggus, vii–xii. Bloomington: Indiana University Press, 1997.

Gates, Henry Louis, Jr. *The Signifying Monkey: A Theory of Afro-American Literary Criticism*. New York: Oxford University Press, 1988.

Gemery, Henry A., and Jan S. Hogendorn. "The Economic Costs of West African Participation in the Atlantic Slave Trade: A Preliminary Sampling for the Eighteenth Century." In *The Uncommon Market: Essays in the Economic History of the Atlantic Slave Trade*, edited by Henry A. Gemery and Jan S. Hogendorn, 143–61. London: Academic, 1983.

Giles, Paul. "Narrative Reversals and Power Exchanges: Frederick Douglass and British Culture." *American Literature* 73, no. 4 (2001): 779–810.

Ginsberg, Elaine K. "Introduction: The Politics of Passing." In *Passing and the Fictions of Identity*, edited by Elaine K. Ginsberg, 1–18. Durham, N.C.: Duke University Press, 1996.

Glissant, Edouard, *Caribbean Discourses: Selected Essays*. Charlottesville: University of Virginia Press, 1989.

Gordley, James. *The Philosophical Origins of Modern Contract Doctrine*. New York: Oxford University Press, 1991.

Gougeon, Len. "Abolition, the Emersons, and 1837." *New England Quarterly* 64, no. 3 (1981): 345–64.

———. "Emerson and Abolition: The Silent Years, 1837–1844." *American Literature* 54, no. 4 (1982): 560–75.

Gould, Philip. *Barbaric Traffic: Commerce and Antislavery in the 18th Century Atlantic World*. Cambridge, Mass.: Harvard University Press, 2003.

Graff, Harvey, J. *The Legacies of Literacy: Continuities and Contradictions in Western Culture and Society*. Bloomington: Indiana University Press, 1986.

Greene, Jack P. *Pursuits of Happiness: The Social Development of Early Modern British Colonies and the Formation of American Culture*. Chapel Hill: University of North Carolina Press, 1988.

Greeson, Jennifer Rae. "The 'Mysteries and Miseries' of North Carolina, New York City, Urban Gothic Fiction, and Incidents in the Life of a Slave Girl." *American Literature* 73, no. 2 (2001): 277–309.

Grimes, William. *Life of William Grimes . . . Written by Himself*. In *Five Black Lives: The Autobiographies of Venture Smith, James Mars, William Grimes, The Rev. G. W. Offley, and James L. Smith*. Edited by Arna Bontemps, 59–128. Middleton, Conn.: Wesleyan University Press, 1971.

Gronniosaw, James Albert Ukawsaw. *A Narrative of the Most Remarkable Particulars in the Life of James Albert Ukawsaw Gronniosaw, An African Prince, As Related by Himself (Bath, 1772)*. In *Unchained Voices: An Anthology of Black Authors in the English-Speaking World of the 18th Century*, edited by Vincent Carretta, 32–58. Lexington: University of Kentucky Press, 1996, 2004.

Gueye, Adama. "The Impact of the Slave Trade on Cayor and Baol: Mutations in the Habitat and Land Occupancy." In *Fighting the Slave Trade: West African Strategies*, edited by Sylviane A. Diouf, 50–61. Athens: Ohio University Press, 2003.

Gusdorf, Georges. "Conditions and Limits of Autobiography." In *Autobiography: Essays Theoretical and Critical*, edited by James Olney, 28–48. Princeton, N.J.: Princeton University Press, 1980.

Gyekye, Kwame. "Person and Community in African Thought." In *The African Philosophy Reader*, edited by P. H. Coetzee and A. P. J. Roux, 317–36. New York: Routledge, 2002.

Habermas, Jürgen. *The Structural Transformation of the Public Sphere: An Inquiry into a Category of Bourgeois Society*, translated by Thomas Burger. Cambridge, Mass.: MIT Press, 1991.

Hamilton, Alexander, James Madison, and John Jay. *The Federalist, or the New Constitution*. 2nd ed. Edited by Max Beloff. New York: Basil Blackwell, 1987. First published in 1948.

Hammett, Dashiell. *The Maltese Falcon*. New York: Knopf, 1929.

Hancock, David. *Citizens of the World: London Merchants and the Integration of the British Atlantic Community, 1735–1785*. New York: Cambridge University Press, 1995.

Hardt, Michael. "The Withering of Civil Society." *Social Text* 14, no. 4 (1995): 27–44.

Harms, Robert. *The Diligent: A Voyage through the Worlds of the Slave Trade*. New York: Basic, 2002.

Hartman, Saidiya. *Scenes of Subjection: Terror, Slavery, and Self-Making in Nineteenth-Century America*. New York: Oxford University Press, 1997.

Hegel, Georg Wilhelm Friedrich. *The Philosophy of History*. Mineola, N.Y.: Dover, 1956.

Hegeman, Susan. *Pattern for America: Modernism and the Concept of Culture*. Princeton, N.J.: Princeton University Press, 1999.

Higginbotham, Leon, Jr. "The Ancestry of Inferiority." In *How Did American Slavery Begin?* Readings (Historians at Work), edited by Edward Countryman, 85–98. Boston: Bedford/St. Martin's, 1999.

Higginson, Thomas Wentworth. *Army Life in a Black Regiment*. New York: Norton, 1984. Originally published in 1870 by Fields, Osgood (Boston).

Hill, Robert A. Introduction to *Ethiopian Stories*, by George S. Schuyler, 1–50. Compiled and edited by Robert A. Hill. Boston: Northeastern University Press, 1994.

Hill, Robert A., and R. Kent Rasmussen. Afterword to *Black Empire*, edited by George S. Schuyler. Boston: Northeastern University Press, 1991.

Hinds, Elizabeth Jane Wall. "The Spirit of Trade: Olaudah Equiano's Conversion, Legalism, and the Merchant's Life." *African American Review* 32, no. 4 (1998): 635–47.

Hobbes, Thomas. *Leviathan*. Edited by Richard E. Flathman and David Johnston. New York: Norton, 1997.

Hobson, Charles. "The Negative on State Laws: James Madison and the Crisis of Republican Government." *William and Mary Quarterly* 36 (1979): 215–35.

Hodder, F. H. "The Authorship of the Compromise of 1850." *Mississippi Valley Historical Review* 22, no. 4 (1936): 525–36.

Hodes, Martha. *White Women, Black Men: Illicit Sex in the Nineteenth-Century South*. New Haven, Conn.: Yale University Press, 1997.

Holt, Thomas C. "Marking: Race, Race-Making, and the Writing of History." *American Historical Review* 100, no. 1 (1995): 1–20.

Hudson, Nicholas. *Writing and European Thought, 1600–1830*. Cambridge: Cambridge University Press, 1994.

Hughes, Langston. *The Big Sea: An Autobiography*. New York: Alfred A. Knopf, 1940.

———. *Fine Clothes to the Jew*. New York: Knopf, 1927.

———. "The Negro Artist and the Racial Mountain." *The Nation* 122, no. 3181 (1926): 692–94.

———. *Not without Laughter*. New York: Simon & Schuster, Scribner's Paperback Fiction, 1995; Macmillan, 1968. Citations refer to the Scribner's Paperback Fiction edition.

———. *The Ways of White Folk*. New York: Vintage Classics, 1991. Originally published in 1934 by Random House.

———. *The Weary Blues*. New York: Knopf, 1926.

Hugill, Peter J. *World Trade since 1431: Geography, Technology, Capitalism*. Baltimore, Md.: Johns Hopkins University Press, 1993.

Inikori, Joseph E. "Slavery and Atlantic Commerce, 1650–1800." *American Economic Review* 82, no. 2 (1992): 151–57.

———. "The Struggle against the Transatlantic Slave Trade: The Role of the State." In *Fighting the Slave Trade: West African Strategies*, edited by Sylviane A. Diouf, 170–98. Athens: Ohio University Press, 2003.

Israel, Jonathan I. *The Dutch Republic: Its Rise and Fall, 1477–1806*. New York: Oxford, 1995.

Jacobs, Harriet. *Incidents in the Life of a Slave Girl by Harriet Jacobs (aka Linda Brent)*. Rockville, Md.: Arc Manor, 2008.

Jacobson, Matthew Frye. *Barbarian Virtues: The United States Encounters Foreign Peoples at Home and Abroad, 1876–1917*. New York: Hill and Wang, 2000.

Jařab, Josef. "Modernity, Modernism, and the American Ethnic Minority Artist." In *Race and the Modern Artist*, edited by Heather Hathaway, Joseph Jařab, and Jeffrey Melnick. Oxford, U.K.: Oxford University Press, 2003.

Jennings, Francis. *The Creation of America: Through Revolution to Empire*. New York: Cambridge University Press, 2000.

Johns, Adrian. *The Nature of the Book: Print and Knowledge in the Making*. Chicago: University of Chicago Press, 1998.

Johnson, Barbara. Translator's introduction to *Dissemination*, by Jacques Derrida. Translated, with an introduction and additional notes, by Barbara Johnson. Chicago: University of Chicago Press, 1981.

Kant, Immanuel. *Critique of Pure Reason*. Translated by Norman Kemp Smith. Boston: Bedford/St. Martin's, 1965. Originally published 1929.

Kawash, Samira. *Dislocating the Color Line: Hybridity and Singularity in African-American Narrative*. Stanford, Calif.: Stanford University Press, 1997.

Keunz, Jane. "American Racial Discourse, 1900–1930: Schuyler's *Black No More*." *NOVEL: A Form of Fiction* 30, no. 2 (1997): 170–92.

Knight, Franklin W. *The Caribbean: The Genesis of a Fragmented Nationalism*. New York: Oxford University Press, 1990.

Kumar, Krishan. "Civil Society: An Inquiry into the Usefulness of an Historical Term." *British Journal of Sociology* 44, no. 3 (1993): 375–95.

Lears, T. Jackson. *Fables in Abundance: A Cultural History of Advertising in America*. New York: Basic, 1994.

Lebovics, Herman. "The Uses of America in Locke's Second Treatise of Government." *Journal of the History of Ideas* 47, no. 4 (1986): 567–81.

Lejeune, Philippe. *On Autobiography*. Translated by Katherine Leary. Minneapolis: University of Minnesota Press, 1989.

Linebaugh, Peter, and Marcus Rediker. *The Many-Headed Hydra: Sailors, Slaves, Commoners, and the Hidden History of the Revolutionary Atlantic*. Boston: Beacon, 2000.

Litwack, Leon F. *North of Slavery: The Negro in the Free States 1790–1860*. Chicago: University of Chicago Press, 1961.

Locke, John. *An Essay Concerning Human Understanding: Collated, Annotated, with Prolegomena, Biographical, Critical, and Historical by Alexander Campbell Fraser*. New York: Dover, 1959.

———. *Two Treatises of Government*, edited by Peter Laslett. New York: Cambridge University Press, 1960.

López, Ian F. Haney. *White by Law: The Legal Construction of Race*. New York: New York University Press, 1996.

López-Alves, Fernando. *State Formation and Democracy in Latin America 1810–1900* (Durham, N.C.: Duke University Press, 2000).

Lorde, Audre. *Sister Outsider: Essays and Speeches by Audre Lorde*. Freedom, Calif.: Crossing, 1984.

Lovejoy, Paul. *Transformations in Slavery: A History of Slavery in Africa*. Cambridge: Cambridge University Press, 1979.

Lowance, Mason I., Jr. *A House Divided: The Antebellum Slavery Debates in America, 1776–1865*. Princeton, N.J.: Princeton University Press, 2003.

Macpherson, C. B. *The Political Theory of Possessive Individualism: Hobbes to Locke*. New York: Oxford University Press, 1985. First published in 1962 by the Clarendon, Oxford.

Madison, James. *Notes of Debates in the Federal Convention of 1787*. New York: Norton, 1987.

Maginnes, David R. "The Case of the Court House Rioters in the Rendition of the Fugitive Slave Anthony Burns, 1854." *Journal of Negro History* 56, no. 1 (1971): 31–42.

Mancall, Peter C. *Hakluyt's Promise: An Elizabethan's Obsession for an English America*. New Haven, Conn.: Yale University Press, 2007.

Marrant, John. "A Narrative of the Lord's Wonderful Dealings with John Marrant, a Black (London, 1785)." In *Unchained Voices: An Anthology of Black Authors in the English Speaking World of the 18th Century*, edited by Vincent Carretta, 110–33. Lexington: University of Kentucky Press, 1996, 2004.

Marren, Susan M. "'Between Slavery and Freedom': The Transgressive Self in Olaudah Equiano's Autobiography." *PMLA (Publications of the Modern Language Association)* 108, no. 1 (1993): 94–105.

Marsters, Kate Ferguson. Introduction to *Travels in the Interior Districts of Africa, by Mungo Park*, edited by Kate Ferguson Marsters, 1–28. Durham, N.C.: Duke University Press, 2000.

Martin, Henri-Jean. *The History and Power of Writing*. Chicago: University of Chicago Press, 1994.

Marx, Karl. *Capital*. Vol. I. Moscow: Progress, 1954.

———. *Pre-Capitalist Economic Formations*. With an introduction by Eric J. Hobsbawm. New York: International, 1965.

Marx, Karl, and Frederick Engels. *The German Ideology*. Edited with an introduction by C. J. Arthur. New York: International, 1970; first published 1947.

Mathias, Peter. "Risk, Credit and Kinship in Early Modern Enterprise." In *The Early Modern Atlantic Economy*, edited by John McCusker and Kenneth Morgan, 15–35. New York: Cambridge University Press, 2000.

Maynard, Douglas H. "The World's Anti-Slavery Convention of 1840." *Mississippi Historical Review* 47, no. 3 (1960): 452–71.

Mbembe, Achille. "Necropolitics." *Public Culture* 15, no. 1: 11–40.

McBride, Dwight A. *Impossible Witnesses: Truth, Abolitionism, and Slave Testimony*. New York: New York University Press, 2001.

McCusker, John. "The Business of Distilling in the Old World and the New World during the Seventeenth and Eighteenth Centuries: The Rise of a New Enterprise and Its Connection with Colonial America." In *The Early Modern Atlantic Economy*, edited by John McCusker and Kenneth Morgan, 186–224. New York: Cambridge University Press, 2000.

———. *Essays in the Economic History of the Atlantic World*. New York: Routledge, 1997.

McDowell, Deborah. "In the First Place: Making Frederick Douglass and the Afro-American Tradition." In *African American Autobiography: A Collection of Critical Essays*, edited by William L. Andrews, 192–217. Englewood Cliffs, N.J.: Prentice Hall, 1993.

Meinig, D. W. "America as Continuation." *The Atlantic World in the Age of Empire*, edited by Thomas Benjamin, Timothy Hall, and David Rutherford, 29–37. Boston: Houghton Mifflin, 2001.

Miller, James A. Foreword to *Black No More*, by George S. Schuyler, 1–11. Boston: Northeastern University Press, 1989. First published in 1931 by Macaulay, New York.

Miller, Joseph C. *Way of Death: Merchant Capitalism and the Angolan Slave Trade 1730–1830*. Madison: University of Wisconsin Press, 1988.

Miller, William Lee. *Arguing about Slavery: John Quincy Adams and the Great Battle in the United States Congress*. New York: Vintage, 1998. First published in 1995 by Knopf, New York.

Mills, Charles W. *Blackness Visible: Essays on Philosophy and Race*. Ithaca, N.Y.: Cornell University Press, 1998.

———. *The Racial Contract*. Ithaca, N.Y.: Cornell University Press, 1997.

Mintz, Sidney. *Sweetness and Power: The Place of Sugar in Modern History*. New York: Penguin, 1985.

Morgan, Edmund. *American Slavery, American Freedom: The Ordeal of Colonial Virginia*. New York: Norton, 1975.

Morrison, Toni. *Beloved*. New York: Knopf, 1987.

Nash, Gary. "The Hidden History of Mestizo America." In *Sex, Love, Race: Crossing Boundaries in North American History*, edited by Martha Hodes, 10–34. New York: New York University Press, 1999.

Neocleous, Mark. "From Civil Society to the Social." *British Journal of Sociology* 46, no. 3 (1995): 395–408.

Nichols, Charles H. "Who Read the Slave Narratives?" *Phylon Quarterly* 20, no. 2 (1959): 149–62.

Nichols, Roy F. "The Kansas-Nebraska Act: A Century of Historiography." *Mississippi Valley Historical Review* 43, no. 2 (1956): 187–212.

Ninkovich, Frank. *The United States and Imperialism*. Oxford: Blackwell, 2001.

Nogee, Joseph. "The Prigg Case and Fugitive Slavery, 1842–1850: Part I." *Journal of Negro History* 39, no. 3 (1954): 185–205.

Northrup, David. *Africa's Discovery of Europe: 1450–1850*. New York: Oxford University Press, 2002.

Ohline, Howard A. "Slavery, Economics, and Congressional Politics, 1790." *Journal of Southern History* 46, no. 3 (1980): 335–60.

Olney, James, ed. "Autobiography and the Cultural Moment: A Thematic, Historical, and Bibliographical Introduction." In *Autobiography: Essays Theoretical and Critical*, edited by James Olney, 3–27. Princeton: Princeton University Press, 1980.

———. *Autobiography: Essays Theoretical and Critical*. Princeton: Princeton University Press, 1980.

———. "I Was Born: Slave Narratives, Their Status as Autobiography and as Literature." In *The Slave's Narrative*, edited by Charles T. Davis and Henry Louis Gates Jr., 148–74. New York: Oxford University Press, 1985.

Omi, Michael, and Howard Winant. *Racial Formation in the United States: From the 1960s to the 1990s*. New York: Routledge, 1994.

Onuf, Paul S. *Statehood and Union: A History of the Northwest Ordinance*. Bloomington: Indiana University Press, 1987.

Orlin, Lena Cowen. "Fictions of Early Modern Probate Inventory." In *The Culture of Capital: Property, Cities, and Knowledge in Early Modern England*, edited by Henry S. Turner, 51–83. New York: Rutledge, 2002.

Park, Mungo. *Travels in the Interior Districts of Africa*. Edited with an introduction by Kate Ferguson Marsters. Durham, N.C.: Duke University Press, 2000.

Pegis, Anton C. "Some Recent Interpretations of Ockham." *Speculum* 23, no. 3 (1948): 452–63.

Pennington, James C. "The Fugitive Blacksmith or Events in the History of Tames W. C. Pennington, Pastor of a Presbyterian Church, New York. Formerly a Slave in the State of Maryland." In *Great Slave Narratives*, edited by Arna Bontemps, 193–268. Boston: Beacon, 1969.

Perelman, Michael. *The Invention of Capitalism: Classical Political Economy and the Secret History of Primitive Accumulation*. Durham, N.C.: Duke University Press, 2000.

Phillips, Carla Rahn. "The Spanish Treasure Fleets." In *The Atlantic World in the Age of Empire*, edited by Thomas Benjamin, Timothy Hall, and David Rutherford, 135–38. Boston: Houghton Mifflin, 2001.

Pickard, John B. "John Greenleaf Whittier and the Abolitionist Schism of 1840." *New England Quarterly* 37, no. 2 (1964): 250–54.

Piersen, William. *Black Legacy: America's Hidden Heritage*. Amherst: University of Massachusetts Press, 1993.

Pietz, William. "The Problem of the Fetish I," *RES: Anthropology and Aesthetics* 9 (1985): 5–17.

———. "The Problem of the Fetish, II: The Origin of the Fetish." *RES: Anthropology and Aesthetics* 13 (1987): 23–45.

———. "The Problem of the Fetish, IIIa: Bosman's Guinea and the Enlightenment Theory of Fetishism," *RES: Anthropology and Aesthetics* 16 (1988): 105–23.

Polanyi, Karl. *The Great Transformation: The Political and Economic Origins of Our Time*. Boston: Beacon, 2001. First published in 1944.

Poovey, Mary. *A History of the Modern Fact: Problems of Knowledge in the Sciences of Wealth and Society*. Chicago: University of Chicago Press, 1998.

Postma, Johannes. "The Dispersal of African Slaves in the West by Dutch Slave Traders, 1630–1803." In *The Atlantic Slave Trade: Effects on the Economies, Societies, and Peoples in

Africa, the Americas, and Europe, edited by Joseph E. Inikori and Stanley L. Engerman, 283–300. Durham, N.C.: Duke University Press, 1992.

Rachleff, Marshall. "David Walker's Southern Agent." *Journal of Negro History* 62, no.1 (1977): 100–103.

Rael, Patrick. *Black Identity and Black Protest in the Antebellum North*. Chapel Hill: University of North Carolina Press, 2002.

Rakove, Jack. "From One Agenda to Another: The Condition of American Federalism, 1783–1787." In *The American Revolution: Its Character and Limits*, edited by Jack P. Greene, 80–105. New York: New York University Press, 1987.

Rathburn, Lyon. "The Debate over Annexing Texas and the Emergence of Manifest Destiny." *Rhetoric and Public Affairs* 4, no. 3 (2001): 459–93.

Renan, Ernst. "*Qu'est qu'une nation?*" In *Nationalism*, edited by John Hutchinson and Anthony D. Smith, translated by Ida Mae Snyder, 17. Oxford: Oxford University Press, 1994.

Renault, Alain. *The Era of the Individual: A Contribution to a History of Subjectivity*, translated by M. B. DeBevoise and Franklin Philip. Princeton, N.J.: Princeton University Press, 1997.

Rhodes, Chip. *Structures of the Jazz Age: Mass Culture, Progressive Education, and Racial Disclosures in American Modernism*. London: Verso, 1998.

Richardson, David. "Shipboard Revolts, African Authority, and the Transatlantic Slave Trade." In *Fighting the Slave Trade: West African Strategies*, edited by Sylviane A. Diouf, 199–218. Athens: Ohio University Press, 2003.

Robinson, Cedric. *Black Marxism: The Making of the Black Radical Tradition*. Chapel Hill: University of North Carolina Press, 2000. First published by Zed, London, 1983.

Rodney, Walter. *A History of the Upper Guinea Coast, 1585–1800*. Oxford: Clarendon, 1970.

Rodriguez, Jaime E. "The Spanish and Spanish American Revolutions." In *The Atlantic World in the Age of Empire*, edited by Thomas Benjamin, Timothy Hall, and David Rutherford, 235–45. Boston: Houghton Mifflin, 2001.

Romero, Lora. *Homefronts: Nineteenth-Century Domesticity and Its Critics*. Durham, N.C.: Duke University Press, 1997.

Roosevelt, Theodore. *Address of President Roosevelt at the Lincoln Dinner of the Republican Club of the City of New York, Waldorf-Astoria Hotel, February 13, 1905*. Washington, D.C.: Government Printing Office, 1905, 16–17. Available at http://ia600303.us.archive.org/9/items/addresspresideooroosev/addresspresideooroosev.pdf (accessed May 27, 2013).

Rorty, Richard. *Philosophy and the Mirror of Nature*. Princeton, N.J.: Princeton University Press, 1979.

Rosen, Hannah. "'Not That Sort of Women': Race, Gender, and Sexual Violence." In *Sex, Love, Race: Crossing Boundaries in North American History*, edited by Martha Hodes, 167–93. New York: New York University Press, 1999.

Rosenberg, Emily. *Financial Missionaries to the World: The Politics and Culture of Dollar Diplomacy, 1900–1930*. Cambridge, Mass.: Harvard University Press, 1999.

Rowe, John Carlos. *At Emerson's Tomb: The Politics of Classic American Literature*. New York: Columbia University Press, 1997.

Samuels, Wilfred D. "Disguised Voice in *The Interesting Narrative of Olaudah Equiano, or Gustavus Vassa, the African*." *Black American Literature Forum* 19, no. 2 (1985): 64–69.

Scarry, Elaine. *The Body in Pain: The Making and Unmaking of the World.* New York: Oxford University Press, 1985.

Schultz, Elizabeth. "Natural and Unnatural Circumstances in Langston Hughes's *Not without Laughter.*" *Callaloo* 25, no. 4 (2002): 1177–87.

Schuyler, George S. *Black No More.* Boston: Northeastern University Press, 1989. First published in 1931 by Macaulay, New York.

———. *Ethiopian Stories.* Compiled and edited by Robert A. Hill. Boston: Northeastern University Press, 1994.

———. "The Negro-Art Hokum." *The Nation* 122 (1926): 682–83.

———. *Slaves Today.* College Park, Md.: McGrath, 1969. First published in 1931 by Brewer, Warren, & Putnam, New York.

Sebok, Anthony J. "Judging the Fugitive Slave Acts." *Yale Law Journal* 100, no. 6 (1991): 1835–54.

Shalhope, Robert E. "Republicanism and Early American Historiography." *William and Mary Quarterly* 39 (1982): 334–56.

Sharnmas, Carole. "The Revolutionary Impact of European Demand for Tropical Goods." In *The Early Modern Atlantic Economy,* edited by John McCusker and Kenneth Morgan, 163–85. New York: Cambridge University Press, 2000.

Singal, Daniel Joseph. "Towards a Definition of American Modernism." *American Quarterly* 39, no. 1 (1987): 7–26.

Singer, Linda. *Erotic Welfare: Sexual Theory and Politics in the Age of Epidemic.* New York: Routledge, 1993.

Sloan, Herbert E. "Hamilton's Second Thoughts: Federalist Finance Revisited." In *Federalists Reconsidered,* edited by Doron Ben-Atar and Barbara B. Oberg, 61–76. Charlottesville: University of Virginia Press, 1998.

Smith, Adam. *An Inquiry into the Nature and Causes of the Wealth of Nations, Books I-III.* New York: Penguin, 1982.

Smith, Rogers M. *Civic Ideals: Conflicting Visions of Citizenship in U. S. History.* New Haven, Conn.: Yale University Press, 1997.

———. "Constructing American National Identity." In *Federalists Reconsidered,* edited by Doron Ben-Atar and Barbara B. Oberg, 19–40. Charlottesville: University of Virginia Press, 1998.

Smith, Sidonie. *Subjectivity, Identity, and the Body: Women's Autobiographical Practices in the Twentieth Century.* Bloomington: Indiana University Press, 1993.

Smith, Valerie. *Self-Discovery and Authority in Afro-American Narratives.* Cambridge: Harvard University Press 1987.

Solomon, Julie Robin. *Objectivity in the Making: Francis Bacon and the Politics of Inquiry.* Baltimore, Md.: Johns Hopkins University Press, 1998.

Soumonni, Elisee. "Lacustrine Villages in South Benin as Refuges from the Slave Trade." In *Fighting the Slave Trade: West African Strategies,* edited by Sylviane A. Diouf, 3–14. Athens: Ohio University Press, 2003.

Spillers, Hortense. *Black, White, and in Color: Essays on American Literature and Culture.* Chicago: University of Chicago Press, 2003.

Starling, Marion Wilson. *The Slave Narrative: Its Place in American History*. Washington, D.C.: Howard University Press, 1988. First published in 1981 in New York by G. K. Hall.

Stauffer, John. *The Black Hearts of Men: Radical Abolitionists and the Transformation of Race*. Cambridge, Mass.: Harvard University Press, 2002.

Steele, G. R. "The Money Economy: Mercantilism, Classical Economics and Keynes' General Theory." *American Journal of Economics and Sociology* 57, no. 4 (October, 1998): 485–98.

Stephanson, Anders. *Manifest Destiny: American Expansion and the Empire of Right*. New York: Hill and Wang, 1995.

Stepto, Robert B. "Narration, Authentication, and Authorial Control in Frederick Douglass' Narrative of 1845." In *Afro-American Literature: The Reconstruction of Instruction*, edited by Dexter Fisher and Robert B. Stepto, 178–91. New York: MLA Press, 1979.

Stevens, Jacqueline. *Reproducing the State*. Princeton, N.J.: Princeton University Press, 1999.

Stewart, James Brewer. "The Emergence of Racial Modernity and the Rise of the White North, 1790–1840." *Journal of the Early Republic* 18, no. 2 (1998): 181–217.

———. "Modernizing 'Difference': The Political Meanings of Color in the Free States, 1776–1840." *Journal of the Early Republic* 19, no. 4 (1999): 691–712.

Stinchcombe, Arthur L. *Sugar Island Slavery in the Age of Enlightenment: The Political Economy of the Caribbean World*. Princeton, N.J.: Princeton University Press, 1995.

Stoler, Ann. *Race and the Education of Desire: Foucault's* History of Sexuality *and the Colonial Order of Things*. Durham, N.C.: Duke University Press, 1995.

Strange, Susan. *The Retreat of the State—The Diffusion of Power in the World Economy*. Cambridge: Cambridge University Press, 1996.

Taylor, Paul C. *Race: A Philosophical Introduction*. Cambridge, U.K.: Polity, 2005.

Thomas, Hugh. *The Slave Trade: The Story of the Atlantic Slave Trade, 1440–1870*. New York: Simon and Schuster, 1997.

Thornton, John. "The Birth of the Atlantic World." In *The Atlantic World in the Age of Empire*, edited by Thomas Benjamin, Timothy Hall, and David Rutherford, 18–29. Boston: Houghton Mifflin, 2001.

Timmermans, Benoit. "The Originality of Descartes's Conception of Analysis as Discovery." *Journal of the History of Ideas* 60, no. 3 (1999): 433–47.

Tise, Larry E. *Proslavery: A History of the Defense of Slavery in America, 1701–1840*. Athens: University of Georgia Press, 1987.

Ullman, Sharon R. *Sex Seen: The Emergence of Modern Sexuality in America*. Berkeley: University of California Press, 1997.

Van Deburg, William L. "William Lloyd Garrison and the 'Pro-Slavery Priesthood': The Changing Beliefs of an Evangelical Reformer, 1830–1840." *Journal of the American Academy of Religion*. 43, no. 2 (1975): 224–37.

Verger, Jacques. *Men of Learning in Europe at the End of the Middle Ages*, translated by Lisa Neal and Steven Rendell. South Bend, Ind.: University of Notre Dame Press, 2000.

Vishneski, John S., III. "What the Court Decided in *Dred Scott v. Sandford*." *American Journal of Legal History* 32, no. 4 (1988): 373–90.

Walker, David. *Appeal to the Colored Citizens of the World, but in Particular, and Very Expressly to Those of The United States of America*. New York: Hill and Wang, 1965.

Wallerstein, Immanuel. *Historical Capitalism, with Capitalist Civilization*. London: Verso, 1983.

Walters, Ronald G. "The Erotic South: Civilization and Sexuality in American Abolitionism." *American Quarterly* 25, no. 2 (1973): 177–201.

Watson, Steven. *The Harlem Renaissance: Hub of African American Culture, 1920–1930*. New York: Pantheon, 1995.

Weber, Max. *The Protestant Ethic and the Spirit of Capitalism*. New York: Routledge, 1992. Translated by Talcott Parsons. First published in 1930 by G. Allen & Unwin, London.

Weintraub, Karl Joachim. *The Value of the Individual: Self and Circumstance in Autobiography*. Chicago: University of Chicago Press, 1976.

Weisbord, Robert G. "Black America and the Italian-Ethiopian Crisis." *Historian* 34, no. 2 (1972): 230–41.

Wiecek, William. "Slavery and Abolition before the United States Supreme Court." *Journal of American History* 65, no. 1 (1978): 34–59.

Williams, Bernard. Introduction to *Meditations on First Philosophy*, by René Descartes. Translated by John Cottingham. New York: Cambridge University Press, 1986.

Wintz, Cary D. *Black Culture and the Harlem Renaissance*. Houston, Tex.: Rice University Press, 1988.

Wood, Gordon. *Black Majority: Negroes in Colonial South Carolina from 1670 through the Stono Rebellion*. New York: Norton, 1974.

Wood, Marcus. *Blind Memory: Visual Representations of Slavery in England and America, 1780–1865*. New York: Routledge, 2000.

Wood, Peter H. "Strange New Land: 1619–1776." In *To Make Our World Anew: A History of African Americans*, edited by Robin D. G. Kelley and Earl Lewis, 53–102. New York: Oxford University Press, 2000.

Wyatt-Brown, Bertram. "The Abolitionists' Postal Campaign of 1835." *Journal of Negro History* 50, no. 4 (1965): 227–38.

Wynter, Sylvia. "Sambos and Minstrels." *Social Text* 1, no. 1 (1979): 149–56.

Zerubavel, Eviatar. *Terra Cognita: The Mental Discovery of America*. New Brunswick, N.J.: Transaction Publishers, 2003. First published in 1992 by Rutgers University Press.

Zilversmit, Arthur. *The First Emancipation: The Abolition of Slavery in the North*. Chicago: University of Chicago Press, 1967.

Zizeck, Slavoj. *The Sublime Object of Ideology*. London: Verso, 1989.

Index

LINDON BARRETT (1961–2008) was a professor of English and African American studies at the University of California, Riverside, and the University of California, Irvine. He was the author of *Blackness and Value: Seeing Double* and the associate editor of the journal *Callaloo* from 1997 to 2000. JUSTIN A. JOYCE is a postdoctoral fellow at Northwestern University. DWIGHT A. MCBRIDE is dean of the graduate school and associate provost as well as the Daniel Hale Williams Professor of African American Studies and English at Northwestern University. JOHN CARLOS ROWE is USC Associates' Professor of the Humanities and professor of English and American studies and ethnicity at the University of Southern California.

THE NEW BLACK STUDIES SERIES

Beyond Bondage: Free Women of Color in the Americas
Edited by David Barry Gaspar and Darlene Clark Hine
The Early Black History Movement, Carter G. Woodson, and Lorenzo Johnston Greene *Pero Gaglo Dagbovie*
"Baad Bitches" and Sassy Supermamas: Black Power Action Films *Stephane Dunn*
Black Maverick: T. R. M. Howard's Fight for Civil Rights and Economic Power *David T. Beito and Linda Royster Beito*
Beyond the Black Lady: Sexuality and the New African American Middle Class *Lisa B. Thompson*
Extending the Diaspora: New Histories of Black People
Dawne Y. Curry, Eric D. Duke, and Marshanda A. Smith
Activist Sentiments: Reading Black Women in the Nineteenth Century *P. Gabrielle Foreman*
Black Europe and the African Diaspora *Edited by Darlene Clark Hine, Trica Danielle Keaton, and Stephen Small*
Freeing Charles: The Struggle to Free a Slave on the Eve of the Civil War *Scott Christianson*
African American History Reconsidered *Pero Gaglo Dagbovie*
Freud Upside Down: African American Literature and Psychoanalytic Culture *Badia Sahar Ahad*
A. Philip Randolph and the Struggle for Civil Rights *Cornelius L. Bynum*
Queer Pollen: White Seduction, Black Male Homosexuality, and the Cinematic *David A. Gerstner*
The Rise of Chicago's Black Metropolis, 1920–1929 *Christopher Robert Reed*
Living with Lynching: African American Lynching Plays, Performance, and Citizenship, 1890–1930 *Koritha Mitchell*
Africans to Spanish America: Expanding the Diaspora
Edited by Sherwin K. Bryant, Rachel Sarah O'Toole, and Ben Vinson III
Rebels and Runaways: Slave Resistance in Nineteenth-Century Florida *Larry Eugene Rivers*
The Black Chicago Renaissance *Edited by Darlene Clark Hine and John McCluskey Jr.*
The Negro in Illinois: The WPA Papers *Edited by Brian Dolinar*
Along the Streets of Bronzeville: Black Chicago's Literary Landscape *Elizabeth Schlabach*
Gendered Resistance: Women, Slavery, and the Legacy of Margaret Garner *Edited by Mary E. Fredrickson and Delores M. Walters*
Racial Blackness and the Discontinuity of Western Modernity
Lindon Barrett, edited by Justin A. Joyce, Dwight A. McBride, and John Carlos Rowe

The University of Illinois Press
is a founding member of the
Association of American University Presses.

Composed in 10.75/13 Arno Pro
by Lisa Connery
at the University of Illinois Press
Manufactured by Sheridan Books, Inc.

University of Illinois Press
1325 South Oak Street
Champaign, IL 61820-6903
www.press.uillinois.edu